The
Left-hander's
Book of
Days

The Left-hander's Book of

DAYS

Leigh W. Rutledge

A DUTTON BOOK

DUTTON
Published by the Penguin Group
Penguin Putnam Inc., 375 Hudson Street, New York, New York 10014, U.S.A.
Penguin Books Ltd, 27 Wrights Lane, London W8 5TZ, England
Penguin Books Australia Ltd, Ringwood, Victoria, Australia
Penguin Books Canada Ltd, 10 Alcorn Avenue, Toronto, Ontario, Canada M4V 3B2
Penguin Books (N.Z.) Ltd, 182–190 Wairau Road, Auckland 10, New Zealand

Penguin Books Ltd, Registered Offices: Harmondsworth, Middlesex, England

First published by Dutton, a member of Penguin Putnam Inc.

First Printing, August, 1999
10 9 8 7 6 5 4 3 2 1

All photographs courtesy of Photofest.

REGISTERED TRADEMARK—MARCA REGISTRADA

LIBRARY OF CONGRESS CATALOGING-IN-PUBLICATION DATA
Rutledge, Leigh W.
    The left-hander's book of days / Leigh W. Rutledge.
        p.   cm.
    ISBN 0-525-94348-X (alk. paper)
    1. Celebrities—Biography—Miscellanea.   2. Left- and right-handedness.
3. Birthday books.   I. Title.
CT105.R85   1999
920.02—dc21
    [B]   98-54340
                                                                CIP

Printed in the United States of America
Set in Goudy and Matrix
Designed by Eve L. Kirch

To Bill Jump

Acknowledgments

For their help in providing me with information or assistance, I would like to thank: the Academy of Motion Pictures Arts and Sciences Library in Beverly Hills, Cecil Adams, Mrs. Mabel Beardsley, Peter Borland, Richard Donley, Randy Fizer, Robert Haag, Paul Hause, Danne Hughes, Bill Jump, Skyler Maxwell, the National Association of Left-Handed Golfers, the National Baseball Hall of Fame and Museum, Paramount Pictures, Kari Paschall, the Professional Bowlers Association of America, Jennifer Rudolph-Walsh, Edward Rutledge, Dr. Elizabeth Rutledge, Charlotte Simmons, Sam Staggs, Roger Striffler, and Stephanie Tade.

Introduction

In his widely read 1876 book *The Delinquent Male*, Italian psychiatrist Cesare Lombroso, director of the lunatic asylum at Pesaro, boldly asserted that men who are left-handed are psychological degenerates prone to crimes of violence, and that if society had one whit of sense they'd all be locked up. A few years later, he published a companion volume, *The Delinquent Female*, in which he made the same assertions about women. Left-handers had heard it all before.

The great lie of life, of course, is that almost everyone is normal, and that only a few unfortunate wayward souls are "different." And like children eagerly connecting the dots in the Sunday newspaper supplement puzzles, we all, just as eagerly, try to connect those differences to the misfortunes of life. Hence, through the ages, left-handers have been blamed for the failure of harvests, the sinking of ships, plagues, wars, pestilence, and the degeneration of the human race. When science and rationalism first attempted to supplant superstition at the beginning of this century, the lyrics changed but the song remained the same. In 1937, a British child psychologist, Sir Cyril Burt, warned that "not infrequently, the left-handed child shows widespread difficulties. . . . [A]wkward in the house, and clumsy in their games, they are fumblers and bunglers at whatever they do." Like Michelangelo. Or Steve Young.

The *reality* is that almost everyone is "different," and that only a few, unfortunate, wayward souls are normal. Thank God.

This book is a celebration of being different. Differences make life fascinating. They also make life move forward. Or, as Martin Luther

King, Jr., once observed, in one of the most profound pronouncements of his life:

> The salvation of mankind lies in the hands
> of the creatively maladjusted.

It's safe to presume that if you've picked up this book, you're either left-handed, or interested in left-handedness, or forgot to bring your reading glasses to the bookstore. If you're left-handed, you're part of one of the most interesting minorities in history, as the following pages will demonstrate.

Defining left-handedness is not always as simple as it seems. It's frequently a subjective judgment. A person may write left-handed but do everything else—throw a ball, light a cigarette, eat dinner—with his or her right hand. Likewise, a person may write with the right hand (and may not even have been "switched" as a child) but do everything else with his or her left. Handedness—like other forms of behavior—exists on a spectrum, with varying shades between the two extremes. And to some neurophysiologists, writing is not even the most significant expression of handedness. Some scientists believe that *throwing* is (presumably since it harks back to the days when we protected ourselves against saber-toothed tigers). Others believe that the most certain sign of handedness is which hand an individual uses to fire a gun (since it involves survival) or to handle fire (since it also, at one time, involved survival).

Our choices in this book are based on a sometimes generous definition of "left-handedness"—though, in at least 90 percent of the cases, these are people who have been observed writing with their left hand, or have acknowledged having been switched from writing with their left hand.

One *very* important note of qualification. We're not exactly prepared, after having compiled this book, to state unequivocally that every person on the planet lies about their birthday—not just the year but the actual day itself—but we're closer to that assertion than at any other time in our careers. Anyone doing research quickly learns that so-called unimpeachable facts from so-called unimpeachable sources may vary widely. In the case of one internationally famous actress in these pages, we soon realized that she herself was probably responsible for the fact that, as the years progress, the year of her birth keeps getting moved up, so that she always stays forty-something. Likewise, there is often confusion and disagreement about the actual *day* of a person's birth. Numerous unimpeachable reference sources list inconsistent dates of birth for Cloris Leachman, George Michael, W. C. Fields, the queen mother Elizabeth, Gerald Ford, King George VI, and Whoopi Goldberg, to name just a handful. In the case of W. C. Fields, for example, one biographer has speculated that Fields himself constantly gave erroneous dates of birth, to keep nosy reporters from being able to research his past too assiduously.

Left-handers Born in
January

*January: First month of the year, named after the Roman
god Janus, god of doorways and beginnings*

1

Today is New Year's Day throughout the Western
world. On this day, in 1863, Abraham Lincoln signed
the Emancipation Proclamation. In 1892, Ellis Island
first opened as a processing center for millions of
immigrants entering the United States.

John Stubbes *(birthday unknown), British writer*

Since the only two possibly left-handed celebrities born on this day
were the corrupt and badly dressed J. Edgar Hoover (no man in history
had less of a figure for an evening gown) and the even more corrupt
and badly attired Ugandan dictator Idi Amin (remember him dressed
as a cowboy "welcoming" the Entebbe hostages?), let's instead begin
the New Year by contemplating the fate of sixteenth-century English
scold John Stubbes, a right-handed individual forced, by royal decree,
to live the last years of his life as a left-hander. Stubbes, whose actual
birth date is unknown (encyclopedias like to say he "flourished"
around 1570), was an acidic essayist and pamphleteer who took aim at
the politics and social mores of his day. When Stubbes turned his attention to Queen Elizabeth and wrote an essay attacking her policies
and insulting her judgment, the queen was outraged: she had him arrested and dragged to the Tower of London, where his writing hand
was lopped off. The unfortunately named Stubbes was then compelled
to live the remainder of his life as a left-hander.

On this day, in 1959, lunar explorer *Luna I* became the first object to escape the gravitational field of the earth.

Sally Rand (1903–1979), *U.S. burlesque artist*

Before there were lap-dances, the *Sports Illustrated* swimsuit issue, and a Hooters in every county, there was the incomparable left-handed artistry of Sally Rand, mistress of the fan dance, "the Balloon Ballerina." Since the left-handed brain tends to be nonverbal, it's no surprise so many left-handers are drawn to performance art. Rand never spoke a word onstage—but she spoke volumes with her body. She was a stripper, in the days when "stripper" meant something more complicated and aesthetic than using one's body as a tetherball around a greased pole. She had style, she had élan, she often stripped to Debussy and other classical composers; and she raised public indecency to such a respectable art form that she became "America's Treasure" and was the eagerly sought dinner guest of Washington politicians, society mavens, millionaire industrialists, labor leaders, and film directors. Wearing a flesh-colored body stocking (at least, she always *said* she wore a body stocking), she danced with two seven-foot pink ostrich-feather fans, one in each hand; the audience got flashing glimpses of the petite body behind the fans, but no one was ever really sure *what*, or how much, they had actually seen. Suspenseful uncertainty was the key to her act—and her success. "The Rand is quicker than the eye!" Sally liked to joke. (The act itself required enormous ambidexterity, as well as wrists of steel: a seven-foot ostrich-feather fan in motion can have the weight of a stack of bricks.) By the 1960s, Rand had evolved into such a mainstream cultural icon she was asked to perform for the Mercury astronauts at a lavish indoor barbecue thrown by Vice President Lyndon Johnson in Texas. When Sally took the stage that night, no one sent the children off to play, or covered their eyes: the chance to see an artist like Sally Rand was like an opportunity to see Sarah Bernhardt or Isadora Duncan in the flesh. (Literally.) Rand—who maintained her svelte figure all her life—continued stripping well into her seventies; however, as she got older she relied on increasingly intense backlighting to maintain the illusion of youth. Left-handers may be nonverbal, but they're not stupid.

Today is Genshi-Sai, "First Beginning," in Japan. On this day, in 1987, Aretha Franklin became the first woman inducted into the Rock-and-Roll Hall of Fame.

Joyce Jameson (1932–1987), U.S. actress

The face is familiar even if the name is not. Left-hander Jameson appeared in dozens of films and television shows, from the 1950s until the mid-1980s, often in nameless but memorable parts: the Telephone Operator, the Chorus Girl, the Soulful Prostitute, the Blond Downstairs. Sexy, smart, but always with an edge of introspective vulnerability, she was a cross between Diana Dors and Donna Reed. Among her best-known films were *The Apartment* (1960), *Good Neighbor Sam* (1964), and *The Outlaw Josey Wales* (1976). She also made countless guest appearances on various television shows, ranging from *The Twilight Zone* in 1959 to *The Waltons* in 1972. The year of her birth, listed above, is only an estimate, since—like many another left-handed beauty—she kept her age a secret: obituaries discreetly noted that "she was *about* 55 years old" at the time of her death.

Bobby Hull (b. 1934), Canadian hockey Hall of Famer

Nicknamed "the Golden Jet" for his speed and blond good looks, left-hander Hull played for the Chicago Blackhawks, the Winnipeg Jets, and the Hartford Whalers before retiring in 1981. A brother, Dennis, and a left-handed son, Brett (see August 9), also played professional hockey.

On this day, in 1884, the first volume of the *Oxford English Dictionary* was published. In 1885, the first successful appendectomy was performed, at a hospital in Iowa.

Michael Stipe *(b. 1960), U.S. rock star*

Left-handed, idiosyncratic lead singer of R.E.M.: "By nature I will find hope in everything. Even if it's the most incredibly hopeless situation or circumstance. That's just me. . . . I'll never be able to see things any other way."

On this day, in 1925, Nellie Taylor Ross became the first woman governor in the United States, when she was sworn into office in Wyoming. In 1961, *Mr. Ed* debuted on television.

Diane Keaton *(b. 1946), U.S. actress*

In this era of political correctness it's probably inappropriate to generalize and say that Diane Keaton epitomizes a certain kind of charming, funny, dizzy but *very* savvy left-hander. So instead we'll simply point out that her 1996 hit comedy, *The First Wives Club,* was one of the most left-handed films in recent memory. Not only were two of the stars, Keaton and Goldie Hawn, left-handed, but they were supported by a cast brimming with talented southpaws: Sarah Jessica Parker, Dan Hedaya, Victor Garber, and Bronson Pinchot. Keaton, vibrant and lovely, is traversing her fifties with a style that's a model for anyone plagued by midlife crisis. Or, as her on-screen mother Eileen Heckart told her in *Wives Club,* "You're not getting any younger. Or thinner. You know what I think you need? Absolutely nothing."

On this day, in 1981, Mark David Chapman pleaded not guilty by reason of insanity to the charge of murdering John Lennon.

Joan of Arc *(1412–1431), French national heroine*

Joan's left-handedness has been surmised on the basis of portraits showing her with her sword in her left hand. That the vast majority of these portraits were drawn well after the fact leaves considerable room for doubt. Was she truly left-handed, or only portrayed that way to bolster her enemies' assertion that she was a witch, or at the very least an unrepentant heretic? Like so much about her life, the question will probably never be answered.

Lou Harris *(b. 1921), U.S. pollster*

If insatiable curiosity is a distinctive trait of left-handers, then pollster Lou Harris epitomizes the breed. For almost fifty years, Harris and his associates have probed, questioned, and dissected the private lives and political views of Americans with the highly regarded and eagerly read Harris opinion polls.

Today is Nanakusa, the ancient Japanese festival honoring the healing power of plants. On this day, in 1949, scientists announced they had taken the first photograph of a gene.

Dustin Diamond *(b. 1977), U.S. actor*

The popular TV series *Saved by the Bell* should have been called *Saved by the Screech*. In episode after episode, Screech—"TV's most lovable nerd"—rescued his friends from detention, suspension, and the wrath of Mr. Belding. Screech was played by left-hander Dustin Diamond. The hit TV series first ran in 1988 and has continued in syndication. Diamond reprised the role in a spin-off series, *Saved by the Bell: The New Class*, as well as in two *Saved by the Bell* movies.

8

On this day, in 1878, David Edward Hughes gave the first public demonstration of his new invention, the microphone.

Prince Albert Victor, Duke of Clarence
(1864–1892), British royal

Left-handed son of King Edward VII (and the grandson of Queen Victoria, who was also left-handed), Albert was handsome, irresponsible, sadistic, oversexed, indolent, and feebleminded—not exactly a recommendation for heir to the throne. He contracted syphilis at the age of sixteen, and suffered a number of debilitating physical problems resulting from it. A marriage—to Mary of Teck—was arranged for him, but he died, at the age of twenty-eight, from pneumonia the day before the wedding. It was a blessing: he was first in line to succeed his father. More than a hundred years after his death, he is best remembered as one of the most likely suspects in the Jack the Ripper slayings. (See August 7.)

9

On this day, in 1793, Jean-Pierre Blanchard made the first balloon flight in the United States, from Philadelphia to Gloucester County, New Jersey.

Crystal Gayle *(b. 1951),*
U.S. country singer

Younger sister of Loretta Lynn, Gayle is renowned for four things: her left-handedness, her beautiful eyes, her music—which includes such chart-toppers as "Don't It Make My Brown Eyes Blue" and "I'll Get Over You"—and her exquisitely long hair, described by one enthusiastic critic as "a five-foot-long, Rapunzel-like pathway to country music Paradise."

On this day, in 1920, the League of Nations—forerunner of the United Nations—was founded.

Willie McCovey (b. *1938*), U.S. baseball player

McCovey played first base for the San Francisco Giants from 1959 to 1980 and quickly earned the nickname "Stretch" for his confounding ability to snap up odd, imperfect, or downright freakish throws. At bat, the Herculean slugger led the National League in RBIs, home runs, and slugging percentage in 1968 and 1969. ("When the ball meets McCovey's bat," one sportswriter remarked, "it's like witnessing a head-on collision between sixteen-wheelers on the freeway.") He hit a total of 521 home runs during his career and had a .270 career average, with a peak of .354 in his maiden year, 1959. He was elected to the Baseball Hall of Fame in 1986.

On this day, in 1974, Susan Rosenkowitz, of Cape Town, South Africa, gave birth to the first sextuplets to survive in modern times.

Alexander Hamilton (*1755–1804*), U.S. politician
and first secretary of the treasury

Hamilton isn't specifically known to have been left-handed, and during the past two hundred years he hasn't shown up on lists of famous left-handers. The only "evidence" that he might have been left-handed is a curious phenomenon visible in numerous engravings and paintings of him at his desk: the quill with which Hamilton presumably wrote is always positioned to the far left of the desktop—a singularly unlikely place for it to be if he had been right-handed.

On this day, in 1773, the first public museum in the United States opened, in Charleston, South Carolina. In 1981, *Dynasty* premiered on prime-time television.

Randy Jones *(b. 1950), U.S. baseball player*

Left-handed pitcher with the San Diego Padres (1973–80) and the New York Mets (1981–82), Jones won the National League's Cy Young Award in 1976. After 1976, he suffered increasing problems with his game, due to escalating arm trouble, and retired in 1982.

On this day, in 1854, the accordion was patented. In 1910, the first public radio broadcast in the U.S. was heard, in New York City.

Bill Smitrovich *(b. 1945), U.S. actor*

Left-hander Smitrovich is best known as the father, Drew Thatcher, in the critically acclaimed television series *Life Goes On*, which first aired in 1989. He is a veteran of dozens of films, including *Independence Day* (1996), *Ghosts of Mississippi* (1996), and *Air Force One* (1997), as well as a frequent guest star on such television shows as *Touched by an Angel*.

14 On this day, in 1952, the *Today* show premiered on NBC. In 1954, Marilyn Monroe married Joe DiMaggio.

Albert Schweitzer (1875–1965), German medical missionary, theologian, and musician

For all the people who sit on their derrieres at night and complain, "There's nothing to watch on television," here's a lesson from the life of indefatigable left-hander Albert Schweitzer. Raised in an age before whining (or couch-potatoism) became de rigueur, Schweitzer received his first doctorate, in philosophy, when he was twenty-four; his second doctorate, in theology, when he was twenty-five; and a third, in medicine, when he was thirty-eight. In 1905, he announced his intention to give up his comfortable life in France and become a missionary in Africa. He and his wife, Helene, then made the arduous journey to the Gabon province of French Equatorial Africa, where they established a missionary hospital (and later a leper colony), largely with their own savings. For almost fifty years afterward, Schweitzer devoted himself to jungle medicine. He was not a perfect man: according to contemporaries, he could be inconsistent, egotistical, and paternalistic. (One African complained, "I'd rather die unattended than be humiliated at Dr. Schweitzer's hospital.") And then there's the ever sticky question of Christian missionaries invading other people's countries and trying to talk them out of their indigenous beliefs. Still, Schweitzer's name was virtually synonymous with humanitarianism, and in 1952 he was awarded the Nobel Peace Prize. In his *spare* time, Schweitzer wrote more than half a dozen books (including the internationally acclaimed *Quest for the Historical Jesus*); he was also a distinguished organist, widely regarded as one of the most perceptive interpreters of the music of Johann Sebastian Bach. He died, at the age of ninety, in his adopted African homeland: his final fear wasn't of death but that he hadn't accomplished enough with his life, especially in warning the world against the proliferation of nuclear weapons in the 1950s and 1960s. Schweitzer, who preached the sanctity of all living things, was also an ardent animal lover who acquired a small cat named Sizi during his years in Africa. Sizi developed a habit of falling asleep on Schweitzer's left arm whenever he was trying to work at his desk. The left-handed doctor eventually taught himself to write with his right hand so he wouldn't disturb the winsome creature.

Cecil Beaton *(1904–1980), British photographer, writer, and designer*

Perhaps best known for designing Audrey Hepburn's flamboyant hats and gowns in the 1965 film *My Fair Lady*, and for his glamorous photography of film celebrities and the British royal family, Beaton—like many left-handers—believed in iconoclasm, showmanship, and subverting the status quo. He advised young people, "Be daring, be different, be impractical: be anything that will assert integrity of purpose and imaginative vision against the play-it-safers, the creatures of the commonplace, the slaves of the ordinary. Routines have their purposes, but the merely routine is the hidden enemy of high art."

Jason Bateman *(b. 1969), U.S. actor*

The left-handed teen idol, whose pinup photos adorned the bedroom walls of teenage girls in the 1980s, appeared in the popular sitcoms *Silver Spoons* and *Valerie*.

15 Today is Martin Luther King, Jr.'s birthday. On this day, in 1967, the Green Bay Packers beat the Kansas City Chiefs in the first Super Bowl.

Paul Badura-Skoda *(b. 1927), Austrian pianist*

Badura-Skoda—who still maintains an active concert schedule in his seventies (an age when many concert pianist's hands have long since been weakened by "burnout")—is one of the world's foremost interpreters of the music of Mozart.

On this day, in 1893, Queen Liliuokalani—the last monarch of the Hawaiian Islands—was deposed by U.S. military forces, at the behest of American business interests in Honolulu.

William Hope *(b. 1956), U.S. actor*

Hope is best known as the ineffectual Lieutenant Gorman in the 1986 James Cameron hit *Aliens*; he has also been in *HellBound: Hellraiser II* (1988), *Shining Through* (1992), *The Saint* (1997), and a number of other films.

On this day, in 1955, the first nuclear-powered submarine, the *Nautilus*, began its maiden voyage.

Benjamin Franklin *(1706–1790), U.S. statesman and investor*

An American Leonardo, Franklin invented bifocals, the lightning rod, and the Franklin stove, wrote the classic *Poor Richard's Almanac*, advanced his century's understanding of electricity and climatology, and helped draft and shape the Declaration of Independence (which he later signed) and the U.S. Constitution. Could this tireless, erudite man—the man who penned such parsimonious maxims as "A penny saved is a penny earned"—really bear any resemblance to the jaunty, bawdy, cheerfully prancing figure that Howard da Silva portrayed in the popular musical *1776*? Well, yes. Franklin was as renowned for his eye for the ladies (and his love of parties and dancing) as he was for standing in thunderstorms and flying kites. He penned the now classic "Letter to Young Men on the Proper Choosing of a Mistress," and by his own admission he frequently pursued the sexual companionship of "low women." He and his wife, Deborah, were never officially married—she had been deserted by her first husband, divorce was not an option—and within their common-law family they raised not only two of their own children but an illegitimate son, the result of one of Franklin's liaisons with a prostitute. Among his innumerable accomplishments, when he found a moment from socializing and inventing, Franklin sought to eliminate any bias in the nation's schools against left-handedness. In a 1785 essay titled "A Petition to Those Who Have Superintendency of Education," he noted the turmoil, prejudice, and rebukes he had suffered growing up as a left-hander in a predominantly right-handed world, and suggested that distinctions made between using the left or right hand were as spurious as a distinction between using the left or the right eye.

Jim Carrey (b. 1962),
Canadian comic actor

Rubber-faced, hyperkinetic superstar of such blockbuster hits as *Ace Ventura: Pet Detective* and *The Mask*, Jim Carrey is an acquired taste. His detractors suggest it's the kind of taste acquired after a lobotomy; his advocates insist he's the legitimate heir to a comedy lineage that includes Charlie Chaplin and Buster Keaton. Whatever one's opinion, Carrey is, for the moment, a phenomenon, and an entirely left-handed phenomenon at that. Studies have long suggested that left-handers are more comfortable and creative with visual imagery than with words. Or, as psychologist Dr. Lauren Harris put it, "Lefties are superior in creativity, tonal memory, spatial ability, originality, and elaboration of thinking"—which is another way of saying that, given half a chance, they tend to be brilliant improvisational comics.

Tex Fletcher (1910–1987), U.S. singing cowboy

Fletcher performed on radio in the 1930s and 1940s, appeared on the first test broadcast of NBC-TV, and made one film, *Six-Gun Rhythm*, in the 1940s. His left-handed guitar was a one-of-a-kind, custom-built model, made in 1934, and is currently on display in the Martin Guitar Museum in Nazareth, Pennsylvania.

18

On this day, in 1778, Captain James Cook became the first European to step foot on the Hawaiian Islands.

Cary Grant (1904–1986),
British-U.S. actor

Grant's first piano teacher will be remembered as the only person who tried to interfere with his left-handedness when he was growing up in Bristol, England. Described by the actor as an "unhandsome, irascible" woman, she went to his house "specifically, I think, to rap the knuckles of my left hand with her ruler." Her methods may have bruised his fingers, but they did nothing to diminish his ardor for the piano, or performing in general. Blessedly, Grant's other teachers left him alone. Later in life, Grant read a book claiming that switched left-handers frequently developed stammers. "I realized," he told an interviewer with characteristic understatement, "how very lucky I was. . . . If I'd grown up with a stammer, it might have proved something of a hindrance to my film career."

Danny Kaye (1913–1987), U.S. actor

Breezy, energetic comic actor remembered chiefly for his roles in such films as *The Secret Life of Walter Mitty* (1947) and *White Christmas* (1954), and for his tireless work on behalf of UNICEF in the 1950s and 1960s.

19

On this day, in 1953, Lucy Ricardo gave birth to Little Ricky, in a much anticipated episode of *I Love Lucy.*

Tippi Hedren (b. 1935), U.S. actress

The cool, blond actress found fame under Alfred Hitchcock's direction in the 1963 thriller *The Birds*. That Hitchcock became obsessed with her beauty, and gleefully subjected her on the set, day after day, to a sadistic and none-too-subtly erotic auto-da-fé-ather, is well documented; he *enjoyed* watching her tied down and pecked, scratched, and sideswiped by deranged crows and seagulls. Less than a decade later, Hedren's career faltered: the title of her lone film credit in 1970—*Satan's Harvest*—says it all. She found fulfillment a few years later when she abandoned acting almost entirely and turned her energy instead to animal conservation (a passion shared, curiously, by another blond, left-handed Hitchcock alumna, Kim Novak). In the mid-1970s, Hedren established the Shambala Preserve—a 180-acre compound for abused and abandoned tigers, cheetahs, and other large cats—outside Los Angeles. Her captivating 1985 book, *The Cats of Shambala*, chronicles her transformation from amateur animal activist to serious conservationist. As far as being left-handed is concerned, she says, "It hasn't made a difference to me at all"—except that she has difficulty telling left from right. "When somebody tells me to turn right, I go left," she told *Lefthander* magazine in 1992. "I can't get left and right straight. . . . You have to keep your sense of humor."

Michael Crawford (b. 1942), British actor

Crawford achieved international stardom in the title role of the stage musical *The Phantom of the Opera*, for which he won Broadway's Tony Award in 1988.

Phil Everly (b. 1939), U.S. singer

One half of the Everly Brothers, the popular singing duo of the fifties and sixties responsible for such hits as "Bye Bye Love," "Wake

Up Little Susie," and "Cathy's Clown." (See February 1 for the other half.)

Today marks the beginning of the astrological sign Aquarius. On this day, in 1969, Richard Nixon was sworn in as the thirty-seventh President of the United States.

Edwin "Buzz" Aldrin
(b. 1930), U.S. astronaut

Aldrin is one of only twelve human beings who have walked on the moon. Let me state that again: *Aldrin is one of only twelve human beings who have walked on the moon.* That the individual Apollo astronauts have mostly faded into obscurity—a kind of American celebrity shadowland where *really* important people, like the members of the Supreme Court, are virtually unknown to the general population—borders on disgrace. Anyone who has actually seen the mercilessly tiny modules that carried the astronauts across a quarter million miles of cold, empty space—no AAA or convenience stores, no "Gee, I think I'll stop and stretch my legs for a minute," no escape—understands the enormity of their achievement. (One tourist viewing an exact replica of the Lunar Lander at Cape Canaveral remarked, "And I get nervous just walking into an elevator. . . .") Aldrin—a brilliant, complicated man—was plagued by depression and alcoholism when the landmark 1969 *Apollo 11* mission was over. He recovered and wrote movingly of his experiences in the book *Return to the Earth*, and has since devoted himself to space and engineering research. How big a role did his left-handedness play in any of this: the decision to become an astronaut, the journey into space, the emotional struggles afterward? It's difficult to know, but one thing is certain: he was not alone.

Of those twelve Apollo astronauts who risked their lives to walk on the moon between 1969 and 1972, one third were left-handed.

George Burns (1896–1996), U.S. entertainer

George Burns could make anything funny. Burns on the dyslexia that plagued his school years: "I stayed in the fourth grade so long I wound up dating my teacher, Mrs. Hollander." Burns on his spelling difficulties: "I spell 'cat' with a capital K and two t's." How do we know for sure that George Burns was left-handed? Because he always smoked his cigar with his left hand, and anyone who knew George Burns knew he'd *never* trust a cigar to anything but his dominant hand.

On this day, in 1793, King Louis XVI of France was guillotined. In 1924, Lenin died in Moscow.

Telly Savalas (1924–1994), U.S. actor

Savalas was best known as the snarling, bald-headed lead of the hit TV series *Kojak* from 1973 to 1978.

On this day, in 1901, Queen Victoria died, ending her sixty-three-year reign, the longest in British history.

Balthazar Getty (b. 1975), U.S. actor

Great-grandson of J. Paul Getty, he has appeared in supporting roles in the films *Lord of the Flies* (1990), *Natural Born Killers* (1994), and *White Squall* (1996). Also a rap artist, he performs onstage under the name "B-Zar."

23 On this day, in 1977, *The Brady Bunch* debuted on network television. In 1997, Madeleine Albright became the first woman secretary of state in U.S. history.

Petr Korda (b. 1968), Czech tennis champion

One of the highest-ranked men's singles players in the world, left-handed tennis champion Petr Korda has won, among other things, the 1993 Compaq Grand Slam Cup, the 1996 Qatar Open, and the 1998 Australian Open, and has earned almost $10 million in career prize money.

24 On this day, in 1848, gold was discovered at Sutter's Mill in California, igniting the California Gold Rush. In 1922, the Eskimo Pie was patented.

Mark Eaton (b. 1957), U.S. basketball player

Eaton—a seven-foot-four-inch, 286-pound left-hander nicknamed "the Manwich"—played center for the Utah Jazz from 1982 to 1992.

25 On this day, in 1915, Alexander Graham Bell made the first transcontinental phone call, from New York to San Francisco. In 1945, Grand Rapids, Michigan, became the first city in the U.S. to add fluoride to public drinking water.

Christine Lakin (b. 1979), U.S. actress

The left-handed television actress has appeared in the made-for-cable film *The Jackal and the Rose* (1990) and the series *Step by Step* (1991).

On this day, in 1837, Michigan was admitted to the Union. In 1885, the Siege of Khartoum ended.

Scott Glenn *(b. 1942), U.S. actor*

Rugged and intense star of such hit films as *Urban Cowboy* (1980); *The Right Stuff* (1983), in which he played astronaut Alan Shepard; *The Silence of the Lambs* (1991); and *Backdraft* (1991).

On this day, in 1870, the first college sorority was founded, at Asbury University in Indiana.

Lewis Carroll *(1832–1898), British author*

"Living backwards!" Alice repeated in great astonishment. "I never heard of such a thing!"
—Through the Looking Glass (1871)

Lewis Carroll was the kind of left-hander who could make other left-handers look almost right-handed. A brilliant mathematician, photographer, and storyteller, Carroll—a shy man with a stammer—inhabited a cerebral universe of startling flexibility, in which up was down, right was left, and the backwards world one glimpsed in a mirror was as real as anything in "real" life. His was the kind of right-brain perspective that saw virtually all conventions as merely arbitrary: toys to be played with. His two classic novels—*Alice's Adventures in Wonderland* and *Through the Looking Glass*—dazzle the reader with riddles, puzzles, exquisite wordplay, and elaborate paradoxes. The phenomenal success of these books, with both children and adults, has mystified literary theorists for years. Or, as the staid *Encyclopaedia Britannica* earnestly notes, "There is no answer to the mystery of *Alice*'s success. . . . The book is not an allegory; it has no hidden meaning or message, either religious, political, or psychological. . . . [I]ts only undertones are some touches of gentle satire." What the *EB* and other scholars have apparently missed is that the book is popular precisely *because* it has no hidden meanings or allegorical significance. Like a free-for-all of left-handed lawlessness, it celebrates the cheerful, unceasing dismantling of logic, rigid values, etiquette, and predictability. It simply pulls reality apart and stands the universe upside down on its head.

On this day, in 1547, King Henry VIII died, at the age of fifty-five. In 1985, *People* magazine chose Mel Gibson as its first "Sexiest Man Alive."

August Piccard (1884–1962), *Swiss physicist and inventor*

Piccard revolutionized hot-air ballooning for scientific research purposes by building balloons with airtight, pressurized cabins that could penetrate the isothermal layer of the atmosphere. He also revolutionized deep-sea diving by applying the same principles to the design of depth-resistant cabins to penetrate the ocean.

On this day, in 1886, German engineer Karl Benz patented the first automobile with an internal combustion engine. In 1919, Prohibition began in the United States.

Greg Louganis (b. 1960), *U.S. Olympic diving champion*

A reading disability in grade school—and the subsequent taunts of schoolmates—inspired Louganis to seek refuge in gymnastics and

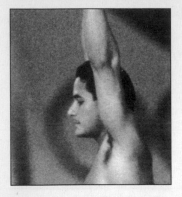

dancing, which eventually led to his participation in diving classes as well. Several years later, the left-handed young athlete went on to win two gold medals for diving at the 1984 summer Olympics in Los Angeles, and in 1988 he won two more medals in Seoul. "I picked up some *fabulous* jewelry over there," he quipped, flashing his medals to an appreciative audience back in the States. He also received the U.S. Olympic Committee's 1988 Olympic Spirit Award. In 1995, Louganis stunned the sports world by acknowledging not only that he's gay but that he is HIV-positive. Courageous men rarely restrict their courage to only one avenue of their lives.

Oprah Winfrey (b. 1954), U.S. talk show host and actress

Oprah's production company is named Harpo Productions—which as any left-hander will immediately recognize is "Oprah" spelled backwards. (Generally, according to researchers, left-handers can read backwards, or backwards *and* upside down, much better than right-handers. This unusual ability indicates a higher degree of certain kinds of latnem ytilibixelf.)

30 On this day, in 1649, King Charles I of England was beheaded. In 1933, Adolf Hitler became Chancellor of Germany.

Phil Collins (b. 1951), British rock star

At times, Collins bears an uncanny physical resemblance to another famous left-hander, Napoleon. Any similarity ends there, however. In an industry known for its guitar-smashing prima donnas and megalomaniac drug addicts, Collins has disproved the aphorism that "nice guys finish last"—he's known for his energy, generosity, and quiet intelligence. No wonder he's won five Grammy Awards and a Golden Globe, not to mention two Academy Award nominations. And no wonder he's been named "Left-hander of the Year" *four times*, in the music category, by the readers of *Lefthander* magazine.

Tony Mullane (*1859–1927*), *U.S. baseball player*

Mullane, a switch-hitter who played for Detroit, Louisville, Cincinnati, Baltimore, and Cleveland between 1881 and 1894, was the first major-league player to switch-*pitch*: that is, to alternate pitching left-handed and right-handed in a single game. The ambidextrous Mullane performed the feat in 1882, while playing for the Louisville Eclipse.

31

On this day, in 1940, the first Social Security check was mailed out.

Patty Costello (*b. 1947*), *U.S. bowling champion*

During a 1971 Professional Bowlers Association tournament in San Jose, California, all sixteen bowlers who survived to the finals were left-handed. Right-handed bowlers threatened to boycott future PBA events: they claimed that the lack of wear on the left side of most bowling lanes gave an unfair advantage to left-handed bowlers. Left-handed bowling champion Patty Costello—one of the top female moneymakers in the history of the sport—believes that right-handers actually have the advantage in bowling. In her book *Bowling*, she maintains that the slight depression on the right side of the lane—if not too extreme—can help right-handed bowlers since it may "guide" the ball to the pins. Whatever the truth, the PBA estimates that approximately 15 percent of professional bowlers are left-handed. In 1972, Costello was named Female Bowler of the Year by the American Bowling Congress.

Left-handers Born in
February

*February: Second month of the year, named after the
Februa, the ancient Roman festival of purification,
held on the fifteenth*

 1 Today is National Freedom Day in the United States. On this day, in 1971, President Nixon began installing secret tape-recording equipment in the Oval Office of the White House.

Gaius Mucius Scaevola *(c. 500 B.C.), ancient Roman hero*

As a young Roman soldier, Gaius Mucius was captured by invading Etruscan forces and taken before their king, Porsena. To demonstrate the unflinching courage of the Roman army—and warn the Etruscans of what awaited them in battle—Mucius thrust his right hand into a blazing fire and held it there until the flesh was entirely consumed. According to legend, he never flinched or uttered a sound. The Etruscans were so impressed by this bombastic show of bravery (or, perhaps aghast at the semipsychotic nature of it), they quickly signed a peace treaty and beat a hasty retreat back to their homeland. Hailed then as the savior of Rome, Mucius was granted a large parcel of government land to retire on, and was given the name by which he was forever known: Scaevola, "the Left-Handed One."

Don Everly (b. 1937), U.S. singer

One half of the Everly Brothers, the popular singing duo of the fifties and sixties responsible for such hits as "Bye, Bye Love," "Wake Up Little Susie," and "Cathy's Clown." (See January 19 for the other half.)

Today is Imbolc, the ancient Wiccan festival celebrating the approach of spring. It is also Groundhog Day. On this day, in 1982, *Late Night with David Letterman* premiered, on NBC.

Brent Spiner (b. 1949), U.S. actor

"Just how fully functional are you?" Denise Crosby asked Lieutenant Commander Data on one of the first episodes of *Star Trek: The Next Generation*. She wasn't talking about his hands, of course. Although well known for his work on Broadway in such musicals as *Sunday in the Park with George*, Brent Spiner achieved his greatest recognition—and developed one of the most ardent followings in Hollywood—with his often poignant portrayal of the android Data, beginning in 1987. While Spiner himself is left-handed, he has portrayed the android as, uh, "fully functional"—that is to say, ambidextrous. Two other members of the *Next Generation* cast were also left-handed: Wil Wheaton (see July 29) and Michael Dorn (see December 19).

Today is Setsubun, the bean-throwing festival, in Japan. On this day, in 1959, rock stars Buddy Holly and Ritchie Valens died in a plane crash in Iowa.

James Michener (1907–1998), U.S. writer

For years, the spectacularly successful author of *The Source* and *Hawaii* appeared on lists of famous left-handers, and in the 1970s he was named "Southpaw of the Year" by the group Southpaws International. As Herman Moore, founder of the organization, later recalled, "We were working from a list that had been provided to us. Several newspapers carried reports of our selections, and shortly afterward I got a call from a reporter in Austin, Texas. He said he had just spoken to James Michener. And Michener told him that the only thing he does with his left hand is occasionally scratch his right elbow." Oh. So why is Michener here at all? To remind us, as T. S. Eliot once observed, that "the only wisdom we can hope to acquire is the wisdom of humility." Tough to admit, but not *all* of the most talented people in the world are left-handed.

Today is Independence Day in Sri Lanka. On this day, in 1974, newspaper heiress Patty Hearst was kidnapped from her home in Berkeley by the radical Symbionese Liberation Army. In 1987, Liberace died of AIDS.

Maurice Flynn (1893–1959), U.S. actor

A handsome, left-handed silent-screen star, Flynn was featured in over two dozen films, including *Bucking the Line* (1921), *Hell's Hole* (1923), *High and Handsome* (1925), and *The Golden Stallion* (1927). Primarily an action hero, he was sometimes billed as "Lefty Flynn." He was married five times.

On this day, in 1776, invisible ink was invented. In 1919, the first commercial airline, Deutsche Luftreederie, began regular service, from Berlin to Leipzig.

Mandy Rice-Davies (b. 1944), British showgirl

What is it that makes so many left-handers irresistible? The beautiful, left-handed model, cabaret dancer, and all-round "good-time girl" Mandy Rice-Davies was involved in events that helped lead to the downfall of Britain's Conservative government in 1963. The scandal—

whose fine points are still buried in classified documents—involved sex, pool parties, high society, drugs, indiscreet love notes, a British defense minister named John Profumo, a Soviet agent named Eugene "Huggy Bear" Ivanov, and a roster of prominent British lords, including Viscount Astor. It resulted in ruined careers, at least one suicide, the resignation of British prime minister Harold Macmillan in the autumn of 1963, and the ascendancy of Britain's Labour party for almost a decade. That a pretty smile and perfect figure could influence the course of millions of lives is the stuff of which left-handed history is made. Rice-Davies went on to become a successful nightclub owner, novelist, and actress.

6

Today is New Zealand Day in—where else?—New Zealand. On this day, in 1952, Elizabeth II became Queen of England.

Babe Ruth (1895–1948), U.S. baseball player

I hit big, or I miss big. I like to live as big as I can.

—Babe Ruth

More than half a century after hitting his last home run on May 25, 1935, Ruth is still one of the most famous and beloved sports figures of all time. He was well known for his various foibles—smoking, drinking, and occasional womanizing—and his training was lax at best; but the weaknesses never overshadowed his achievements. George Herman Ruth was born in Baltimore, and by the time he was seven he was already so unruly his parents sent him to a Catholic boys' school, where the monks taught him to play baseball. Although he wrote right-handed, he pitched and batted left-handed.

By the age of nineteen he was already playing professionally. He started out as a pitcher—perhaps the best left-handed pitcher of all time—but it soon became obvious he was even more valuable as a hitter. His formidable left-handed swing fostered a cavalcade of memorable nicknames: "the Sultan of Swat," "the Colossus of Clout," "the Maharajah of Mash." Year by year, his fame grew. He played for the Yankees from 1920 to 1934, and Yankee Stadium soon became known as "the house that Ruth built." In 1930, when he demanded—and got—an unprecedented $80,000 contract, someone indignantly observed that he was making more money than President Hoover. "I had a better year," Ruth replied. Not only could he hit the ball farther than anyone else (sometimes he swung so hard he almost fell over when he missed), but he did it with stunning frequency. Roger Maris and Hank Aaron eventually bested his single-season and lifetime home-run records, but no one has ever come close to his home-run average: he hit a homer once out of every 11.8 times at bat, 714 home runs in all. Leading the Yankees to seven pennant victories and four World Series triumphs, he seemed invincible, but he made his share of blunders: he was, for example, the only major-league ballplayer to lose a World Series by being tagged out while stealing a base. He was uncouth and at times ill mannered—he hit umpires and occasionally chased a derisive fan—but to his adoring followers, those lapses only contributed to the Babe Ruth mystique. Never ashamed of his own less-than-glamorous origins, he donated much of his time and money to helping underprivileged youngsters, and rarely refused a request to visit the sickbed of a dying child. It was amazing what a visit from the Babe could do for a child's morale.

Bobby Mitchell (1856–1919), U.S. baseball player

Mitchell—who played baseball for only four years—has the distinction of having been the first left-handed pitcher in the major leagues. He played for Cincinnati in 1877 and 1878, for Cleveland in 1879, and for St. Louis in 1882. He had a career win-loss record of 20–23.

Natalie Cole (b. 1949), U.S. singer

Left-handed daughter of singing legend Nat King Cole, she won a Grammy in 1992 for her rendition of "Unforgettable," featuring a posthumously dubbed duet track with her father. The album, *Unforgettable With Love*, eventually sold over five million copies.

Rip Torn (b. *1931*), U.S. actor

Offbeat, left-handed actor who, while never a leading man, has nonetheless established a memorable, long-lasting career in Hollywood in such films as *Tropic of Cancer* (1970), *Cross Creek* (for which he received an Oscar nomination as Best Supporting Actor, in 1983), *Defending Your Life* (1991), and *Men in Black* (1997). He also appeared opposite Garry Shandling on the hit cable-TV series *The Larry Saunders Show*. Torn's outspoken politics and passionate civil rights activism in the 1950s and 1960s led him to acquire his own FBI file and to be out of favor for many years in some show business circles.

Louis Nizer (*1902–1994*), U.S. attorney

Nizer was an extraordinary man: painter, songwriter, caricaturist, a much sought-after master of ceremonies. Like many left-handers, he excelled at a number of pursuits. He was, however, best known as one of the first "superstar" attorneys, a lawyer almost as famous as his clients, which included Mae West and Charlie Chaplin, as well as a number of movie studios. Two of his memoirs, *My Life in Court* and *The Jury Returns*, were number one best-sellers in the 1960s.

 7

On this day, in 1819, the United States acquired Florida from Spain. In 1922, *Reader's Digest* was published for the first time.

Ahmad Ibn Ibrahim Al-Ghazi (*1506–1543*), *Ethiopian ruler*

Not all left-handers are heroes. Witness Ahmad Ibn Ibrahim Al-Ghazi, who, as a Muslim zealot in sixteenth-century eastern Africa, decided that the Christians in Ethiopia must go—either by conversion or by slaughter—and launched a bloody jihad against them, leaving a trail of murder, dismemberment, mutilation, and torture behind him. With the help of his allies—the Turks (who supplied him with firearms)—he conquered most of Ethiopia by 1535. Keeping the conquered lands, however, proved more problematic than expected, and he spent the rest of his life, until his death in battle in 1543, trying to hold on to what he had so bloodily acquired. Once he was dead, the previous ruler of Ethiopia returned to power, and reconverted everyone who had earlier converted to Islam. How can we be sure that this religious crusader was, in fact, left-handed at all? Because even though his given name was Ahmad Ibn Ibrahim Al-Ghazi, he was known to contemporaries as Ahmad Gran: Ahmad "the Left-Handed." Left-handers born on this date can take solace from the fact that Ahmad Gran's actual birth date is the subject of disagreement, and the date listed above is only an estimate.

On this day, in 1984, the Winter Olympics in Sarajevo opened. In 1986, presidential son Ron Reagan danced in his underwear on *Saturday Night Live* in a parody of Tom Cruise in *Risky Business*.

Ted Koppel (b. *1940*), U.S. television journalist

Koppel became a fixture on American television when, at the outset of the Iran hostage crisis in 1979, ABC began broadcasting a nightly update, *America Held Hostage*, hosted by Koppel. Americans, feeling that in the Iran crisis they were witnessing the disintegration of some important part of their world (and U.S. influence), were rapt. When the crisis ended in January 1981, ABC kept the show, no longer known by its now unnecessary name, but instead called, simply, *Nightline*. Though the program occasionally had missteps—Miss Piggy discussing the stock market and pork futures, overzealous movie stars arguing over serious subjects best left to experts—both Koppel and the program soon established themselves as leaders in the burgeoning genre of serious, issue-oriented, television talk shows. *Nightline* was the forum in which Jim and Tammy Faye Bakker pled their case before the American public ("Ted, can I say something? I just want to say, remember, God loves you. He really, really does"), where disgraced presidential candidate Gary Hart tried to make excuses for nonwife Donna Rice sitting in his lap ("This attractive lady, whom I had only recently been introduced to, dropped into my lap. I chose not to dump her off"), where Dan Quayle built his public reputation with such remarks as "I'm not so sure we want all those that graduated number one or number two in their class to be on the federal judiciary. This is a diversified society." Henry Kissinger appeared on the program in 1985 and criticized *Nightline* itself and similar television news shows. "If the Nazis had invited networks to Auschwitz to watch people marching off to the gas chamber, would it be appropriate news coverage to cover that?" he demanded in dismay. Koppel's quick-as-lightning reply was typical of his insight and surefootedness. "Absolutely," he retorted. "Can you imagine what the outrage of the world would have been? I can't imagine that you would think otherwise." Left-hander Koppel has been quoted as saying, "I think left-handed people have a chip on their shoulder, and have something to prove."

On this day, in 1870, the National Weather Service was founded. In 1964, the Beatles appeared for the first time on *The Ed Sullivan Show*.

Karoly Takacs (1910–1976), *Hungarian athlete*

A right-handed army sergeant who served on the Hungarian Olympic sharpshooting teams in 1929 and 1937, Takacs lost the use of his right hand in a grenade accident in 1938. He then taught himself to shoot left-handed, and went on to win Olympic gold medals in rapid-fire pistol shooting in 1948 and 1952.

On this day, in 1888, John Dunlop invented the first bicycle with inflatable tires.

Mark Spitz (b. 1950), U.S. Olympic swimmer

Because it has been linked to better underwater vision, left-handedness is said to give swimmers and divers an advantage. In 1972, left-handed swimming champion Mark Spitz traveled to the Munich summer Olympics intending to sweep all the events in which he was entered. A handsome dental student from California, he had previously won two gold medals, in 1968. He was true to his ambitions in Munich: not only did he win a record seven gold medals—more than any other individual athlete at a single Olympic Games—but he broke four world records.

Lenny Dykstra (b. 1963), U.S. baseball player

The legendary left-handed outfielder—nicknamed "Nails"—played for the New York Mets (1985–89) and the Phillies (1989–96), and batted .325 in his best year, 1990.

On this day, in 1858, Bernadette of Lourdes saw her first vision of the Virgin Mary in a grotto near the town's trash yard.

Ken Kimmons (b. 1965), U.S. actor

Left-handed actor best known as Detective Jake Spanner on the TV series of the same name, in 1989.

12

On this day, in 1898, Englishman Henry Lindfield became the world's first known automobile fatality following an accident on the road between Brighton and London.

Bill Russell (b. 1934), U.S. basketball player

Regarded as the greatest defensive center in the history of basketball, Russell was named NCAA Player of the Year in 1956 and led the U.S. Olympic basketball team to a gold medal in the 1956 games in Melbourne, Australia. Between 1957 and 1969, he played for the Boston Celtics and helped catapult them to eleven NBA title victories. In 1968, *Sports Illustrated* dubbed him "Sportsman of the Year," and he was named "Athlete of the Decade" two years later by the *Sporting News*. He was also named the NBA's Most Valuable Player five times. In 1966, he became the first black NBA head coach.

Joe Garagiola (b. 1926), U.S. baseball player and sportscaster

Left-hander Garagiola played ball for St. Louis, Pittsburgh, Chicago, and New York from 1946 to 1954, but became a household name when, in the 1960s, he was chosen to cohost NBC's *Today* show, with Barbara Walters and Hugh Downs. He remained one of the most prominent television sportscasters for the next thirty years, and also wrote two national best-sellers: *Baseball Is a Funny Game* (1960) and *It's Anybody's Ballgame* (1968).

13

On this day, in 1542, Henry VIII's fifth wife, Catherine Howard, was beheaded. In 1985, actor Sean Penn had his first date with Madonna.

Kim Novak (b. 1933), U.S. actress

What was it about left-handed blonds and Alfred Hitchcock? Five years before he became fixated on the cool and sensual left-hander Tippi Hedren (see January 19), Hitchcock was obsessed with the cool and sensual left-hander Kim Novak: he cast her as the beguiling Madeleine in the unforgettable 1958 thriller *Vertigo*. Although he never subjected her to the same sadistic rigors as Hedren (there being no birds in the plot, only inner demons and an occasional nun), it's said he did make her repeat, over and over, the scene in which she jumps into San Francisco Bay—just for the "pleasure" of seeing her repeatedly soaked, from head to toe, in Edith Head's elegant and expensive wardrobe. Novak—frequently underrated as an actress—was a charming, earthy, often ravishing screen presence who starred in numerous other hits, including *The Man with the Golden Arm* (with Frank Sinatra), *Picnic* (in which she uttered the immortal line, "Oh, I'm so tired of just being pretty"), and *Bell, Book, and Candle* (as an urban witch in love with Jimmy Stewart). People tend to forget that in 1956 she was named the country's number one box-office attraction. Like Hedren, though, she, too, finally abandoned Hollywood—except for an occasional "guest star" appearance, as in the 1980 Agatha Christie murder mystery *The Mirror Crack'd*—and found fulfillment surrounded by animals; in this case, horses, which she raises, with her veterinarian husband, in Carmel Valley, California.

14

Today is Valentine's Day. On this day, in 1929, rival mob factions clashed in a warehouse in Chicago, resulting in the St. Valentine's Day Massacre. In 1972, *Grease* opened on Broadway.

Dave Dravecky *(b. 1956), U.S. baseball player*

Dravecky worked his way up from the minor leagues to eventually become a starter for the San Diego Padres. In 1987, the left-handed pitcher was traded to the Giants, and that same year, as he was preparing for playoffs against the St. Louis Cardinals, he suddenly noticed a small, seemingly insignificant bump on his left shoulder. He ignored it, but over the next few months it grew. It turned out to be a cancerous tumor. Shortly after the growth was removed, doctors told him he had "zero chance" of ever pitching again. He refused to give in. "I have a passion for the game, for competition, for winning," he told an interviewer. Despite the fact that almost half the muscle tissue in his pitching arm had been removed along with the tumor, he embarked on a ten-month intensive rehabilitation program. In August 1989, with the cancer seemingly in remission, Dravecky returned to the mound. Giants fans gave him a standing ovation, and he proceeded to pitch, for seven innings, a near perfect one-hit game against the Cincinnati Reds. It was in Montreal five days later that one of the most memorable comebacks in baseball history came to an abrupt and agonizing end. During the sixth inning of the game, Dravecky threw a wild pitch—and collapsed in agony on the mound. He had broken his left shoulder: the sound of the bone snapping was so loud the catcher could hear it. A new diagnosis of cancer followed a short time later, and there were renewed rounds of surgery, as well as radiation therapy; but finally, the entire left arm and shoulder had to be amputated. The cancer, thankfully, did not spread. Dravecky gives much of the credit for his recovery to his devoted wife and children. In great demand as a public speaker, he has traveled the country describing his ordeal and trying "to give others hope." Although he probably won't be remembered as one of baseball's greatest left-handed pitchers, he'll certainly be remembered as the bravest.

15

On this day, in 1898, the U.S. battleship *Maine* exploded and sank under still mysterious circumstances in Havana Harbor.

Matt Groening (b. *1954*),
U.S. cartoonist

Left-hander Groening enlivened the world with, among other things, *The Simpsons*: a bombastic, hellish view of the middle-class nuclear family. The cartoon gave a decidedly left-handed spin to the concept of "family values." Its most famous star, Bart Simpson, was a renegade southpaw often forced to stay after school and write contrite sentences like I WILL NOT INSTIGATE REVOLUTION on the blackboard. Outside cartoonland, Bart became so popular he was named one of *People* magazine's "25 Most Intriguing People of 1990." "Bart," says Groening, "is trapped in a world where everyone else is struggling to be normal. Bart's response to being normal is 'No way, man!' He is irreverent; he never learns his lesson and is never repentant." Bart, after all, is an acronym for "brat."

Melissa Manchester (b. *1951*), *U.S. singer*

The daughter of a member of the Metropolitan Opera Orchestra, Manchester started her career as one of the original Harlettes, singing backup for Bette Midler's outrageous New York City cabaret act. She went on to become a Grammy Award–winning singer on her own, with such hits as "Midnight Blue," "You Should Hear How She Talks About You," and "Don't Cry Out Loud."

16 Today is Independence Day in Lithuania. On this day, in 1841, the first filibuster in the U.S. Senate began. In 1937, nylon was first patented.

John McEnroe (b. 1959),
U.S. tennis player

Sportswriter Rex Lardner once offered this pithy assessment of left-handed tennis players: "Left-handers are very offensive-minded. They keep the right-hander off-balance because they hit from the wrong side, and they move to the net instinctively to cut off his bewildered returns. They are especially powerful in serving to the ad court and in making slashing cross-court serve returns from the ad court." In 1979, left-hander McEnroe—"offensive-minded" with opponents *and* line judges and umpires—won the men's singles of the U.S. Open against Vitas Gerulaitis; he won it three more times after that, and won the men's singles at Wimbledon four times as well. He finished his career with 77 championships in singles and 77 more in doubles, including 9 Grand Slam titles. Renowned for his, uh, "artistic" temperament, he once railed at spectators and reporters at Wimbledon, "You are the pits of the world! Vultures! Trash!"

On this day, in 1600, astronomer Giordano Bruno was burned at the stake by the Catholic Church for suggesting, among other things, that not only were there other planets throughout the universe but they were probably inhabited by a multitude of other life-forms.

Richard Karn (b. 1957), U.S. actor

The handsome, portly, *very* patient sidekick to Tim Allen on the hit series *Home Improvement*, Karn has also been seen in the films *Desperately Seeking Susan* and *House of Games*. "I think one of the clearest memories of grade school for me," the left-hander once said, "was when we were learning how to write. I remember the teacher saying, 'Everybody point your pencil erasers towards the window.' I said to her, 'But mine's pointing towards the door'—and she said, 'Well, that's okay,' and it made me feel kind of special."

On this day, in 1861, Jefferson Davis was inaugurated as the president of the Confederacy. In 1930, the planet Pluto was discovered.

Ila Borders (b. 1975), U.S. baseball player

For the better part of the twentieth century, it was an undisputed maxim of baseball that a woman's place was in the kitchen (and, okay, the secretarial pool), but never, ever, not in a thousand years, at home plate. To make matters worse, the virtually all-male bastion of professional sports was, if not an arena of indifference to feminists, then at least one that had a low priority. It took, not surprisingly, a left-hander to change the rules. The only woman ever to have won a baseball scholarship to college (Southern California College, in 1994), left-hander Borders went on, the following year, to become the first woman to pitch a winning college game, against California Claremont-Mudd. In 1997, she made sports-page headlines across the country when she was signed to the Northern League's St. Paul Saints, the first and only woman in the league. Later that year, she was traded to the otherwise all-male Duluth-Superior Dukes. "I knew what I wanted ever since I was a little girl," she told one interviewer. "And I knew I was never going to let anything get in my way. And that included what people say, or do, or anything. My dad taught me not to be a wimp. To put up or shut up. My family has supported me along the way and never babied me." Interestingly, although Borders pitches left-handed, she bats right-handed.

Matt Dillon (b. 1964),
U.S. actor

Pugnacious star of *Rumble Fish* (1983), *The Flamingo Kid* (1984), *Drugstore Cowboy* (1989), and other films, including 1998's *There's Something About Mary*. His popularity as a teen idol was so intense in the 1980s that a magazine running a contest with one of Dillon's used T-shirts as the grand prize was deluged with entries; one individual submitted a total of 180. (The winner was a man from Los Angeles.)

George Kennedy (b. 1925), U.S. actor

Durable, brawny character actor, winner of an Academy Award as Best Supporting Actor for his performance in *Cool Hand Luke* in 1967. Kennedy has also been memorable in *Airport* (1970), *Earthquake* (1974), *Death on the Nile* (1978), and as police detective Ed Hocken, straight man to Leslie Nielsen, in *The Naked Gun* film series.

On this day, in 1942, President Roosevelt ordered the internment of all Japanese-Americans for the duration of World War II.

Ernie Gonzalez (b. 1961), U.S. golf pro

One of only five left-handed golfers to win on a PGA tour, Gonzalez won the Pensacola Open in 1986. (See also March 14 and August 13.)

Russ Nixon (b. 1935), U.S. baseball player

A left-handed batter for Cleveland, Boston, and Minnesota between 1957 and 1968, Nixon is, among other things, famous for never having stolen a single base in his twelve-year major-league career.

Today marks the beginning of the astrological sign Pisces. On this day, in 1962, John Glenn became the first American to orbit the earth, three times, in his space capsule, *Friendship 7.*

Phil Esposito (b. 1942), U.S. hockey player

The first National Hockey League player to score over a hundred points in a season (126 points in 1969), left-hander Esposito played for the Boston Bruins and was twice named Most Valuable Player, first in 1969 and again in 1974. After retiring, he became president and general manager of the Tampa Bay Lightning.

On this day, in 1965, Black Muslim leader Malcolm X was assassinated.

John Titus (1876–1953), U.S. baseball player

Even among superstitious left-handed baseball players, Titus—who played for Philadelphia between 1903 and 1912—stood out. Nicknamed "Silent John" for his taciturn nature, he felt he could only bat successfully when he was biting on a toothpick. In a 1905 St. Louis–Philadelphia match, pitcher Sandy McDougal successfully knocked the toothpick right out of Titus's mouth: Titus immediately dropped to his knees and began scrambling in the dust for it. He held up the game for several minutes. He then ran to the dugout, but despite his pleas, none of his teammates had a toothpick to give him. Disheartened, he returned to home plate and reluctantly picked up the bat. He was easily struck out. "Without biting on that ol' toothpick," he said afterward, "I ain't able to hit nothing."

Today is George Washington's birthday. On this day, in 1879, the first Woolworth's opened, in Utica, New York. In 1889, North and South Dakota were admitted to the Union.

Christopher Bram (b. 1952), U.S. writer

The acclaimed, left-handed author of the novels *Father of Frankenstein* and *In Memory of Angel Clare* considers himself lucky: he had left-handed parents. When grade school teachers asked if Christopher should be forced to write with his right hand, his parents' reply was emphatic: "No." "They'd been through all that crap themselves," Bram has said, "and they didn't want to put me through it, too." Bram considers himself fortunate in another respect as well. "I was raised just in time for the ballpoint pen," he says. "I didn't have to worry about dragging my hand through the ink every time I wrote something."

Lord Baden-Powell *(1857–1941), founder of the Boy Scouts*

Baden-Powell got the idea for the Boy Scouts in 1907 after taking two dozen boys on a camping trip to Brownsea Island off the southern coast of England. A short time later, he adopted the left-handed handshake as the "official" handshake of the organization. It was said he got the idea from an African tribe whose bravest warriors greeted one another left-handedly.

Dan Seymour *(1915–1993), U.S. actor*

In the 1948 classic *Key Largo*, Dan Seymour—playing the gangster thug Angel—can be seen shaving mob boss Edward G. Robinson left-handed with a straightedge razor. It's a nerve-racking scene: Robinson is impatient, he's angry at the insulting things Humphrey Bogart is saying to him, he's squirming, the razor seems to be just missing a vein in his throat, the camera closes in on the sharp edge of the blade, Robinson starts to snarl, twitch, he finally explodes in rage out of the chair, the razor blade gets out of his way just in time. The blade and Seymour's left hand are used to underscore the tension of the situation: nine people, five of them desperate mobsters, trapped in an island hotel during a hurricane. The role was typical of Dan Seymour's career. A widely respected but largely anonymous character actor, he was the veteran of dozens of Hollywood productions and made a career primarily playing corrupt and thuggish individuals. He can be seen as Abdul in *Casablanca*, as Captain Renard in *To Have and Have Not*, and as Comanche Paul in *Rancho Notorious*. To TV watchers, he is probably best known as the villainous Maharajah on several episodes of *Batman*.

Chuck O. Finley *(1918–1997), U.S. baseball team owner*

A confirmed and proud eccentric, Finley acquired the Oakland A's in 1960 and immediately worked to boost the team's fortunes with one idiosyncratic promotional idea after another. He dressed the team in flashy, colorful uniforms; he installed a mechanical rabbit behind home plate to pop out of a hole in the ground and deliver fresh balls to umpires; he bought sheep to graze just beyond right field during ball-games (he said he liked the look of them); he had the team's baseballs dyed orange. Loud, contentious, and hot-tempered, he also argued in-cessantly with managers, players, umpires, fans, and baseball commis-sioners, and throughout his career he was embroiled in a number of nasty lawsuits. Some of his innovations—though jarring to a tradition-bound game—eventually became widely accepted. It was Finley who was first responsible for the idea of the designated hitter and night games in the World Series. At the time of his death in 1996, one of his former players, Catfish Hunter, eulogized, "He was ten to twenty years ahead of his time."

On this day, in 1836, Santa Anna began his assault on the Alamo. In 1940, Woody Guthrie composed his song "This Land Is Your Land."

Peter Fonda (b. 1940), U.S. actor

There's no way around it: *Easy Rider* looks as dated these days as an old WAR IS BAD FOR FLOWERS AND OTHER LIVING THINGS bumper sticker, and the dialogue is as painful to listen to as being trapped in an elevator full of stoned college students. ("Hey, dude . . ." "Yeah, dude . . ." "You, like, are you, how are you, dude?" "Hey, dude, good." "Yeah, dude?" "Yeah, dude.") Still, in 1969, the independently made, counterculture saga seemed to many critics to be a revolution in film-making, and it catapulted Peter Fonda and his buddy, director Dennis Hopper, to instant stardom. Fonda's career floundered for years after that: films like *Dirty Mary Crazy Larry*, *Wanda Nevada* (in which Fonda wins Brooke Shields in a poker game), and *Death Bite* are not exactly the stuff that Hollywood immortality is made of. Still, Fonda managed a surprising comeback: in 1998, he garnered an Academy Award nomination for his performance in the film *Ulee's Gold*.

On this day, in 1942, Voice of America transmitted its first radio broadcast.

Gene Benson (1914–?), *U.S. baseball player*

Left-hander Benson played for the Bacharach Giants, one of the Negro National League teams (before professional baseball became integrated), starting in 1934. From 1937 to 1947, he played for the Philadelphia Stars, with a career batting average of .300. During his best season, 1946, he batted .370.

On this day, in 1870, the first African-American U.S. senator, Hiram R. Revels from Mississippi, took his seat in Congress.

Enrico Caruso (1873–1921), *Italian opera singer*

Caruso thrilled audiences around the world with his rich, extraordinary tenor voice. Back in the days when opera was still a working-class entertainment, as mainstream as country-western music is today, Caruso enthralled listeners with renditions of "Vesti la giubba" from *I Pagliacci* and arias from *La Bohème*. His private life thrilled people as well. Engaged to be married at an early age, he ran off at the last minute with another woman, a ballerina, instead. He had two sons out of wedlock, the result of a turbulent affair with an aging soprano. In 1906, he was arrested for pinching a woman's buttocks at the Central Park Zoo. He was convicted and fined, but the episode never dented his popularity.

On this day, in 1522, the last Aztec emperor, Cuauhtemoc, died. In 1993, a terrorist bomb exploded at the World Trade Center.

J. T. Snow *(b. 1968), U.S. baseball player*

A left-handed thrower—and a switch-hitter at bat—Snow started his major-league career in 1992. He has played for New York, California, and San Francisco, and has established himself as one of the best defensive first basemen in the game.

Today is Independence Day in the Dominican Republic. On this day, in 1789, the most famous racehorse in history, *Eclipse*, died in Britain.

Joanne Woodward *(b. 1930), U.S. actress*

Widely esteemed actress, winner of an Academy Award as Best Actress for her powerful performance in *The Three Faces of Eve* (1957). She was nominated again in 1969 for her role in the drama *Rachel, Rachel*, directed by her husband, Paul Newman, and 1991 for *Mr. & Mrs. Bridge*

28 On this day, in 1983, the final episode of the TV series *M*A*S*H* was aired.

Linus Pauling (1901–1994), U.S. biochemist

Genius in left-handedness is often expressed not in verbal finesse or wit but in a startling, nonverbal ability to imagine complicated structures from all angles instantly. Hence, it comes as no surprise to learn that a higher-than-normal percentage of architects are left-handed. It should come as no great surprise either that the brilliant biochemist Linus Pauling—a man who devoted his life to studying the architecture of matter—was left-handed as well. Pauling spent a lifetime probing the intricacies of molecular structure, and was especially fascinated by the question of how structure dictated the interactive properties of both inanimate and animate matter. In 1954, he was awarded the Nobel Prize for Chemistry for his discoveries. Eight years later, he was awarded a second Nobel Prize, this time for Peace. (He was only the second person in history to win two Nobel Prizes; Madame Curie was the first.) Pauling received the Nobel Peace Prize for his other obsession: a tireless effort to curb nuclear proliferation in the 1950s. In 1958, he presented the United Nations with a petition signed by over eleven thousand scientists urging an end to nuclear testing in the world. He was instrumental in securing a test ban treaty in 1963. The man who understood more about the structure of matter than anyone else on the planet also understood how fragile that structure is.

Milton Caniff (b. 1907), U.S. comic-strip artist

Originator of the popular comic strips *Terry and the Pirates* (which debuted in newspapers in 1934) and *Steve Canyon* (which first appeared in 1947).

Mercedes Ruehl *(b. 1954), U.S. actress*

Award-winning star of stage and screen, left-hander Ruehl won a Tony for her performance in the play *Lost in Yonkers* and an Oscar for her performance in the 1991 film *The Fisher King*.

Left-handers Born in
March

March: Third month of the year—when spring begins in the northern hemisphere—named after Mars, the Roman god of war

On this day, in 1961, the Peace Corps was created by President Kennedy.

Louis II *(846–879), French king*

There isn't much that's memorable about the brief reign of this inconsequential French monarch: he became king at the age of thirty-one and died two years later, having done little to improve either the lot of his subjects or the power and wealth of his kingdom. The most interesting thing about him is the sobriquet with which contemporaries branded him: Louis the Stammerer. The stammer was apparently the result of having been switched from left-handedness at an early age. Louis was, incidentally, the son of King Charles II, known to history as Charles the Bald. He was followed on the throne by: Louis the Blind (Louis III), Louis the Do-Nothing (Louis V), Louis the Fat (Louis VI), Louis the Quarreler (Louis X), and Charles the Mad (Charles IV).

Alan Thicke *(b. 1947), Canadian actor*

Thicke achieved international celebrity as psychiatrist-cum-perfect-dad Dr. Jason Seaver in one of the most popular sitcoms of the 1980s, *Growing Pains.*

On this day, in 1967, the luxury liner *Queen Elizabeth* was retired from active service.

Mel Ott (1909–1958), *U.S. baseball player*

Ott—who joined the major leagues when he was only seventeen—threw right-handed but batted left-handed. He played for the New York Giants between 1926 and 1947. When he stood at the plate, he looked like any other left-handed batter—until he swung. When the ball was pitched, Ott lifted his right leg high into the air, then slammed it to the ground as the ball met the bat. In this foot-stomping fashion, he hit 511 home runs during his career.

On this day, in 1931, "The Star-Spangled Banner" officially became the national anthem of the United States.

Ronald Searle (b. 1920), *British cartoonist*

Cartooning seems to come naturally to left-handers: witness Milt Caniff (*Terry and the Pirates*), Matt Groening (*The Simpsons*), Cathy Guisewhite (*Cathy*), and a host of other left-handed cartoonists. Left-hander Searle published his first work in the 1930s, but it wasn't until 1941 that he hit comic gold with a series of cartoons portraying the bizarre and fiendish schoolgirls of an imaginary British educational institution, St. Trinian's. Run by a dotty and oblivious headmistress, Miss Amelia Fritton, St. Trinian's was more mental institution than prim English academy: its hallowed halls were rife with gambling, sex, murder, depravity, and mayhem. The series of cartoons lasted until 1953. It raised eyebrows, elicited denunciations—and kept people laughing for a dozen years. In 1954, Searle's left-handed vision of scholastic bedlam was turned into the first of four popular movies, *The Belles of St. Trinian's*. In keeping with the cheerfully subversive spirit of the material, dour British actor Alistair Sim—best known as

Scrooge in the 1951 film version of *A Christmas Carol*—was recruited to don a dress and a wig and play headmistress Fritton. The whacked-out film, like Searle's cartoons, was a smash success.

On this day, in 1857, James Buchanan became the United States' first and only bachelor president.

Tom Lampkin *(b. 1964), U.S. baseball player*

Lampkin started his major-league career in 1988 as a catcher for the Cleveland Indians. He has since played for San Diego, Milwaukee, San Francisco, and St. Louis. In 1992, he led Pacific Coast League catchers with eleven double plays. Two years later, he had 595 putouts. As a left-handed batter, he reached his career high in 1997, with seven home runs.

On this day, in 1982, John Belushi died of a cocaine and heroin overdose in a Hollywood hotel room.

Rex Harrison
(1908–1990), British actor

Legendary leading man of stage and screen who appeared in more than forty films from 1930 to 1983, Harrison was adept at comedy (*Unfaithfully Yours*), sentimental romance (*The Ghost and Mrs. Muir*), historical drama (*Cleopatra*—he was the best thing in it), and musicals (*Doctor Dolittle*—he was the best thing in *it*). He won an Oscar as Best Actor in 1964, for his role as Henry Higgins in *My Fair Lady*.

On this day, in 1930, frozen foods appeared for the first time on U.S. grocery shelves. In 1981, Walter Cronkite retired as anchor of the *CBS Evening News*.

Michelangelo (1475–1564), Italian sculptor, painter, and poet

On a late spring afternoon in 1933, a U.S. Customs agent in New York City peered into a recent shipment of art books from Europe and clucked his tongue in dismay. The books—which had been shipped from Italy—contained oversized, full-color depictions of male and female nudes. The bulging muscles of the males, the Amazonian quality of the women, the livid colors, the almost unbearably intense rendering of human flesh: all of it meant only one thing in the customs agent's mind—pornography—and he ordered the shipment to be seized and held. A few days later, a very embarrassed U.S. Treasury Department relinquished the books and apologized to the Italian government. It turned out that the assistant customs inspector on the dock that day had never heard of Michelangelo, and the Treasury Department wanted the world to know that art books of Michelangelo's *Last Judgment* were *not* considered pornography in the United States. Thus, the right-handed sensibility of control, conformity, and order clashed with the left-handed sensibility of expression, license, and individuality on a New York dock in the days of the Great Depression. No quick summary of Michelangelo and his work is adequate. Better for everyone to march to the local library and delve into a thick, thirty-pound coffee-table book on his life and work. Michelangelo was twenty-nine when he sculpted his *David*, an eighteen-foot sculpture—later dubbed *Il gigante* by astonished Florentines—carved from a single damaged slab of Carrara marble. (The sling used to kill Goliath is held in David's left hand, incidentally.) When he was thirty-three, he began painting the ceiling of the Sistine Chapel for Pope Julius II. The resulting frescoes—which Michelangelo labored at for nearly three years—portrayed Adam as having received life through the left hand, and only further enhanced the artist's widespread reputation as *Il divino* ("the Divine One"). It was said that Michelangelo, who was ambidextrous, switched hands back and forth to avoid cramps while painting the ceiling. From 1536 to 1541, he labored over *The Last Judgment*, a fresco of the Day of Wrath, on one of the walls of the chapel. He continued sculpting and painting right up until the week of his death. Six days before he died, at the age of eighty-eight, he was at work sculpting the *Rondanini Pietà* with hands that were said by then to resemble gnarled tree roots. "God," said one of his contemporaries, "designed the world from sketches provided by Michelangelo."

Pete Gray *(b. 1915), U.S. baseball player*

When Gray was a boy, his right arm had to be amputated just above the elbow after it was crushed under the wheels of a milk truck. Despite his disability, he later played for the minor leagues, and in 1945—when ballplayers were in short supply, due to World War II conscription—he became the first and only one-armed player in major-league baseball history. He played more than seventy games for the St. Louis Browns, and batted, one-handed, .218.

On this day, in 1724, Pope Innocent XIII died. In 1862, the Civil War Battle of Pea Ridge was fought.

Sir Edwin Landseer *(1802–1873), British painter*

Landseer liked to astonish party guests by drawing a deer with his left hand while simultaneously sketching a horse with his right. What particularly amazed people was that both sketches were dramatically detailed, perfectly realistic, and extraordinarily beautiful.

8

Today is International Women's Day. On this day, in 1976, one of the largest meteorites ever recovered, weighing 3,902 pounds, fell near Kirin, China.

Kathy Ireland (b. 1963),
U.S. supermodel

Three-time cover model of the *Sports Illustrated* swimsuit issue, left-hander Ireland has her own line of clothing and workout equipment at Kmart, has a fitness video (*Kathy Ireland's Total Fitness Workout*), has appeared in television commercials for Lays potato chips and Cheerios, and has had roles in over a dozen feature films: *Mr. Destiny* (1990), *The Player* (1992), and others.

Carl Philipp Emanuel Bach (1714–1788), German
composer

Left-hander Carl Philipp Emanuel was the only one of Johann Sebastian Bach's twenty children to achieve nearly as much fame and popularity as the family patriarch. A composer of religious music, symphonies, and works for the harpsichord and the clavier, he enjoyed enormous acclaim in his lifetime. He is still regarded as the leading composer of the preclassical era. He was also the author of numerous treatises on music theory and performance, including his influential *Essay on Keyboard Instruments*, which Haydn proclaimed to be "the school of schools."

On this day, in 1862, the Battle of the *Monitor* and the *Merrimack* was fought.

Terry Mulholland *(b. 1963), U.S. baseball player*

Left-handed pitcher for San Francisco, Philadelphia, Seattle, and New York, beginning in 1986. In his best year, 1993, he had a 3.25 ERA; in his worst, 1994, a 6.49. Mulholland throws left-handed but bats right-handed.

On this day, in 1922, Mahatma Gandhi was arrested for sedition by the British for advocating an independent India.

Bix Beiderbecke *(1903–1931), U.S. jazz musician*

The life of the influential left-handed jazz composer and trumpeter served as the inspiration for Dorothy Baker's classic novel *Young Man with a Horn*, later made into a slick Hollywood melodrama starring Kirk Douglas and Doris Day. Reckless, ambitious, and hard-driven, Beiderbecke was expelled from high school at eighteen, had become an alcoholic by twenty-three, and spent the last five years of his life in and out of sanatoriums. His masterpieces include "I'm Comin' Virginia," "A Good Man Is Hard to Find," and "In a Mist." Although he officially died of pneumonia, at twenty-eight, the breakneck pace of his life—punctuated by booze, sex, and an aversion to sleep—led a friend to remark, "Bix died of *everything*."

Dean Campbell *(b. 1946), U.S. businessman*

The founder of Lefthanders International, in 1975—as well as the publisher of *Lefthander* magazine—Dean authored the so-called Bill of Lefts, a ten-article document guaranteeing justice and liberty for all left-handers, which was "ratified" in his magazine's offices on International Left-handers Day—August 13—in 1978.

On this day, in 1985, Mikhail Gorbachev became President of the Soviet Union. In 1993, Janet Reno was confirmed as U.S. attorney general.

Albert Salmi (1928–1990), U.S. actor

Salmi was a grizzled, tough, often hammy character actor, a veteran of hundreds of movies and television programs, including the films *The Brothers Karamazov* (1958), *Escape from the Planet of the Apes* (1971), and *Caddyshack* (1980), as well as the TV shows *Bonanza* and *The Twilight Zone*. He became especially well known for his portrayal of Tucker, the Space Pirate, in two episodes of *Lost in Space*. His was one of many faces—virtually always unconnected to a name in the public's mind—instantly recognizable as soon as they flash on the screen. "Oh yeah—that's, that's ... *Who* is that?" There are worse fates than this uniquely twentieth-century form of fame and anonymity, as Salmi himself illustrated in 1990, when, at the age of sixty-two, he murdered his wife and then committed suicide.

On this day, in 1940, the Russo-Finnish War ended. In 1980, a jury found serial killer John Wayne Gacy guilty of thirty-three murders and sentenced him to die in the Illinois electric chair.

Daryl Strawberry (b 1962), U.S. baseball player

Described by one sportswriter as "one of baseball's most feared sluggers," the Straw Man—as fans called him—saw his best years between 1983 and 1991, when he hit 26 or more home runs each season in nine consecutive seasons for the New York Mets. In fact, the left-handed outfielder hit 39 home runs for the Mets in 1987; he repeated the performance in 1988, and hit 37 more (along with 108 RBIs) in

1990. His decline—both professionally and personally—began shortly after that, and by 1995 Strawberry's name was constantly in the headlines, usually in connection with bad news. The Los Angeles District Attorney's office filed criminal charges against him for failure to pay almost half a million dollars in child support to his ex-wife and children. (Strawberry eventually reached a settlement with the court and paid $260,000.) He pleaded guilty to tax evasion and was sentenced to six months' house arrest. He was released from the San Francisco Giants after testing positive for cocaine. (He had twice earlier, in 1990 and 1994, undergone rehabilitation for drug use.) When the New York Yankees decided to risk signing Strawberry in June 1995, White House drug czar Lee Brown was blunt: "The Yankees have struck out by signing Daryl Strawberry. They are sending the worst possible message to the youth of America. That if you use drugs you can be rewarded with big money in big-time sports." Sidelined by a bad knee and other problems, Strawberry saw his fortunes plummet further. By the end of the 1997 season, he had seen only 29 at bats and had hit no home runs.

13 On this day, in 1781, the planet Uranus was discovered. In 1884, the Siege of Khartoum began.

Frances Fisher (b. 1952), U.S. actress

The five-foot-four native Texan started her career in the daytime soap operas *The Edge of Night* and *The Guiding Light*. She made her feature film debut, opposite Karen Black and Michael Emil, in the critically excoriated 1983 comedy *Can She Bake a Cherry Pie?* Since then, she has repeatedly proven herself a solid, gifted actress in such films as *Welcome Home, Roxy Carmichael* (1990), *L.A. Story* (1991), *Unforgiven* (1992), and the 1991 TV movie *Lucy and Desi: Before the Laughter*, in which she portrayed Lucille Ball. However, she is best known as Kate Winslet's brittle, clutching mother in the 1997 blockbuster *Titanic*.

14

On this day, in 1793, Eli Whitney patented the cotton gin. In the nineteenth century, the Great Blizzard of '88 left four hundred people dead and parts of the East Coast buried under five feet of snow.

Albert Einstein (1879–1955), *German physicist*

Albert Einstein wrote with his right hand and played the violin right-handed (he was a passionate amateur violinist), yet he frequently shows up on lists of famous left-handers. The reason is simple: he exhibited many key characteristics of a "switched" left-hander. Einstein grew up in a Germany that abhorred nonconformity. That abhorrence extended to the classroom, where any and all measures were taken to "convert" left-handed pupils. Was Einstein one of these unfortunate youngsters? Some modern researchers think so. For one thing, Einstein didn't even learn to speak until an unusually late age; by the time he was nine, he still wasn't very articulate. For another, he was, in his early years, such a slow learner that his parents feared he might be mentally deficient. ("He'll never make a success of anything," one of his teachers concluded.) Several of Einstein's biographers—chief among them, Ronald Clark—have disputed suggestions that Einstein was in any way dyslexic. Instead, they attribute his early slowness to a generally taciturn nature and to the fact that he was painfully bored in the German public school system. Besides, they point out, how could a boy who read Darwin and Kant at thirteen (and understood them better than most adults) possibly be dyslexic? The puzzle of Einstein's handedness will probably never be solved. Still, there are tantalizing clues. For example, Einstein *was* apparently left-eye dominant (yes, people have a dominant eye as well as a dominant hand): photographs consistently show him looking through telescopes and microscopes with his left eye. The odds favor the supposition that if he was left-eyed, he was left-handed as well. Or was Einstein simply "cross-dominant"—that is, right-handed but left-eyed? Such individuals are often said to be more creative, especially when it comes to using their spatial sense and visualizing difficult concepts—two things at which Einstein undeniably excelled.

Taylor Hanson (b. 1983), U.S. pop star

Lead singer of the group Hanson, left-hander Taylor also plays keyboard, bongo, and tambourine.

On this day, in 44 B.C., Julius Caesar was assassinated. In 1892, the escalator was patented.

Ruth Bader Ginsburg (b. 1933), U.S. Supreme Court justice

She looks like everyone's high school English teacher: was there ever a hairdo that cried out more for a pencil sticking up in the middle of it? Make no mistake, though—gracious, well spoken, and thoughtful as she is, this is *not* a woman to sit idly on a summer's day daydreaming about Byron or reading odes to Grecian urns. In 1954, she graduated first among the women in her class at Cornell University. She attended Harvard Law School from 1956 to 1958, and graduated at the top of her class from Columbia University Law School in 1959. The resistance she encountered in the course of her search for employment suitable to her intellect and her credentials after graduation eventually moved her to found the Women's Rights Project of the American Civil Liberties Union. In 1980, she was nominated to the U.S. Court of Appeals, and in 1993 she was sworn in as only the second woman on the U.S. Supreme Court. Endowed with a passionate, ferocious intelligence, she has, in the intervening years, established herself as the "conscience" of the Court: like many left-handers, she is less interested in orderly adherence to anyone else's idea of constitutional propriety and more committed to justice and enlightened change.

On this day, in 1968, the My Lai massacre—in which U.S. soldiers in Vietnam tortured and murdered over four hundred men, women and children in a South Vietnamese village—occurred.

Victor Garber (b. *1949*), *Canadian actor*

Veteran of numerous films—including *Jeffrey* and *The First Wives Club* (he played Goldie Hawn's sleazy film producer ex-husband)—as well as a supporting star in numerous Broadway shows, in which he is frequently cast as a heavy. But perhaps he is best known from *Titanic* (1997)—he played Thomas Andrews, her designer.

Todd MacFarlane (b. *1961*), *Canadian comics artist*

The left-handed creator of *Spawn* originally intended to be a baseball player. He played for the Canadian League, and was about to break into the U.S. minor leagues when an injury abruptly ended his ballpark career. He turned then to his other great love, comics.

Today is St. Patrick's Day. On this day, in 1897, boxer Jim Corbett lost the world heavyweight boxing title when he was knocked out by Robert Fitzsimmons in the fourteenth round.

Steve Harvey (b. *1957*), *U.S. comedian*

Left-handed stand up comic, nominated in 1998 for an Image Award—annually presented by the NAACP—as star of the television sitcom *The Steve Harvey Show*, which began airing in 1996.

Today is the feast day of St. Edward the Martyr. On this day, in 1925, a dozen major tornadoes swept through six states, including Illinois, Missouri, and Indiana, leaving 792 people dead.

Richard Condon (1915–1996), U.S. writer

Left-hander Condon was the best-selling author of *The Manchurian Candidate* and *Prizzi's Honor*.

F. W. de Klerk (b. 1936), former president of South Africa

The last white president of South Africa, left-hander de Klerk officially dismantled apartheid in 1991 and transferred the reins of power to former political prisoner and African National Congress leader Nelson Mandela three years later. He and Mandela shared the Nobel Peace Prize in 1993.

Peter Graves (b. 1926), U.S. actor

Best known as Mr. Phelps on the television series *Mission: Impossible*, from 1967 to 1973, and as the host of the A&E series *Biography* in the 1990s, Graves has also appeared in more than two dozen films, including *Red Planet Mars* (1952), *Beneath the 12-Mile Reef* (1953), and *The Court-Martial of Billy Mitchell* (1955).

On this day, in 1831, the City Bank of New York was robbed of $245,000—the first bank robbery in U.S. history.

Bruce Willis (b. 1955), U.S. actor

The left-handed star of the films *Die Hard*, *Death Becomes Her*, and *The Fifth Element* suffered from mild dyslexia and stuttering as a boy.

In school, he discovered that the stammer mysteriously disappeared whenever he got up and performed in front of an audience. "When I acted I was being a different person," he told interviewer David Sheff in 1996. "The emotional trigger that caused me to stutter—I don't know what it was—but it stopped when I would act. Finally, I told myself I wasn't going to be affected by it, and I grew out of it."

20

On this day, in 1852, *Uncle Tom's Cabin,* by Harriet Beecher Stowe, was published.

Sarah Jessica Parker *(b. 1965), U.S. actress*

Left-handed actress seen in *Footloose* (1984), *Honeymoon in Vegas* (1992), *Ed Wood* (1994), and *The First Wives Club* (1996): "I have this thing about hands. It's one of the first things I look at. I make a big thing about clean hands and feet. I'm compulsive."

Hal Linden *(b. 1931), U.S. actor*

Linden starred in the hit TV series *Barney Miller* from 1975 to 1982.

21

Today marks the beginning of the astrological sign Aries. On this day, in 1152, Eleanor of Aquitaine married King Henry II of England. In 1935, Persia changed its name to Iran.

Matthew Broderick (b. 1962), U.S. actor

Likable, talented star of stage and screen, winner of a Tony Award as Best Actor in a Musical for his performance in the 1996 Broadway revival *How to Succeed in Business Without Really Trying*. Broderick has also starred in the films *WarGames* (1983), *Ferris Bueller's Day Off* (1986), *Torch Song Trilogy* (1988), *Glory* (1989), *The Freshman* (1990), and *Mrs. Parker and the Vicious Circle* (1994), among others. He is married to fellow left-hander Sarah Jessica Parker.

22

On this day, in 1958, film producer Michael Todd, husband of actress Elizabeth Taylor, was killed in a plane crash in New Mexico.

Marcel Marceau
(b. 1923), French mime

Marcel Marceau gave new meaning to the phrase "Not another peep out of you" when he started performing in the 1950s. Back then, mimes were still a novelty, an object of fascination, and Americans eagerly tuned in to *The Ed Sullivan Show* and other venues to watch Marceau—the only mime most of them had ever seen—perform. In the forty years since his professional debut, his eloquent silence—and his success—have inspired a small army of imitators.

Pat Robertson *(b. 1930), U.S. televangelist and businessman*

Multimillionaire, conservative televangelist, founder of the Christian Broadcasting Network (later changed to the more benign-sounding "Family Channel"); also a presidential candidate in the 1988 campaign.

On this day, in 1857, the first passenger elevator was installed, in a department store in New York City.

Ramesses II *(reigned 1304–1237 B.C.), Egyptian pharaoh*

Ramesses is known to have been left-handed from the bas-reliefs and portraits carved during his reign.

On this day, in 1989, the oil tanker *Exxon Valdez* ran aground in Alaska's Prince William Sound.

Tommy Hilfiger *(b. 1952), U.S. fashion entrepreneur*

An acid-dropping hippie in the sixties—"Anything traditional did not make sense to me"—Hilfiger seemed as *un*destined for American fashion superstardom as anyone could be. Still, it was precisely his nonconforming nature that started him down that career path. "We couldn't find bell-bottoms or mod clothes in Elmira, New York," he told *Playboy* in 1997. "So in 1969 two friends and I put some money together and drove to New York City, where we bought a bunch of jeans. We brought them back to Elmira and sold them to our friends." His unruliness—"I wasn't a serious kid. I was silly, always stirring the pot, always making trouble at home with my sisters or brothers, always creating a little bit of havoc"—had its roots in severe dyslexia. "I still have a problem," he acknowledged, "identifying certain letters and numbers. But in those days, I couldn't figure out what was wrong. I felt really bad about myself in school. . . . I used my class-clown routine so they wouldn't think I was completely stupid." That the dyslexic rebel ultimately made a world-class fortune marketing primarily mainstream clothes, boldly imprinted with *words*, seems more than a little ironic.

Steve McQueen *(1930–1980), U.S. actor*

McQueen appeared in the popular TV series *Wanted: Dead or Alive* from 1958 to 1961, but was most famous for his film roles, which included *The Blob* (1958), *The Magnificent Seven* (1960), *The Great Escape* (1963), *The Sand Pebbles* (for which he was nominated for an Oscar, in 1966), *Bullitt* (1968), and, in what was perhaps his greatest performance, *Papillon* (1973).

25 On this day, in 1985, Sally Field accepted her Oscar for Best Actress with the immortal words, "You like me! You really like me!"

James Lovell *(b. 1928), U.S. astronaut*

Lovell's abortive 1970 mission to the moon, *Apollo 13*, ended in near catastrophe, but, as part of *Apollo 13*, as well as *Gemini 7*, *Gemini 12*, and *Apollo 8*, he has achieved a remarkable distinction: he has traveled more miles than any other human being in history.

Mike Aulby *(b. 1960), U.S. bowling champion*

Winner of nearly two dozen PBA championships between 1979 and 1996, and the only player to have achieved bowling's Grand

Slam: victories in the Brunswick World Tournament of Champions, the PBA National Championship, the BPAA U.S. Open, the ABC Masters, and the Bayer/Brunswick Touring Players Championship. He was inducted into the PBA Hall of Fame in 1996.

Paul Michael Glaser *(b. 1942), U.S. actor*

Left-hander Glaser is best known as Detective Dave Starsky in the popular television police drama *Starsky and Hutch*, which ran from 1975 to 1979.

Tom Glavine *(b. 1966), U.S. baseball player*

One of the most popular baseball players of the 1990s, left-hander Glavine has also been one of the most successful. He compiled an impressive 144–78 win-loss record pitching for the Atlanta Braves between 1988 and 1997, and was instrumental in propelling the Braves to victory in the 1995 World Series.

26 On this day, in 1979, Anwar Sadat and Menachem Begin signed the landmark Egyptian-Israeli peace accord.

Chip Zien *(b. 1957), U.S. actor*

Best known for his work on Broadway—in *Into the Woods*, *Falsettos*, and *Grand Hotel*—Zien is also a veteran of the TV series *Love, Sidney* and *Almost Perfect*, as well as feature films, including *Howard the Duck* (1986) and *Mrs. Parker and the Vicious Circle* (1994).

On this day, in 1794, the U.S. Navy was established. In 1855, kerosene was invented.

Louis XVII (1785–1858?), son of Louis XVI and Marie Antoinette and heir to the French throne

Wandering about Paris and Versailles in her strange, dated clothes and her ornate, wide-brimmed hats, the lady known as Jenny Savalette de Lange aroused only mild curiosity while she was alive. She was, according to her contemporaries, no beauty: she was gaunt and tall, with hard, aristocratic features and a sullen, almost masculine look. It was commented that she bore a slight resemblance to King Louis XVI, who—with his wife, Marie Antoinette—had been beheaded, six decades earlier, during the Reign of Terror that followed the French Revolution. She always carried an umbrella, as if shielding her face from close scrutiny. When she finally died at Versailles on May 6, 1858, her body was quietly handed over to two elderly women to prepare it for burial. It was then discovered that Jenny was, in fact, a man. Apparently, for more than fifty years, no one had known her secret; she remained aloof from her neighbors, she had few friends, and she never married (although local gossip claimed she had had lovers). She had lived most of her life on an inexplicably magnanimous government pension—though no one could figure out how she'd gotten the pension, or why. Bureaucratically speaking, she did not even exist: there were no official records of her birth in any hall or archive. Stories soon began to spread that Jenny was actually Louis XVII, the left-handed son of Marie Antoinette and left-handed King Louis XVI. Captured by French revolutionaries along with his mother and father as they tried to flee France in 1791, the ten-year-old Louis had allegedly died in prison of tuberculosis shortly after his parents were guillotined. However, his last months in prison had been veiled in secrecy, and for years afterward there were stories that the boy had actually escaped with the help of a conspiracy of monarchists who planned to restore him one day as rightful heir to the throne of France. Over the years, more than thirty people claimed to be the young prince. In the case of Jenny Savalette de Lange, nothing could ever be proved and the mystery was never solved, despite the efforts of numerous people to find out exactly who she was and where she had come from. Jenny was quietly buried—it apparently never occurred to anyone to investigate the issue of her handedness—and her death certificate stated simply that she was "an unknown man . . . a bachelor." (See also August 23.)

On this day, in 1979, Margaret Thatcher became Prime Minister of England.

Willie Foster *(1901–1976), U.S. baseball player*

Foster played for the Negro Leagues from 1920 to 1935, ten of those years with the American Giants, where, as one of the greatest left-handed pitchers in the leagues' history, he distinguished himself with a legendary fastball. In 1927, he set a league record with 18 wins against 3 losses, and he led the Giants to the Negro World Series in 1926 and 1927. He was inducted into the Baseball Hall of Fame in 1996.

On this day, in 1912, explorer Robert Scott died in Antarctica, on the second expedition to reach the South Pole.

The "Left-Handed Whopper" *(1998)*

Although there's at least one well-known left-hander born on this day—baseball pitcher Eric Gunderson—the day seems more properly to belong to the first fast-food menu item specifically designed for southpaws: Burger King's Left-Handed Whopper. In late March 1998, the fast-food giant announced plans to introduce a new version of its famous hamburger "with all the condiments rotated 180 degrees, thereby redistributing the weight of the sandwich so that the bulk of the contents will skew to the left." "We have always been proud of the fact," said a Burger King spokesman, "that we offered 1,024 ways to order our flagship Whopper sandwich. Now we are offering 1,025 ways. It's the ultimate 'Have It Your Way' for our left-handed customers." The corporation took out a full-page ad in *USA Today* to introduce the new sandwich to consumers, and the Associated Press trumpeted its arrival with a press story announcing, "Left-handed burger eaters will be left out no longer." Not everyone was happy. Managers at some Burger King franchises complained they hadn't been given sufficient notice—not to mention equipment or instructions—to prepare the new burger. They needn't have worried. It was all a hoax. On April 1, Burger King announced that the entire story—and the ad in *USA Today*—had been an elaborate April Fool's joke dreamt up by some of its marketing executives, giving new meaning indeed to the term "Whopper."

30 On this day, in 1867, the United States purchased Alaska from Russia. In 1981, President Reagan and three other men were shot during an assassination attempt by John Hinckley, Jr.

Celine Dion (b. 1968), *Canadian singer*

One of fourteen children born to a Quebec ditchdigger, left-hander Dion made her singing debut at twelve and her first recording at fifteen. A decade and a half later, in 1998, she had the fastest-selling album in history—*Let's Talk About Love*—and the most popular song ever recorded for a motion picture, "My Heart Will Go On," from *Titanic.* An ardent golf fanatic—"I'm fixing my tour schedule around golf," she confessed in 1998—she was, like many left-handers, unhappy in school when she was growing up. "I hated school," she told one interviewer. "I always hated school and even today, talking about it—I know that school is very, very important, but I don't think school is for everyone and it was definitely not for me." "Since I was very little," she said, "I always hoped and wished that everything was going to be very beautiful in life and especially in show business, and it's turned out exactly the way I thought."

31 On this day, in 1918, the first Daylight Savings Time went into effect. In 1979, the Village People's "In the Navy" began a thirteen-week run in the Top 40.

Shirley Jones (b. 1934),
U.S. actress

Jones built a career starring in wholesome movie musicals like *Oklahoma!* (1955), *Carousel* (1956), and *April Love* (1957). In 1960, she abruptly broke with her popular on-screen image and took the role of a bitter, conniving prostitute in the hard-hitting religion-and-hypocrisy drama *Elmer Gantry*. To the horror of many of her fans, the film was heavily advertised with stills of the onetime good girl in slutty lingerie. She won an Oscar as Best Supporting Actress. "It's hard to be certain," mused one critic, "whether she got the Oscar for the performance, or because Hollywood was flabbergasted at the spectacle of Shirley Jones as a blackmailing whore." In 1970, she reverted to her original image with her role as the *very* wholesome Shirley Partridge in the popular TV series *The Partridge Family*. She's never been seen in public in a slip since.

Gabe Kaplan (b. 1945), U.S. actor

Left-hander Kaplan created, produced, and starred in the hit TV series *Welcome Back, Kotter*, which was based on his own experiences in "remedial" high school classes. He modeled Kotter after one of his own teachers (in actuality, a woman), who had inspired him and other misfit "sweathogs."

Left-handers Born in
April

*April: "The cruelest month," named from the Latin
aperire, meaning "to unfold" or "to blossom"*

1

Today is April Fool's Day. It is also Victory Day in
Spain. On this day, in 1904, the first Rolls-Royce was
completed and road-tested. In 1960, the first
weather satellite was launched.

Cecil Adams *(b. ?), U.S. journalist*

Adams is known to weekly newspaper readers as the author of "The
Straight Dope," a column devoted to arcane questions of fact not likely
to be found in the *Encyclopaedia Britannica* or *The World Almanac*:
What does the H. in Jesus H. Christ stand for? What are the real lyrics
to "Louie Louie"? When a person is executed by lethal injection, do
they swab the arm with alcohol first? Tasteful questions. Obsessive
questions. Left-handed questions. Gerbils, M&Ms, and various forms
of bodily excretion have all figured in his columns at one time or another. "The Straight Dope," which first appeared in 1973, is carried by
more than thirty newspapers throughout the United States and
Canada, and has been anthologized in a number of popular books.
Adams himself is "cagey" about his personal life. He could be thirty or
a hundred and thirty; some people have speculated he doesn't exist at
all, but is the Penelope Ashe of journalism. (Ashe was the reputed author of the outrageously sexy 1960s best-seller *Naked Came the Stranger*;
"she" was actually a group of twenty-five journalists on the Long Island
newspaper *Newsday* who decided to write a trashy best-seller together.)

Adams's official biography states only that "Cecil Adams is the world's most intelligent human being. We know this because: (1) He knows everything, and (2) He is never wrong." It also states that the enigmatic but cocksure journalist is left-handed.

Colonel Alexander Branscom (c. 1880), U.S.
swindler and confidence man

Since no one knows when the elusive, left-handed Colonel Branscom was really born—the colonel himself probably didn't remember, he lied so much about everything—it seems only fitting to celebrate his birthday on April Fool's Day. Branscom—a dapper and irresistibly charming middle-aged Virginian—was missing his right hand; he claimed he'd lost it fighting for the glory of the Confederacy in the Civil War. More likely, he lost it in a back-alley knife fight or after cheating someone at cards. He was a counterfeiter, forger, and all-purpose con man who cheerfully practiced every "gentlemanly" (i.e., nonviolent) form of thievery conceivable. In a typical subterfuge, he would move from city to city posing as a book publisher to bilk unsuspecting advertisers and contractors out of tens of thousands of dollars. His forgeries of checks, letters, and loan agreements were considered flawless. "His expertness with the pen is a marvel," said one awed police chief, "in view of his being obliged to write with his left hand." The colonel's career was halted in 1884, when he was apprehended by New York City police. All the Southern charm in the world couldn't keep him out of prison: he was sent away for a very, very long time.

Sergei Rachmaninoff (1873–1943), Russian
composer and pianist

The rich and sensuous music of Rachmaninoff has thrilled concertgoers for almost a century now, despite the fact that he has come under increasing criticism from scholars and theorists: his music is sublimely accessible, which, as anyone who has suffered through a college course in aesthetics knows, means "unworthy"—at least in the rusty halls of academia. His Piano Concerto No. 2 (the last movement of which was cribbed for a popular song, "Full Moon and Empty Arms," in the 1940s), the rapturously lyrical Second Symphony, and his *Rhapsody on a Theme of Paganini* continue to thrill listeners as much as when they were premiered at the beginning of the twentieth century. In a career lasting more than five decades, Rachmaninoff was also regarded, in the words of one music historian, as "the most formidable pianist of his time." He had the largest known hand span of any human being: one hand could cover twelve white keys on the piano. Rachmaninoff could play a chord of C, E-flat, G, C, and G with his left hand alone.

Samuel R. Delany *(b. 1942), U.S. science fiction writer*

Generally speaking, dyslexia is a reading disorder associated with an inability to interpret letters and words and to integrate their meaning. It often manifests itself as a tendency to read words backwards or to confuse certain letters, such as *b* and *d*, or numbers, such as 6 and 9. However, no definition can evoke the syndrome as vividly as the following graphic description from noted science fiction writer—and dyslexic—Samuel R. Delany: "Imagine looking at a page—but the page is on a turntable, spinning slowly before you. And while it's turning, each word on the page is on its own small turntable, turning in different directions. Then, on top of those one-word turntables, each letter in each word is on a separate turntable. All of them are turning at different speeds, now changing directions, now changing back again, some getting faster, some getting slower. . . . That is what the ordinary page feels like for the young dyslexic." Not all dyslexics are left-handed, but the two traits are frequently linked: it's been estimated that left-handers are eleven times more likely to be dyslexic than right-handers. Some, but not all, dyslexia may be the result of attempts to "switch" a left-handed child to right-handedness. However, the exact cause of the syndrome is still open to controversy, with an increasing number of experts believing that it has a neurophysiological basis. (One startling clue to the nature of the problem is that swimming lessons at an early age seem to lessen dyslexia; the alternating right-brain/left-brain mechanics of swimming apparently strengthen key aspects of communication between the two hemispheres of the brain.) Because of the problems dyslexics have with reading, it is often mistakenly assumed that they are stupid or illiterate. There is, however, absolutely no link between dyslexia and illiteracy, as confirmed by even a brief list of some of the famous people who, like Delany, struggled with it: Virginia Woolf, F. Scott Fitzgerald, Gustave Flaubert, and William Butler Yeats.

On this day, in 1877, the first known "human cannonball" act was performed at a circus in the United States. In 1968, Stanley Kubrick's *2001: A Space Odyssey* was given its world premiere.

Hans Christian Andersen (1805–1875), Danish storyteller

The clever left-handed storyteller Hans Christian Andersen was—to put it delicately—peculiar. For one thing, he was hounded by the certainty he would one day be buried alive, and he propped a note—"I only seem dead"—by his bed every night so that overeager morticians wouldn't take him away by mistake. For another, he was pyrophobic: he had such an extreme horror of fire he packed huge lengths of rope with him whenever he traveled—so he'd have an easy means of escape if he were ever caught in a blaze. His father went insane and died in 1816, when Hans was still only a boy. (His maternal grandfather, meanwhile, was known as the town lunatic.) Andersen himself suffered from debilitating bouts of hypochondria and long, dark sieges of depression. He was high-strung, high-handed, ruthlessly ambitious, and often scathingly malicious to those around him. A better candidate for Prozac is hard to imagine. But then, of course, we might never have had his extraordinary gift to posterity: 156 of the most beautiful and poignant fairy tales ever written (and translated into more than a hundred languages), including "The Princess and the Pea," "Thumbelina," "The Emperor's New Clothes," and, all too appropriately, "The Ugly Duckling."

Charlemagne (742–814), King of the Franks

Charlemagne was the man who pulled together, by conquest, the bickering states and kingdoms of ninth-century western Europe. He then forcibly Christianized all of his conquered subjects, and ruled them as emperor for the next fourteen years. He brought peace, the Bible, and a reasonable level of prosperity to his kingdom. And Latin—he brought *lots* of Latin. For anyone who was forced to study Latin in school and hated every minute of it, Charlemagne is the man to thank: believing that Latin was the only proper language in which to study Christianity (or even *think* about it), he decreed that every school be required to teach the language to every student, a tradition that lasted well into the twentieth century.

Carmen Basilio *(b. 1927), U.S. boxer*

A natural left-hander who boxed right-handed, Basilio beat Tony Marco for the world welterweight title in 1955, and took the middleweight crown from Sugar Ray Robinson two years later. He was inducted into the International Boxing Hall of Fame in 1990. (See also July 6.)

On this day, in 1860, the Pony Express began operating between Missouri and California.

Marsha Mason *(b. 1942), U.S. actress*

Versatile actress, former wife of playwright Neil Simon, Mason is best known for her performances in the films *Cinderella Liberty* (1973), *The Goodbye Girl* (1977), *Chapter Two* (1979), and *Only When I Laugh* (1981), all of which garnered her Academy Award nominations as Best Actress.

On this day, in 1887, the first woman mayor in the U.S. was elected, in Argonia, Kansas. In 1896, the first modern Olympics opened, in Athens.

Anthony Perkins *(1932–1992), U.S. actor*

In the 1960 classic *Psycho*, Anthony Perkins tells a sympathetic Janet Leigh, "Mother, my mother—what is the phrase?—she isn't quite herself today." Obviously not. "She" was actually "he." For the left-handed Perkins, it was the role of a lifetime—and one he could never escape afterward. That his career started with a series of memorable, sensitive, sympathetic performances—in the films *Friendly Persuasion* (for which he was nominated for an Oscar in 1957), *The Matchmaker* (1958), and *On the Beach* (1959)—is hardly remembered by most film-goers. *Psycho* overshadows them all, and Perkins was trapped reprising the role, in one way or another, for the rest of his life.

On this day, in 1815, the Indonesian volcano Tambora erupted, creating such havoc with the world's weather that the following year was known as "the year without a summer."

Hilary Shepard Turner *(b. 1966), U.S. actress*

Left-handed actress, veteran of numerous films and TV shows, from the feature film comedies *Hunk* (1987) and *Troop Beverly Hills* (1989) to *The Golden Girls* and *Star Trek: Deep Space Nine*. Turner is best known as the villainous alien queen Divatox ("Bow down to me, you little peons!") in both the TV show *Power Rangers* and the Power Ranger feature films.

On this day, in 1917, the United States entered World War I, with a declaration of war on Germany. In 1938, Teflon was discovered.

Raphael (1483–1520), Italian painter

It's no coincidence that the three great artists of the High Renaissance—Michelangelo, Leonardo, and Raphael—were either left-handed or ambidextrous. The sheer scale of projects—church ceilings, twenty-foot-high tombs, palace walls—required a kind of grandiloquent obsessiveness typical of left-handers. And lest anyone think of the Renaissance as merely an elevated period of quiet and altruistic cerebral pursuits—something like an extended spiritual retreat in the woods—it should be remembered that it was in fact one of the most cutthroat, competitive periods in the history of art and that its princes and popes craved novelty—albeit, *civilized* novelty—in a way not too dissimilar from the twentieth century's insatiable appetite for variety, amusement, and innovation. Raphael, like his two older contemporaries, had a rebelliousness about him, an inability to accept the status quo and a compulsive drive to reexamine the world and persuade its inhabitants to accept *his* point of view. No wonder, against so many of the pretty, perfunctory, all-too-often sterile Renaissance works decorating chapel walls and papal apartments, Raphael's stunning achievements stand out so vividly: his figures are far more lyrical than others', his faces sweeter and more down-to-earth, his fascination is less with rigid aesthetics or religion-driven artistic dogma and more with feeling, expression, the commonality of all people. Like so many left-handers—whether artists, or baseball players, or actors, or con men—he felt compelled to break the rules.

7 Today is World Health Day. On this day, in 1949, the musical *South Pacific* opened on Broadway. In 1970, *Midnight Cowboy* became the first and only X-rated film to win the Academy Award for Best Picture.

Harry Hay *(b. 1912), U.S. social activist*

Hay is primarily remembered as an active, outspoken member of the U.S. Communist party in the 1940s and as an early agitator for trade unions. He also, in the 1950s, founded the first prominent homosexual rights organization in the U.S., the Mattachine Society. (And he was boyfriends for many years with—you'd better sit down—actor Will Geer, best known as Grandpa Walton on *The Waltons*.) Hay was born left-handed but was forced to switch by his father, an orchard farmer, who whipped him—brutally—whenever he used the "wrong" hand. In one instance, Hay's father beat him so savagely that Harry, barely a teenager, sustained permanent hearing loss in one ear. Hay's teachers were equally unsympathetic to his left-handedness: they forced him to write with his right hand. Ever the anarchist, Harry went back to writing with his left hand once he was out of school and on his own, and remained a southpaw—a leftist lefty—for the rest of his life.

John "Mugsy" McGraw *(1873–1934), U.S. baseball player*

"Mugsy"—a left-handed batter who played for the Baltimore Orioles from 1891 to 1902 and the New York Giants from 1902 to 1906—was known as a pugnacious player: he delighted in baiting umpires, and it wasn't unusual to see him in a cloud of dust on the baseball diamond as he pummeled teammates and opponents alike. Although he ended his career with an impressive .334 batting average, it isn't his prowess at bat he is most remembered for. In the spring of 1894, in the middle of a game between Baltimore and Boston, McGraw became incensed at the Boston third baseman and started slugging it out with him. It didn't take long for the entire roster of both teams to jump in, and as the players were hammering away at one another, spectators in the stands started fighting as well. In the ensuing free-for-all, someone set fire to the stadium, and the ballpark burned to the ground, taking nearly two hundred surrounding buildings with it. Despite his notoriety, McGraw eventually became manager of the Giants and led the team to nine National League pennants and three World Series victories. His players nicknamed him "Little Napoleon" for his dictatorial, take-no-prisoners style of management.

On this day, in 1974, Hank Aaron broke Babe Ruth's record by hitting his 715th home run. In 1988, televangelist Jimmy Swaggart was defrocked by the Assemblies of God Church.

Steve Mizerak *(b. 1944), U.S. billiards champion*

Left-hander Mizerak was the U.S. Open Pool champion four times during the 1970s. He won the 1976 World Open by shooting, left-handed, a perfect 150-ball run—a feat his opponent, Rusty Miller, likened to "swimming the English Channel underwater." Mizerak's talent didn't make him rich (tournament stakes were quite modest). Nor did his sharpshooting make him famous—until he appeared in a series of commercials for Miller Lite beer doing some of the most intriguing trick shots ever recorded on camera.

On this day, in 1865, General Lee surrendered to General Grant at Appomattox. In 1962, *West Side Story* won the Academy Award as Best Picture.

Dennis Quaid *(b. 1954), U.S. actor*

Popular, handsome, often strutting actor known for his light touch and relaxed physicality in such films as *Breaking Away* (1979), *The Right Stuff* (as astronaut Gordo Cooper—"the best damn pilot you ever saw"—in 1983), *Enemy Mine* (1985), *The Big Easy* (1986), *Innerspace* (1987), and *Dragonheart* (1996).

10

On this day, in 1997, NASA announced that data from the Jupiter-orbiter *Galileo* suggested that one of Jupiter's moons, Europa, had conditions favorable to the development of life.

Chuck Connors (1921–1992), U.S. actor

Former professional baseball player—for the Brooklyn Dodgers, the Chicago Cubs, and other teams between 1949 and 1951—Connors turned to acting in the early 1950s and achieved fame primarily on television, in the title role of the hit Western series *The Rifleman*, from 1958 to 1963. As a baseball player, he both batted and threw left-handed.

11

Today is National Heroes Day in Costa Rica. On this day, in 1898, the Spanish-American War began. In 1988, *The Last Emperor* was named Best Picture at the Academy Awards.

Louise Lasser (b. 1939), U.S. actress

Although she appeared in numerous popular films, including *Bananas* and *Everything You Always Wanted to Know About Sex But Were Afraid to Ask* (she played Gina, the woman who can only have sex in public places), the former wife of Woody Allen is best known as the star of the offbeat 1970s satirical soap opera *Mary Hartman, Mary Hartman*, in which she portrayed an angst-ridden, "average" American housewife frequently on the verge of a nervous breakdown over "waxy yellow buildup"—and other domestic disappointments—in her far-from-typical suburban household.

On this day, in 1961, Soviet astronaut Yuri Gagarin became the first human being into space when he and his *Vostok 1* spacecraft made a single orbit around the earth.

Tiny Tim (1925–1996), U.S. performer

The mortician-like, coiffure-impaired entertainer desperately needed a good creme rinse, but he nonetheless skyrocketed to national fame in the 1960s for strumming a ukulele left-handed and singing falsetto renditions of "Tiptoe Through the Tulips" on *Rowan and Martin's Laugh-In*. Later, to the astonishment of many (who presumed he had to be gay), he married his girlfriend, Miss Vicki, live on Johnny Carson's *Tonight Show*. It was one of the highest-rated episodes in *Tonight Show* history. Obscurity awaited him. He had bit parts in films like *One Trick Pony* (1980) and *Blood Harvest* (1987), but remained as fixed a cultural icon of the sixties as peace stickers and FLOWER POWER buttons. Interestingly, while he played the ukulele left-handed, he played guitar right-handed. (Tiny Tim's birthday is also listed, in various sources, as December 30.)

On this day, in 1895, Alfred Dreyfus became the first prisoner incarcerated on Devil's Island. In 1997, Tiger Woods won the PGA Masters tournament.

Eudora Welty (b. 1909), U.S. writer

Welty is one of the great stylists in American literature, and if her name isn't quite a household word it's probably due to the fact that she—like that other supreme American stylist Willa Cather—didn't spend a lot of time fighting in foreign revolutions, or deep-sea fishing in Cuba, or chasing bulls in Barcelona. Americans, always a bit ticklish about "the arts," often prefer their writers to be as unwriterly as possible. Still, Welty's short stories have only grown in stature with time, and they belie—*decimate* would be a better word—the notion that all left-handers are "lexicographically challenged." Like most left-handers of her generation, Welty was forced, by schoolteachers, to write with her right hand. Her father, unfortunately, approved of the switch. "He pointed out," Welty writes in her poignant memoir *One Writer's Beginnings*, "that everything in life had been made for the convenience of right-handed people, because they were the majority, and he often used 'what the majority wants' as a criterion for what was best." Ironically, Welty's mother was left-handed, as were five of her uncles  and her maternal grandmother. (Her maternal grandfather, a lawyer, was ambidextrous: he could, according to Welty, "write with both hands at the same time, also backwards and forwards and upside down, different words with each hand.") "My continuing passion," Welty once wrote of her vision of life, "is to part a curtain, that invisible shadow that falls between people—the veil of indifference to each other's presence, each other's wonder, each other's human plight."

Ron Perlman (b. 1950), U.S. actor

The left-handed actor is best known as "the Beast" on the popular TV series *Beauty and the Beast* in the late 1980s.

14

On this day, in 1865, President Lincoln was assassinated. In 1902, the first J.C. Penney's opened, in Kemmerer, Wyoming.

Rod Steiger (b. 1925), U.S. actor

Steiger won a Best Actor Oscar for his performance in the 1967 melodrama *In the Heat of the Night*, and was nominated for Academy Awards on two other occasions: for *On the Waterfront* in 1954 (in which he played Marlon Brando's brother) and *The Pawnbroker* in 1965.

15 Today is the deadline for filing income tax returns in the United States. On this day, in 1912, the *Titanic* sank.

Leonardo da Vinci *(1452–1519), Italian scientist and artist*

Trying to summarize the life of left-hander Leonardo da Vinci in a single, pithy paragraph is like trying to explain quantum physics on a matchbook cover. Here, then, are the basic facts:

- He painted the Mona Lisa, which, after centuries of speculation, may simply have been a portrait of Leonardo himself in the guise of a woman. In 1986, art historian Lillian Schwartz used computers to analyze every aspect of the painting, arguably the most famous in the world. She discovered that the features of Leonardo's other self-portraits aligned almost perfectly with the major features of the Mona Lisa. She made no speculation as to whether the painting was meant as a prank or an exercise, or was merely an accident of the unconscious.

- He painted the spectacular fresco *The Last Supper* in the refectory of the monastery of Santa Maria delle Grazie in Milan. The fresco, despite recent valiant efforts at restoration, is still in danger of being lost forever, since Leonardo used experimental pigments to paint it.

- He excelled at architecture, engineering, sculpting, and painting, and advanced astonishingly prescient theories in ballistics, aviation, biology, deep-sea diving, embalming, fluid mechanics, and weaponry design. And, yes, he came up with the idea for the helicopter (and drew a diagram of it in his notebooks) five hundred years before the fact.

- He left behind numerous portfolios full of observations on life, nature, and human anatomy, all written in "mirror writing," a minute backwards script that ran from right to left. Said the sixteenth-century Italian art historian Vasari, "He wrote backwards in rude characters, and with the left hand, so that anyone who is not practiced in reading them, cannot understand them." Some of

Leonardo's contemporaries speculated that he used the baffling script to conceal potentially heretical thoughts about God and nature. Modern theorists continue to argue about the significance of the mirror script but rarely seem to consider the possibility that Leonardo—who took an astonishing pleasure in almost everything he did—did it, yes, for privacy, but also simply because he *could*. God, as that other left-hander Lenny Bruce once ruefully observed, likes to have fun, too.

Robert Walker, Jr. *(b. 1940), U.S. actor*

The offbeat actor was switched to right-handed penmanship as a boy but continued to be left-handed for most other activities, including painting and drawing. Walker is best known for his performance in the title role of the 1964 film *Ensign Pulver*, as well as for appearances in *The War Wagon* (1967), *The Happening* (1967), and *Easy Rider* (1969).

Hans Conried *(1917–1982), U.S. actor*

Memorably staid character actor best remembered for his appearance as "the Elocution Instructor" on an episode of *I Love Lucy*, and for his narration of the popular series *Fractured Fairy Tales* in the 1960s. He was also the voice of Snidely Whiplash on *The Bullwinkle Show*.

Emma Thompson *(b. 1959), British actress*

Radiant, multifaceted actress, winner of an Oscar for Best Actress for her performance in *Howards End* (1992) and another Oscar, for Best Screenplay, for her adaptation of Jane Austen's *Sense and Sensibility* (1995).

16

On this day, in 1926, the first in-flight movie—*The Lost World*—was shown on a commercial flight from London to Paris.

Charlie Chaplin
(1889–1977), British actor, director, and screenwriter

It's astonishing that Charlie Chaplin could laugh about anything: his childhood was like something out of *Oliver Twist*. Abandoned at an early age at an orphanage for destitute children, he suffered constant deprivations, cold, and hunger, and was incessantly whipped for small infractions of the rules. When he forgot to make his bed the day before Christmas, the orphanage staff punished him by withholding his Christmas present: an orange and a few pieces of candy. More to the point, he was regularly punished for being left-handed. Whenever he tried to write with his left hand, his teachers rapped him over the knuckles. Chaplin defied them, until one teacher finally beat the offending hand black and blue; only then did the boy acquiesce and teach himself to write with his right hand. "The only benefit of that episode," one biographer noted, "was a dubious one: all his life Chaplin was ambidextrous." (Go rent *City Lights*, the 1931 Charlie Chaplin masterpiece in which Chaplin's left hand provides the key to the film's staggeringly emotional conclusion. The film—ranked as one of the ten greatest of all time—and the finale, described by one critic as "the most poetic thirty seconds in the history of cinema," are an enduring testament to Chaplin's genius.)

Peter Ustinov *(b. 1921), British actor and writer*

Multitalented figure—author, director, actor, diplomat—the son of a Russian journalist and a French painter, Ustinov is perhaps best known to recent audiences as detective Hercule Poirot in the films *Death on the Nile, Evil Under the Sun,* and *Appointment with Death.* He won Academy Awards for his performances in *Spartacus* (1960) and *Topkapi* (1964), but is a veteran of over sixty films, ranging from breezy comedies—*One of Our Dinosaurs Is Missing* (1976), *The Great Muppet Caper* (1981)—to hard-hitting dramas like *Billy Budd* (1962) and *Lorenzo's Oil* (1992). He has also done work for the United Nations, and has been the goodwill ambassador for UNICEF since 1971. He was knighted in 1990.

17

Today is Flag Day in American Samoa. On this day, in 1790, Benjamin Franklin died. In 1964, the Ford Mustang was introduced to the American public.

Norman "Boomer" Esiason *(b. 1961),*
U.S. football player

Left-handed quarterback for the Cincinnati Bengals, Esiason is ranked ninth all-time in the NFL, with 36,442 passing yards and 2,851 completions. He was named the NFL's Man of the Year in 1995. Off the playing field, he is a national figure in the fight against cystic fibrosis. More than just another wealthy sports celebrity looking to temper his image with well-publicized "good works," Esiason has a son, Gunnar, afflicted with the condition. Through tireless activism, Esiason has raised more than $2.5 million in money for research against the disease through the Boomer Esiason Heroes Foundation. Esiason is also a published novelist; his first novel, *Toss*, was published in 1998.

18

On this day, in 1775, Paul Revere made his famous midnight ride to warn American colonists that "the British are coming!" In 1906, San Francisco was devastated by the most destructive earthquake in its history.

Clarence Darrow (1857–1938), U.S. defense attorney

If at the beginning of the twentieth century there were still people who thought left-handers were the minions of Lucifer, then in July 1925 the citizens of Dayton, Tennessee, must have thought that the Satanic Majesty himself had arrived in their quiet and conservative town. Not only was renowned defense attorney Clarence Darrow left-handed, but he had come to Dayton to defend John T. Scopes, a high school teacher arrested for teaching evolution in the public schools. The eleven-day courtroom battle that followed pitted Darrow's skepticism and agnosticism against the crowd-pleasing religious theatrics of beloved lawyer William Jennings Bryan. Darrow lost the case—and the law itself wasn't repealed until 1967—but he won in the broader judgment of history. The case was typical of his stubborn, relentless rebelliousness: Darrow took unpopular cases as a matter of deep conscience. "I had little respect for the opinion of the crowd," he wrote in his 1932 autobiography, *The Story of My Life*. "My instinct was to doubt the majority view." Denounced from pulpits, excoriated by traditionalists, threatened on more than one occasion with bodily injury at the hands of vigilante mobs, Darrow defended socialists, anarchists, thrill-seeking murderers, atheists, labor leaders, terrorists, and assassins. He did it out of a deep-rooted conviction that the law is all that stands between civilization and the jungle, and that the litmus test of humanity is how society treats its most reprehensible and despised members. It was not a popular point of view. In a typical case—the Sweet Case of 1926—Darrow defended an African-American family thrown into jail for fighting back against a white mob that tried to evict them from their Detroit home for no reason other than prejudice. (The law at the time did not look kindly on blacks defending themselves for any reason.) Darrow won their acquittal—and strengthened his reputation as a "godless," "dangerous" man. Despite his brilliance and his unswerving principles, his cynicism and repeated battles with public opinion took their toll. "Had I known about life in advance," he said, looking back, "and been given a choice in the matter, I most likely would have declined the adventure. . . . There are times when I feel otherwise, but on the whole I believe that life is not worthwhile."

On this day, in 1988, Sonny Bono became the mayor of Palm Springs, California. In 1995, a truck bomb ripped through the federal building in Oklahoma City, killing 168 people and injuring more than 500.

Don Adams *(b. 1926), U.S. actor*

The left-handed comic actor found fame as Agent Maxwell Smart on the hit TV series *Get Smart*, from 1965 to 1970, but—like Anthony Perkins in *Psycho*—was straitjacketed in the role for the rest of his career. He often expressed weariness at the hordes of individuals, each one thinking he or she was the first to do so, who came up to him at airports, bars, or on the street, speaking into a shoe in their hand (Maxwell Smart's shoe-phone was one of his trademarks) and uttering the words, "Would you believe . . ."

On this day, in 1940, the first electron microscope was publicly demonstrated. In 1949, cortisone was discovered.

Ryan O'Neal *(b. 1941), U.S. actor*

Left-hander O'Neal has had several moments of glory in his long career: in the 1972 comedy *What's Up Doc?* with Barbra Streisand, in the 1973 comedy *Paper Moon*, and even in the 1970 soap opera hit *Love Story*, for which he was nominated for a Best Actor Oscar. His greatest moment came in the visually stunning 1975 epic *Barry Lyndon*: it was a strangely haunting performance (even if disconcerting to those who could never see him as anything but callow Rodney

Harrington on *Peyton Place*), and since the film—one of Stanley Kubrick's numerous masterpieces—is almost guaranteed a very long life, O'Neal is certain to enjoy a measure of immortality as well.

Don Mattingly *(b. 1961), U.S. baseball player*

Though naturally ambidextrous, Mattingly made an early choice to bat and throw exclusively with his left hand in order to better his chances of making it into the major leagues. The strategy worked. He batted .343 in 1983 and .352 in 1986 and became one of the most powerful home-run sluggers in the major leagues: in 1987, he set a new major-league record by hitting six grand slams. Considered one of the game's best first basemen, he was also the last major-league left-hander to have played second and third base. He retired in 1996.

21 Today marks the beginning of the astrological sign Taurus. On this day, in 1509, Henry VIII became King of England. In 1910, Mark Twain died.

Elizabeth II *(b. 1926),*
Queen of England

Like her son Charles, her grandson William, and her mother, Elizabeth, the queen is left-handed—which also gives her something in common with the entertainer who does the best impression of her, Carol Burnett. Unlike Carol Burnett, her father, great-grandfather, and her great-great-grandmother, Queen Victoria, were also left-handed.

22 Today is Queen Isabella Day in Spain. On this day, in 1823, roller skates were invented. In 1969, the first human eye transplant was successfully performed.

Eddie Albert *(b. 1908), U.S. actor*

Enter the title *Green Acres* on the Internet Movie Database and you'll find the keywords *comedy/farm/small-town/surreal*. What *could* be more surreal than two penthouse-dwelling Manhattanites transplanted to a place called Hooterville, where hay fever, Arnold the pig, and Fred and Doris Ziffel awaited them? Left-hander Eddie Albert was the star, but it was Eva Gabor, as the irrepressibly ditsy Lisa Douglas, who usually stole the show. Wardrobed in diaphanous gowns and oversized jewelry, she kept trying to apply the mind-set of jet-setting, socialite New York to her new hayseed, rural environment, often with bizarre results. Hooterville was a counterclockwise world in which everything seemed to run backwards to her inclinations. A classic fish-out-of-water saga if ever there was one—and something every left-hander could identify with.

Glen Campbell *(b. 1936), U.S. singer*

Popular singer of the 1960s and 1970s, Campbell had numerous hits, including "Wichita Lineman" and "Rhinestone Cowboy." He also appeared in several films, notably *True Grit* (1969) and *Norwood* (1970).

Charlotte Rae *(b. 1926), U.S. actress*

Rae is best known as Mrs. Garrett on the hit TV series *The Facts of Life*, which ran from 1979 to 1986.

23 Today is St. George's Day in England. On this day, in 1996, hundreds of personal items from the estate of Jacqueline Kennedy Onassis went on the auction block in New York City, eventually netting $34.5 million.

Alphonse Bertillon (1853–1914), French criminologist

Working for the Paris police, Bertillon developed a method of cataloging convicted criminals (later superseded by fingerprinting) that incorporated precise body measurements, photographs, and minute physical descriptions. The cumbersome method, called *bertillonage*, was widely adopted by police throughout Europe; all that remains of it today is the mug shot, which Bertillon was the first to use. Bertillon also fancied himself, among other things, an expert handwriting analyst. He should've stuck to mug shots: it was partly on his grossly mistaken testimony that French army captain Alfred Dreyfus was convicted and sent to Devil's Island, in one of the most scandalous miscarriages of justice in the nineteenth century. In his own life, the left-handed criminologist was plagued, like many left-handers, by indecipherable penmanship; in fact, it was his "horrifying" handwriting that led him to find a wife. Due to repeated complaints from colleagues, Bertillon was forced to hire a full-time secretary to recopy his manuscripts before they could be submitted to publishers. Amelie Notar, the Austrian girl who took the unenviable position, eventually became Madame Bertillon.

24

On this day, in 1800, the Library of Congress was established. In 1981, the first personal computer was introduced, by IBM.

Jean-Paul Gaultier *(b. 1952), French fashion designer*

The man who gave the world Madonna's cone bra, and who turned underwear into outerwear, has a decidedly left-handed approach to fashion: rules are made to be broken, and breaking them should be fun. "Beauty does not always appear where you think it should," he once told an interviewer. "Even in the ugliest of circumstances, it's all around us in one form or another. I think if we learned that, we'd make great strides toward the eradication of prejudices. If people loved things that were different rather than fearing things that were different, beauty would blossom everywhere."

Shirley MacLaine

(b. 1934–this life), U.S. actress

Next time you, or someone you know, is tempted to dismiss left-hander MacLaine as "that flaky high priestess of reincarnation," pull out the following list of films, pausing for a moment on each to remember the pleasure it gave you: *Around the World in Eighty Days* (1956), *The Matchmaker* (1958), *Some Came Running* (Oscar-nominated performance, 1959), *The Apartment* (Oscar-nominated performance, 1960), *The Children's Hour* (1962), *My Geisha* (1962), *Irma La Douce* (Oscar-nominated performance, 1963), *Sweet Charity* (1969), *The Turning Point* (Oscar-nominated performance, 1977), *Being There* (1979), *Terms of Endearment* (Oscar-winning performance, 1983), *Steel*

Magnolias (1989), *Postcards from the Edge* (1990), and *Guarding Tess* (1994). (MacLaine also received a sixth Oscar nomination in 1975, for the documentary *The Other Half of the Sky: A China Memoir*, which she wrote, produced, and codirected.) Whether or not she's had multiple lives on a spiritual plane that spans the centuries, she's had multiple lives in *this* century as an actress, dancer, nightclub performer, writer, spiritual guru, and film producer. Given her remarkable accomplishments in entertainment, most people couldn't care less, one way or the other, who she was in ancient Egypt, medieval Europe, or anywhere else.

25

On this day, in 1982, the *Jane Fonda Workout* videotape went on sale. In 1990, the Hubble space telescope was deployed.

Edward R. Murrow *(1908–1965), U.S. journalist*

The pioneering CBS News journalist, acclaimed for the trend-setting weekly programs *See It Now* (starting in 1951) and *Person to Person* (1953–60), not only had a profound impact on the field of television journalism but influenced U.S. politics with his exposé of Senator Joseph McCarthy in 1954 (his investigative work led to the termination of McCarthy's largely undocumented witch-hunt for Communists in U.S. government circles and Hollywood) and his 1960 documentary *Harvest of Shame*, which exposed, in compelling detail, the appalling circumstances of migratory farm workers.

Albert King *(b. 1923), U.S. blues musician*

The guitarist and blues innovator achieved a magical mix of electric guitar and traditional blues, with a smooth, wailing style that directly influenced such later stars as Jimi Hendrix, Eric Clapton, and Stevie Ray Vaughan.

26

On this day, in 1977, Studio 54 opened in New York City.

Carol Burnett *(b. 1933),*
U.S. comedienne and actress

Left-handers have always tended toward an absurdist view of the world. Right-handers may try to reason everything out, dissecting the fine points of existence, but left-handers are more likely to laugh at the "everything" *and* the dissection of it. It's hard to imagine a right-hander coming up with a parody of *Gone With the Wind* in which the heroine, renamed Starlett, grabs the living room drapes, rod and all, and throws them over her shoulders to make a grand impression on Rhett Butler. Carol Burnett has, throughout her career, basked in the absurd. As *New York Times* critic Robert Berkvist once noted, "She has a keen sense of the absurd, a genius for exaggeration, impeccable timing, and a wonderously plastic face." Another critic noted that she had a "genius for inhabiting a limitless range of characters, especially the blissfully loony." The daughter of divorced alcoholics, Burnett was raised by her grandmother in Los Angeles; her trademark left-handed earlobe tug, which she started using on television in 1955, was meant as a greeting to Granny White, who, like Carol, was left-handed.

On this day, in 1865, Cornell University was chartered. In 1947, Norwegian explorer Thor Heyerdahl set sail from Peru for Tahiti on his raft, the *Kon-Tiki*.

Earl Anthony (b. *1938*), U.S. bowler

Called "the greatest bowler in pro tour history," left-hander Anthony won forty-two PBA Tournament championships, was named Bowler of the Year three times, and won the PBA National Championship.

On this day, in 1789, Fletcher Christian seized control of the H.M.S. *Bounty* and led a mutiny against Captain William Bligh. In 1987, the nuclear power plant at Chernobyl began meltdown.

Jay Leno (b. *1950*), U.S. talk show host

The left-handed star of *The Tonight Show* was, in his own words, "mildly dyslexic" growing up. "I got C's and D's in school," he told *Playboy* magazine in 1996. "You'll hear me mix up words in the monolog sometimes. And one thing about mildly dyslexic people— they're good at setting everything else aside to pursue one goal. I go five nights a week, every week, no days off, no sick days." Leno has also said he gets only three or four hours of sleep a night. "Most creative-type people appear to be left-handed," he's asserted.

29 Today is the emperor's birthday in Japan. On this day, in 1803, the Louisiana Purchase was made. In 1913, the modern zipper was patented.

Jerry Seinfeld (b. *1955*), *U.S. comic*

Since Seinfeld has said that the real Jerry and the TV Jerry are the same guys, what can be said about him that everyone doesn't already know? "They know me better than they know Dan Rather," he once said. "You couldn't predict what Dan Rather would do in most situations, but I think you could with me." One of the things that irritates him most is when strangers on the street try to make him laugh. "Could you explain that to me, please?" he once asked an interviewer. "What the hell is that phenomenon? If I meet singers, I don't go, 'Hey, what do you think of this?' and sing."

Henri Poincaré (*1854–1912*), *French mathematician, astronomer, and philosopher*

The ambidextrous Poincaré was one of the greatest mathematicians of the nineteenth century, as well as a brilliant writer in the field of philosophy of science. As a young man in school, he excelled at both composition and math but was poor in sports and art. He also had a photographic memory—which came in handy since he was so painfully nearsighted that not even corrective lenses could entirely compensate for the deficiency. Among friends and colleagues, he was renowned for his ability to perform long, complicated mathematical calculations instantly in his head. Poincaré not only made huge contributions to the fields of celestial mechanics, topology, and algebra, he wrote eloquently, at length, on the role of the unconscious and of pure intuition in scientific research and discovery.

Today is Walpurgisnacht in Germany, Scandinavia, and various other countries. On this day, in 1931, the Empire State Building was completed.

Cloris Leachman (b. *1926*), *U.S. actress*

Not all left-handers have indecipherable handwriting, and not everyone with bad penmanship is left-handed. Still, the two traits sometimes seem to go together. Small wonder, since virtually every aspect of writing—right down to the spiral notebooks with those oh-so-painful rings on the left—is geared toward the right-handed majority. Like many left-handers, Oscar-winning actress Cloris Leachman was no stranger to less-than-satisfactory penmanship grades in school. "In those days," she once recalled, "I would smudge everything as I'd write. I still have to sign autographs with my hand up in the air like the body of a tarantula."

Ian Ziering (b. *1964*), *U.S. actor*

The handsome, athletic, left-handed actor has become a modern-day heartthrob as a result of his portrayal of Steve Sanders on the hit TV show *Beverly Hills 90210*.

Left-handers Born in
May

*May: Fifth month of the year, named after Maia,
Roman goddess of fire*

Today is May Day, a festival of spring celebrated throughout the world. On this day, in 1967, Elvis Presley married Priscilla Beaulieu. In 1973, *Playgirl* magazine debuted.

Arthur William Patrick Albert, Duke of Connaught and Strathearn (1850–1942),
British royal

If any family in history attests to the genetic origins of left-handedness, it's the British royal family, that zany, madcap, irrepressible brood of subversives, insurrectionists, and blue-blooded party animals. Okay, we exaggerate—omit *madcap*. Queen Victoria—herself left-handed (see May 24)—had nine children, several of them also left-handers. Arthur William Patrick Albert was her third son, and his mother's favorite. If there was an interesting or eccentric thing about him, history books have conspired to conceal it. He was an able administrator and military man, he served competently in Egypt (commanding the First Guards Brigade at Tel al Kebir), and served in India and Ireland as well. In 1911, his mother made him governor-general of Canada. He wasn't popular in the position—the Canadians found him too officious and meddlesome—and he left the post in 1916. After that, he increasingly withdrew from public life and into obscurity. But like his mother—and dozens of her ancestors and descendants—he was left-handed, though switched to right-handedness at an early age. One can only hope that behind closed doors he led a secret and more typically left-handed life of wearing lampshades on his head and scribbling outrageous cartoons of his mum.

On this day, in 1945, Karl Donitz succeeded Adolf Hitler as President of the Third Reich and supreme commander of the Nazi military, after Hitler committed suicide in Berlin; Donitz's presidency only lasted a few days.

Eddie Collins (1887–1951), U.S. baseball player

The left-handed batter for Philadelphia and Chicago started playing major-league ball in 1906 and had the longest major-league career of any twentieth-century player: twenty-five years, ending in 1930, when he was forty-three. He batted above .300 for eighteen of those years, and ended his major-league stint with a .333 career average; his best year was 1920, when he batted .372. His teammates nicknamed him "Cocky" for his unfailing confidence at bat.

On this day, in 1988, Madonna made her Broadway debut in the play *Speed-the-Plow*.

Eppa Jeptha Rixey (1891–1963), U.S. baseball player

His name, a teammate once observed, "sounds like a cross between a Greek letter fraternity and a college yell." The six-foot-five left-handed pitcher—who originally planned to be a chemist, before being discovered by the coach of the University of Virginia baseball team—played major-league ball for twenty-one years, for the Phillies and the Cincinnati Reds. His career included 4,494 innings pitched,

39 shutouts, and 266 lifetime victories. Not especially known for his batting, he hit only three home runs during his entire major-league stint. When he called his fiancée after hitting one of them in St. Louis in 1924, she exclaimed, "Something dreadful is about to happen in St. Louis if you hit a home run." The next day, the city was struck by a tornado. Rixley was elected to the Baseball Hall of Fame in 1963.

On this day, in 1904, work began on the Panama Canal. In 1968, McDonald's introduced the Big Mac.

Beatrice Mitchell (1914–1987), *U.S. baseball player*

The seventeen-year-old, left-handed, female pitcher was the only woman known to have pitched against baseball legends Babe Ruth and Lou Gehrig. Signed to the Chattanooga Lookouts, a minor-league team, in 1931, she pitched an exhibition game against the New York Yankees on April 2. She proceeded to strike out both Babe Ruth—who stormed away from the plate enraged—and Lou Gehrig; she then walked Hall of Fame second baseman Tony Lazzeri. Although there were immediate accusations that the exhibition was a publicity stunt, Mitchell maintained to her dying day that she had honestly fanned the two titans of baseball. Given her background, there was little reason to doubt her: despite her age, she had already made a name for herself in both high school and the semipros, and had earned a reputation for a lethal drop pitch. Unfortunately, soon after the April 2 exhibition game, her contract with the Lookouts was voided by baseball commissioner Kenesaw Landis, who declared that the only place for women in baseball was in the bleachers. Although Mitchell continued to amaze spectators at barnstorming games and exhibitions over the next six years, in 1937 she returned to her native Chattanooga and went to work for her father, an optometrist. (See also February 18 and December 21.)

Today is Cinco de Mayo in Mexico. On this day, in 1961, Alan Shepard became the first U.S. astronaut in space, when his *Freedom 7* space capsule made a fifteen-minute suborbital flight.

Lee Richmond (1857–1929), *U.S. baseball player*

The first full-time left-handed pitcher for the major leagues (see also February 6), Richmond was also the first player in major-league history to pitch a perfect game. Nicknamed "the Heartside Heaver" for his left-handedness, Richmond played for the Worcester Brown Stockings from 1879 to 1882, then for the Providence Grays in 1883, and finally for Cincinnati in 1886. Problems with his pitching arm forced his early retirement from the game.

On this day, in 1937, the dirigible *Hindenburg* burst into flames as it attempted to land at Lakehurst, New Jersey. In 1954, Roger Bannister broke the four-minute mile.

Mare Winningham (b. 1959), *U.S. actress*

The Emmy-winning left-handed actress, veteran of more than forty films and television shows, was nominated for an Academy Award for Best Supporting Actress for her performance in the 1995 sibling-rivalry drama *Georgia*, starring Jennifer Jason Leigh. Her other films include *St. Elmo's Fire* (1985), *Turner and Hooch* (with Tom Hanks, in 1989), and *The War* (1994).

On this day, in 1824, Beethoven's Ninth Symphony was premiered, in Vienna. In 1915, the luxury liner *Lusitania* was sunk by a German torpedo during World War I, killing 1,198 passengers.

William Henry Ireland (1777–1835), British

forger

The precocious, ambidextrous son of a noted London engraver, young Ireland demonstrated a talent for deception and fakery at an astonishingly early age: as a boy, he took one of his father's seventeenth-century books and forged a handwritten dedication on the flyleaf—from the book's author to Queen Elizabeth. His father, an expert on autographs and antiquarian books, was completely duped by the forgery. Emboldened by his success—and having recently secured a blank piece of authentic Elizabethan parchment—little William, barely in his early teens, went on to forge a property lease: this time, signed "Wm. Shakespeare." The document (worth a fortune if authentic) fooled not only his father but various Shakespeare scholars, including James Boswell. The strangely gifted boy genius then quietly moved on to bigger and better things: he fabricated an entire, fictitious correspondence between Shakespeare and the Earl of Southampton. His natural ambidexterity was especially helpful in the undertaking: to achieve completely distinctive signatures, he forged all of Shakespeare's letters with his right hand, the earl's replies with his left. *Still* not out of his teens—and completely overwhelmed by his unexpected success so far—he decided to forge an entire, previously unheard-of masterpiece by Shakespeare; the resulting play—a tragedy lugubriously titled *Vortigern and Rowena*—was produced on the London stage by renowned theater impresario Richard Sheridan. The play's opening night—attended by more than two thousand people—proved to be young Ireland's undoing. Doubters in the audience became vocal less than halfway through the performance, and eventually even the actors onstage succumbed to the absurdity of the sophomoric dialogue they were reciting: howls of laughter greeted the ill-fated production, the actors began to play the tragedy for laughs, and Ireland fled, panic-stricken, into the night. "Had the play of *Vortigern* succeeded with the public, and the manuscript been acknowledged as genuine," he later confessed, "it was my intention to have completed a series of plays from the reign of William the Conqueror to that of Queen Elizabeth; that is to say, I should have planned a drama on every reign the subject of which had not been treated by Shakespeare." Ireland eventually published a best-selling book titled *An Authentic Account of the Shakespearean Manuscripts*, in which he acknowledged all of his forgeries and hoaxes.

8

On this day, in 1903, artist Paul Gauguin died in Tahiti. In 1970, the last Beatles album, *Let It Be*, was released.

Harry S Truman

(1884–1972), U.S. president

Truman, like many left-handers, was drawn to iconoclasm of any sort, and perhaps nowhere is that better reflected than in his now legendary use of uncouth, often blatantly scatological language. He once attended a flower show in the nation's capital with his wife, Bess, and inadvertently offended several onlookers with his repeated references to the "good manure" used to raise such splendid blossoms. "Bess," a prim friend finally asked, "couldn't you please get the president to say 'fertilizer'?" Said Bess, without missing a beat, "Heavens, no. It took me twenty-five years to get him to say 'manure.'"

Peter Benchley *(b. 1940), U.S. writer*

Benchley is the best-selling author of *Jaws*, *The Deep*, and *The Island*.

Don Rickles *(b. 1926), U.S. comic*

The left-handed nightclub comic—and occasional actor on television and in films—is known for his relentless insults and intentionally obnoxious style. "At his best," said critic Kenneth Tynan in 1978, "he breaks through the bad-taste barrier into a world of sheer outrage where no forbidden thought goes unspoken and where everything is anarchically liberating." Another, less charitable critic once described him as "the Lizzie Borden of one-liners."

On this day, in 1899, the lawn mower was invented. In 1960, birth control pills were approved for sale in the United States.

Tony Gwynn *(b. 1960), U.S. baseball player*

Gwynn ended each season between 1983 and 1997 above .300, and in 1994 batted .394, the highest major-league average since 1941. In 1997, Gwynn's .340 career average placed him fourteenth on the all-time list, a tie with Lou Gehrig.

On this day, in 1994, Nelson Mandela became the first black president of South Africa.

Gary Owens *(b. 1936), U.S. comic actor*

Owens became an instant celebrity in 1968 as the deadpan announcer—with his hand cupped to his ear—on *Rowan and Martin's Laugh-In*. One of only four regulars who were with the show from its premiere to its cancellation (the other three were the hosts—Dan Rowan and Dick Martin—and Ruth Buzzi), he managed to convey, week after week, the impression of a man one step away from a nervous breakdown but always valiantly clinging to his sanity nonetheless.

On this day, in 1858, Minnesota was admitted to the Union. In 1997, a 7.1 earthquake hit northeastern Iran, killing over 2,500 people and leaving more than 40,000 homeless.

Chang (1811–1874), Siamese twin

The "original" Siamese twins—the generic use of the term was derived from their international fame—Chang was left-handed, Eng was not. It was left-handedness by necessity: Chang stood on his brother's left, and the use of his right hand would have been awkward for both men.

On this day, in 1937, George VI was crowned King of England. In 1959, Elizabeth Taylor married Eddie Fisher.

Bruce Boxleitner (b. 1950), U.S. actor

A durable leading man of television shows and made-for-TV movies, left-hander Boxleitner starred in the popular series *Scarecrow and Mrs. King* (with Kate Jackson), from 1983 to 1987, and in the sci-fi series *Babylon 5*, beginning in 1995.

On this day, in 1846, the Mexican-American War officially began. In 1950, the first Diners Club card was issued.

Armistead Maupin (b. 1944), U.S. writer

Maupin's daily serial, "Tales of the City," debuted in the *San Francisco Chronicle* in May 1976, and was later turned into the best-selling novel *Tales of the City* and its numerous sequels.

Lari White (b. 1965), U.S. country singer

A left-handed guitarist, White was nominated for a TNN/MCN Country Music Award for her duet, "Helping Me Get Over You," with Travis Tritt.

14 On this day, in 1948, Israel became an independent nation. In 1996, Antonio Banderas and Melanie Griffith were married.

David Byrne (b. 1952),
Scottish composer

Students at the Rhode Island School of Design realized there was something unique about fellow undergraduate David Byrne when, for one of his assignments, he gave a performance in which, to an accordion accompaniment, he had his beard and hair shaved off onstage while a beautiful chowgirl flipped large cue cards written in Russian. That was in 1971, and Byrne was eighteen. Shortly afterward, he was asked to leave the school. Byrne's multitalented (and distinctly left-handed) genius defies easy summary. Composer, photographer, author, and even occasionally an actor (he appeared in a short film, *Trying Time*, made by his close friend director Jonathan Demme, and had a part in the 1989 Jeff Daniels comedy *Checking Out*), Byrne won an Oscar for his commanding and haunting score for the film *The Last Emperor* in 1987, gained critical acclaim for his deeply unusual 1995 book of photographs *Strange Ritual*, and has produced albums for such diverse groups as the B-52s and Fun Boy Three. He is best known to the MTV generation as the lead singer of the offbeat group Talking Heads. The word "anarchy"—with its implication of pointlessness—doesn't begin to describe his odd yet likable, and often mesmerizing, perspective, a perspective that takes its cue from the left-handed impulse to disassemble the entire world and then reassemble the tiniest pieces into new and meaningful shapes. "A whole culture can be revealed in some very simple objects," he once said. "You can extrapolate from something very mundane. It's been an interest of mine for a long time." Far from being another shock-o-rama rock star trying to cash in on the institutionalized craziness that is adolescence, Byrne has earnestly taken to heart—and given a very sensible meaning to—the title of one of his most popular songs, "Stop Making Sense."

On this day, in 1940, nylons went on sale in the United States for the first time. In 1971, the Rolling Stones album *Sticky Fingers* entered the nation's Top 40.

George Brett (b. 1953), U.S. baseball player

Between 1975 and 1988, left-hander Brett batted over .300 ten times, and his .390 average for 1980 remains the highest in the major leagues since Ted Williams batted .406 in 1941. After he led the Royals to a World Series victory in 1985, BRETT FOR PRESIDENT bumper stickers were seen all over Kansas City.

On this day, in 1866, root beer was invented. In 1986, the film *Top Gun* opened in U.S. theaters.

John Leitham (b. 1954), U.S. jazz musician

The left-handed, Grammy-nominated bassist has played with Mel Tormé, Doc Severinsen, and Bob Cooper, among others. His second solo CD, released in 1994, was titled *The Southpaw*. His third CD, in 1996, was *Lefty Leaps In*. Fellow bassist Milt Hinton once commented, "John has amazing dexterity and a big sound. He is all over the bass when he plays and the fact that he's a southpaw makes him even more unique." "The funny thing is," Leitham has said, "I'm right-handed for almost everything else. . . . I guess I'm ambidextrous."

Today is Constitution Day in Norway. On this day, in 1875, the first Kentucky Derby was held. In 1954, the U.S. Supreme Court ruled that segregated schools were illegal.

Jody Racicot (b. *1968*), U.S. actor

Left-handed actor seen in the feature films *P.C.U.* (1994) and *Hostile Intent* (1997), as well as on television in the miniseries *The Last Don* and in the TV movies *TekWar: TekLab* and *What Happened to Bobby Earl?*

On this day, in 1927, the first movie-star footprints—those of actress Norma Talmadge—were impressed in the courtyard of Graumann's Chinese Theater in Hollywood. In 1980, Mount St. Helens in Washington began to erupt.

Robert Morse (b. *1931*), U.S. actor

The boyish, left-handed comic actor—popular in numerous films of the 1950s and 1960s, including *The Matchmaker* (with fellow left-hander Anthony Perkins), *The Loved One*, and *A Guide for the Married Man*—is perhaps best known for his Tony Award–winning work on Broadway, in the 1962 musical *How to Succeed in Business Without Really Trying* (a role he re-created in the 1967 film adaptation) and his acclaimed one-man show, *Tru*, based on the life of author Truman Capote.

Reggie Jackson (b. *1946*), U.S. baseball player

During his career, Jackson struck out more times than any other player in major-league history (2,597 times, to be exact), but he more

than made up for it with his 563 home runs. In twenty-one seasons, "Mr. October" was on eleven division-winning teams and participated in five World Series. Although he batted .391 and hit two home runs in the 1978 World Series, his greatest triumph had actually come a year earlier, in the 1977 World Series, when he powered the Yankees to victory over the Dodgers—by hitting a record-breaking five home runs, including three in one game.

19

On this day, in 1536, Anne Boleyn was beheaded. In 1884, the Ringling Bros. Circus made its debut.

David Hart (b. 1955), U.S. actor

Left-handed character actor seen in numerous films, including *Silver Bullet* (1985), *Legal Eagles* (1986), and *Three Wishes* (1995), but most famous as Sergeant Parker Williams on the popular TV series *In the Heat of the Night*, which started airing in 1988.

20

On this day, in 1932, Amelia Earhart became the first woman to fly solo across the Atlantic.

George Gobel (1919–1991), U.S. entertainer

Ask anyone over sixty where the catchphrases "Well I'll be a dirty bird" and "You don't hardly get those no more" came from, and they'll almost certainly know. George Gobel was one of the overnight sensations of 1950s television. With a face that even in youth bore an un-settling resemblance to that of Queen Victoria (the resemblance got more striking as he aged), and with his slightly halting delivery, en-dearing for its lack of pretense, Gobel propelled the live, variety-comedy hour *The George Gobel Show* into Emmy-winning success in its first year, 1954. Gobel himself won an Emmy Award as "Most Out-standing New Personality" that year, and the show won for Best Comedy Writing. Unfortunately, in the show's second season, rival network CBS decided to put a then unknown (and not especially promising) Western drama, *Gunsmoke*, up against it on Saturday nights; within a year it had knocked Gobel out of the Nielsen top ten. *The George Gobel Show* struggled on until its inevitable cancellation, in 1960, but its impact had been enough to make Gobel a star. A tire-less professional, he spent the next three decades—until his death in 1991—in a ubiquitous role as Everyone's Favorite TV Guest Star on *Wagon Train*, *F Troop*, *The Lucy Show*, *Love American Style*, *Fernwood 2-Night*, and countless other shows.

David Wells *(b. 1963), U.S. baseball player*

In May 1998, left-hander Wells became only the thirteenth pitcher in major-league history to pitch a perfect game; he was also the first player in the history of Yankee Stadium to pitch a perfect game in regular play. (Right-hander Don Larsen had pitched one in Yankee Stadium during the 1956 World Series.) "Couldn't happen to a crazier guy, huh?" Wells told the Associated Press after the feat. Until the ac-complishment, Wells was primarily known for his often unruly behav-ior: he broke his pitching hand in a street fight with two strangers in 1997; in 1995, he flouted the no-facial-hair rule of the Reds by sport-ing a mustache (he was forced to shave it off); he wore an authentic $35,000 Babe Ruth baseball cap while pitching one game for the Yan-kees (the Yankees' manager insisted he remove it). He was also known for his repeated arguments (usually related to Wells's weight) with Yankees owner George Steinbrenner. Wells's mother had died shortly before the perfect game Wells pitched against the Minnesota Twins on May 17. He dedicated his achievement to her memory.

Bronson Pinchot *(b. 1959), U.S. actor*

Pinchot's scene-stealing five minutes on-screen in *Beverly Hills Cop*—as Serge, the gay art-gallery worker—made him famous in 1984. Like so many other left-handed comic actors—Sid Caesar, Peter Sellers, Jim Carrey—he excels at larger-than-life caricatures of otherwise everyday people; and like Caesar and Sellers especially, he's a genius at dialects and hilariously verbal contortion. "Of course I remember what you said," he once ad-libbed as Balki Bartokomous, the newly emigrated shepherd from Mypos, on the hit TV show *Perfect Strangers*—"I have a pornographic memory." Balki's favorite line on the show was the oft repeated "Don't be ridikalus"—advice that Pinchot himself has, thankfully, never taken.

21 On this day, in 1881, Clara Barton founded the Red Cross. In 1975, *A Chorus Line* opened at the Public Theater in New York City.

Albrecht Dürer *(1471–1528), German engraver and painter*

Often described as the German Leonardo, Dürer was the foremost northern European artist of the Renaissance. His most famous works include *Melancholia*, *The Knight*, and *St. Jerome in His Study*.

Peggy Cass *(b. 1924), U.S. actress*

Left-hander Cass—with her inimitable, foghorn voice—was a regular on Jack Paar's *Tonight Show* in the late fifties and early sixties, and a regular panelist on *To Tell the Truth* from 1964 to 1967. In 1958, she was nominated for an Oscar for her role as Agnes Gooch, in the film *Auntie Mame*.

22 Today is Thanksgiving Day in Haiti. On this day, in 1967, *Mister Rogers' Neighborhood* premiered on PBS. In 1972, Ceylon changed its name to Sri Lanka.

Barbara Parkins *(b. 1942), U.S. actress*

The svelte, brunette actress first found popularity as Betty Anderson on the TV series *Peyton Place* from 1964 to 1969, and went on to a brief movie career in such films as *The Kremlin Letter* (1970), *The Mephisto Waltz* (1971), and, most notably, *Valley of the Dolls* (1967).

Tommy John *(b. 1943), U.S. baseball player*

Nicknamed "Baseball's Bionic Man," John batted right-handed but pitched left-handed. He severely injured his elbow while pitching for the Los Angeles Dodgers in 1974, and underwent one of the world's first ligament transplants to have it repaired. The procedure involved removing a tendon from the right forearm and transplanting it to the left elbow: hence the joke that he was baseball's first "right-handed southpaw." The operation was successful, and he returned to the mound to win twenty games in 1977. He retired in 1989.

Peter Nero *(b. 1934), U.S. musician and conductor*

The Grammy Award–winning pianist and conductor has sold millions of albums with his distinctive and orchestral arrangements of popular songs, including *Born Free* and *Summer of '42*. He is also the composer of the music for the 1963 film *Sunday in New York*.

On this day, in 1785, Benjamin Franklin invented bi-focals. In 1934, bank robbers Bonnie and Clyde were ambushed and gunned down by law enforcement officers.

Marvin Hagler (b. 1954), U.S. boxer

The world middleweight boxing champion from 1980 to 1987, left-hander Hagler acquired the nickname "Marvelous" Marvin for his handsome looks and smooth style in the ring. He liked the nickname so much he had his first name legally changed to Marvelous in 1982. His pro record was sixty-two wins, three losses, and two draws, with fifty-two knockouts. "There are no nice guys inside those four corners," he once said. "When I step into the ring, I want to remember everything I've had to go through to get there. I become like a monster whose motto is 'Destruct and destroy.' "

Drew Carey (b. 1958), U.S. actor

The left-handed native of Cleveland worked as a stand-up comic for many years before landing his own sitcom—the enormously popular *Drew Carey Show*—beginning in 1995.

On this day, in 1883, the Brooklyn Bridge was completed. In 1964, *Hello, Dolly!* won the Tony Award as Best Musical of the year.

Queen Victoria (1819–1901), Queen of England

A natural left-hander, Victoria was switched to right-handed penmanship as a child, and she soon became noted for—among other things—her idiosyncratic handwriting, which was euphemistically characterized by one contemporary as employing "much freedom." A later biographer wryly noted that as the queen aged, "the freedom increased while the legibility declined."

Bob Dylan (b. 1941), U.S. singer and songwriter

Born Robert Zimmerman in Duluth, Minnesota, left-hander Dylan continues, nearly four decades after his first album, to produce critically acclaimed hits; but his legendary popularity resides primarily in his connection to the 1960s. Dylan produced definitive anthems of the turbulent decade: "Blowin' in the Wind," "A Hard Rain's A-Gonna Fall," "Mr. Tambourine Man," "Like a Rolling Stone," and "The Times They Are A-Changin'."

25 On this day, in 1878, the Gilbert and Sullivan operetta *H.M.S. Pinafore* premiered in London.

Karen Valentine (b. 1947), U.S. actress

So memorable was Karen Valentine in the hit ABC series *Room 222* that thirty years later, most people forget she wasn't even the show's central character. In fact, when Valentine won an Emmy in 1970 for her performance in the series, it was as Best *Supporting* Actress. The show ran for five years, from 1969 to 1974, and made Valentine a household name.

26 On this day, in 1937, the Golden Gate Bridge opened. In 1994, the United States and Vietnam resumed diplomatic relations, twenty years after the end of the Vietnam War.

John Wesley Hardin (1853–1895), U.S. gunslinger

The notorious young outlaw gunned down his first victim—a former slave—when he was fifteen. By the time he was in his early twenties, he had murdered upwards of thirty men, including various other gunslingers eager to test themselves against him. One of his favorite feats involved suddenly crossing his arms and pulling out two Colt

.45s—one from each side of his vest—and firing them simultaneously, both with lethal accuracy.

On this day, in 1919, the pop-up toaster was patented. In 1941, the German battleship *Bismarck* was sunk by a British submarine torpedo.

Wild Bill Hickok (1837–1876), U.S. frontier lawman

Hickok's ambidexterity was legendary. As sheriff of Ellis County, Kansas, he once pursued two murderers to the town of Solomon. The fugitives fled—one running up the street in one direction, the other running down the street in the opposite direction. Hickok simultaneously pulled out the two six-guns he always wore on each hip and fired both at the same time, killing the two men instantly. Later, he treated audiences to similar displays of ambidextral gunplay as part of his traveling "Buffalo Bill's Wild West" exhibition.

On this day, in 1897, Jell-O was introduced.

Marie Dionne (1934–1960), one of the Dionne quintuplets

In May 1934, Ontario farmwife Elzire Dionne and her husband, Oliva, became the stunned parents of five identical daughters: Annette, Cecile, Emilie, Marie, and Yvonne, better known as the Dionne Quintuplets. The girls' birth generated international headlines and the curiosity of the world. Only one of the quintuplets—Marie—was left-handed.

On this day, in 1953, Edmund Hillary became the first human being to climb Mount Everest.

Tony Carreiro (b. 1960), U.S. actor

The left-handed character actor makes an impression even when he's on-screen for less time than it takes a bird to glide across the background of a shot. Whether as a cop in the 1997 Jim Carrey comedy *Liar, Liar* or as a scene-stealing waiter in an episode of *The Golden Girls*, he has the uniquely left-handed ability to stand out against a sea of mostly cookie-cutter right-handers.

On this day, in 1431, Joan of Arc was burned at the stake. In 1921, the Lincoln Memorial in Washington, D.C., was opened.

Michael J. Pollard (b. 1939), U.S. actor

Character actor primarily known for offbeat, nutty roles in *Little Fauss and Big Halsy* (1970), *Roxanne* (1987), *Scrooged* (1988), and *Dick Tracy* (1990). He was nominated for an Academy Award as Best Supporting Actor for his portrayal of C. W. Moss in the 1967 hit *Bonnie and Clyde*.

Gayle Sayers (b. 1943), U.S. football player

Legendary running back for the Chicago Bears, left-hander Sayers joined the team in 1965 and scored 22 touchdowns in his first season; he also tied a National Football League record with 6 touchdowns in one game. He was overwhelmingly voted Rookie of the Year. Named All-Pro from 1965 to 1969, he retired, as a result of knee injuries, in 1971, with a career total of 4,956 yards. "When you step onto that field," he once said, "you cannot concede a thing."

31 On this day, in 1040, Lady Godiva rode naked through the streets of Coventry to protest high taxes. In 1879, Madison Square Garden opened.

Jim Hutton (1933–1979), U.S. actor

The former army soldier—discovered (by film director Douglas Sirk) while stationed with the U.S. military in Germany—specialized in military or light-comedy roles: *Where the Boys Are* (1960), *Period of Adjustment* (1962), *The Trouble with Angels* (1966), and *The Green Berets* (1968). He was the father of actor Timothy Hutton.

Left-handers Born in
June

June: Sixth month of the year, named for Juno, Roman goddess of women, strongly associated with the moon

1

Today is the official start of hurricane season in the United States. On this day, in 1984, Bruce Springsteen's album *Born in the U.S.A.* was released.

Marilyn Monroe *(1926–1962), U.S. actress*

Don't you know that a man being rich is like a girl being pretty? You might not marry a girl because she's pretty, but—my goodness—doesn't it help?

—Marilyn Monroe, *Gentlemen Prefer Blondes* (1953)

No one knows why Marilyn Monroe shows up so often on lists of famous left-handers. She not only writes right-handed in her films but does everything else—including yanking an electric-fan cord out of a door in *The Seven Year Itch*—with her right hand, as well. Is it simply that left-handers want to claim as one of their own one of the most beautiful and enduring stars in film history? Is it because she was impulsive, vulnerable, occasionally flighty, and often very funny, traits frequently associated with left-handedness? Is it because she had a slight stammer? (Not all left-handers have stammers, but the two are sometimes related, especially when a left-handed child is switched to right-handedness.) One Monroe authority has said categorically, "If

she was left-handed, I've never heard about it. It never comes up in any biographical material I've ever seen about her." So *why* is she always included? Like those long-held customs and rituals whose origins have long since faded into complete obscurity— saying "God bless you" when someone sneezes, eating pork and sauerkraut on New Year's Day, giving Christmas presents to relatives one loathes—no one knows. We're just happy she is.

Morgan Freeman (b. *1937*), U.S. actor

The three-time Oscar-nominated actor (*Street Smart*, *Driving Miss Daisy*, and *The Shawshank Redemption*) is the father of four and has ten grandchildren.

Cleavon Little (*1939–1992*), U.S. actor

Little has portrayed a variety of idiosyncratic characters on film— *Vanishing Point*, *Cotton Comes to Harlem*, *Once Bitten* (as Lauren Hutton's glib butler)—and he won a Tony Award for his performance in the Broadway musical *Purlie*. But it's *Blazing Saddles* and the character Black Bart—the mild-mannered convict-turned-frontier-sheriff—for which he is best known remembered.

On this day, in 1981, Barbara Walters asked Katharine Hepburn, in a television interview, what kind of tree she would be if she were a tree.

Edda Barends *(b. 1949), German actress*

Left-handed actress, star of the German films A *Question of Silence* (1985), *Broken Mirrors* (1984), and *Zaterdagavond Café* (1992).

On this day, in 1509, Henry VIII married the first of his six wives, Catherine of Aragon. In 1888, the poem "Casey at the Bat" was first published, in the *San Francisco Examiner.*

Ellen Corby *(b. 1913), U.S. actress*

Corby started her career working as a script girl for a dozen years, in the 1930s, before landing her first feature-film role: as a French maid in the 1945 suspense drama *Cornered*, starring Dick Powell. Thirty years—and more than ninety film performances—later, she achieved her greatest popularity as America's favorite no-nonsense grandmother, Esther Walton, on the hugely successful TV drama *The Waltons*, beginning in 1972.

On this day, in 1844, the great auk became extinct, when the last two reported specimens were clubbed to death by hunters in Iceland.

Scott Wolf *(b. 1968), U.S. actor*

Sad thing about Hollywood: they don't especially like "out-of-the-closet" left-handers. Southpaw actors are routinely advised—by agents, publicists, superstitious friends—to write with their *right* hand on-screen, so as not to alienate anyone in the audience. Just another case of trying to be all things to all people—there may be someone in the backwoods who still thinks left-handers are handmaidens of the Devil. In the 1996 tour de force *White Squall*, Scott Wolf is shown on-screen writing with his left hand for a total of sixty-seven seconds. This must be some kind of record—and no one has yet accused the intensely likable and talented actor of being in league with the dark forces of nature. (The film's director, Ridley Scott, is also left-handed, incidentally.) Wolf became an American heartthrob in the television series *Party of Five*, beginning in 1994. An earlier performance in the 1993 movie *Teenage Bonnie and Klepto Clyde* is not worth mentioning; his critically lauded roles in the films *White Squall*, *The Evening Star*, and *Cross Country* are. Often compared to the young Tom Cruise (but with more warmth and less vehemence), Wolf represents a new generation of left-handed actors, with fewer switched or closeted lefties in their ranks.

Today is World Environment Day. On this day, in 1968, Robert Kennedy was assassinated.

Marky Mark *(b. 1971), U.S. model, rap singer, and actor*

Underwear. Does it really matter what else Marky Mark does: sing, act, receive commendatory reviews in films like *Boogie Nights*? (He is, incidentally, probably the only author in history to have dedicated a book—his 1992 memoir *Marky Mark*—to his penis.) Skivvies are what Marky Mark is all about, so let's celebrate his birthday by talking for a moment about underwear, as well as another point of fashion: the age-old question of why women's blouses button from the left while men's shirts button from the right. The question of buttons first. The answer goes back many years, to a time when men, it was presumed, tended to dress themselves, whereas wealthy women were often dressed by maids: the left-hand row of buttons on a blouse was more convenient for right-handed maids. It's that simple. With that mystery finally solved, we can say with certainty that almost all clothing—including men's underwear—discriminates against left-handers. Boxers are more left-hand friendly than briefs, but only because they're looser. Button flies—on tapered boxers, union suits, or jeans—are strictly a right-handed convenience: no surprise, since the button fly on trousers was introduced in Turkey—a culture deeply ill disposed to left-handedness—shortly before 1700. (According to one historian, "The Turks introduced the fly to Europe between the eighteenth and nineteenth centuries. Its purpose was not only to facilitate urination, but also to facilitate fornication and rape.") And zippers, like almost everything else couture, discriminate against left-handers, to the extent that they force left-handers to become right-handers—that is, unless you want to leave the house looking as undressed as, well, Marky Mark (who is, incidentally, very much left-handed himself).

On this day, in 1850, Levi Strauss produced its first pair of blue jeans. In 1930, the first drive-in movie theater opened, in Camden, New Jersey.

Bill Dickey (1907–1993), *U.S. baseball player*

The New York Yankees catcher played from 1928 to 1946 and helped propel the team to World Series victories in 1932, 1937, 1938, and 1939 with his powerful left-handed swing at bat. His career batting average was .313, with a career high of .362 in 1936; he had over 100 RBIs per year for four consecutive years between 1936 and 1939. As a catcher, he astonished teammates and opponents alike with his infallible memory. Once, in 1943, he found himself sharing an elevator with a serviceman at a hotel in St. Louis. Suddenly, the man in uniform turned to Dickey and remarked, "I bet you don't remember me." Dickey looked him up and down for a moment and finally replied, "I don't recall your name, but I remember we pitched you inside and high." (The serviceman was former Phillies team member Joe Gantenbein, who had played major-league ball for only two years.) Dickey was inducted into the Baseball Hall of Fame in 1954.

On this day, in 1899, ax-swinging, antidrinking activist Carrie Nation laid waste to her first saloon, in Kiowa, Kansas.

The artist formerly known as Prince
(b. 1958), U.S. rock star

Given that the artist formerly known as Prince is left-handed and wrestled with dyslexia in his youth, is it any wonder he replaced his name with a symbol? Is the symbol a bit pompous, a bit flaky, a bit obvious? Of course it is. But no more so than the notion of an Illinois farmboy named Roy Scherer changing his name to *Rock* Hudson, or a skinny singer named William Broad turning himself into Billy *Idol*, or one Doris von Kappelhoff of Cincinnati, Ohio, reinventing herself as Doris *Day*. The entertainment industry has always been a bit pompous, a bit flaky, a bit obvious—that's part of its enduring attraction. Get over it.

On this day, in 1786, ice cream went on sale for the first time in the United States, in New York City.

Robert Preston *(1918–1987), U.S. actor*

First put under contract by Paramount studios in 1938, Preston languished for almost two decades in lackluster, undistinguished supporting roles, often in dreary Westerns like *North West Mounted Police* (Cecil B. DeMille at his worst) and *The Lady of Cheyenne* (opposite, gulp, Loretta Young as a frontier-town feminist). He didn't come into his own until he was almost forty, when he landed the title role in the smash-hit Broadway musical *The Music Man*—for which he won a Tony Award. He repeated the performance in the spectacularly successful film of the play in 1962. Two decades later, when Preston was entering his sixties he was tapped by farceur Blake Edwards for plum parts in the 1981 Hollywood satire *S.O.B.* and in the 1982 musical

Victor/Victoria, with Julie Andrews. It was the latter role—as the charming, cheerfully manipulative gay cabaret singer Toddy—that earned him an Oscar nomination as Best Supporting Actor.

LeRoy Neiman (b. 1927), U.S. sports artist

Named official artist of the Olympic Games in 1972, left-hander Neiman—known for his vibrantly colored, impressionistic paintings and lithographs of sports events, from downhill skiing to pole-vaulting—received the Olympic Artist of the Century Award in 1979. He was also named the Outstanding Sports Artist in America by the Amateur Athletic Union in 1976.

Griffin Dunne (b. 1955), U.S. actor

The son of author Dominick Dunne, left-hander Griffin played the lead in Martin Scorsese's 1985 black comedy *After Hours*; he also appeared in *An American Werewolf in London* (1981), *Amazon Women on the Moon* (1987), and several other films.

On this day, in 1960, Typhoon Mary killed almost two thousand people in the Fukien province of China. In 1963, the film *Cleopatra* opened in New York City.

Cole Porter (1892–1964), U.S. songwriter

Undoubtedly the wittiest and most accomplished lyricist and song-writer of the twentieth century, Porter gave the world a seemingly endless repertoire of snappy, delicious, unforgettable songs, including "Let's Do It," "You're the Top," "Begin the Beguine," "I've Got You Under My Skin," "I Get a Kick out of You," and "In the Still of the Night."

Robert McNamara *(b. 1916), U.S. presidential adviser*

U.S. secretary of defense between 1961 and 1967, McNamara became controversial for his advocacy of the Vietnam War. He withdrew from White House politics in 1968 to become president of the World Bank, a post he held until 1981.

On this day, in 1935, Alcoholics Anonymous was founded.

Judy Garland *(1922–1969), U.S. singer and actress*

When I was a little girl, I was left-handed, but the doctor told my mother I might grow up to be a very dangerous criminal. They make me do things with my right hand now.

—Judy Garland as Hanna Brown in *Easter Parade* (1948)

Not all the news for left-handers is good news. Numerous studies have suggested that left-handers are more sensitive to the effects of tranquilizers and painkillers and may be more prone to alcoholism and drug dependency. The validity of these studies is still controversial. In the case of Judy Garland, it's impossible to know whether left-handedness played any role in the drug addiction that laid waste to most of her adult years and eventually led to her death from an overdose of sleeping pills in June 1969, when she was forty-seven. There is certainly no lack of alternative explanations: pushed into stardom before she had even reached her teens, she quickly became one of America's favorite movie stars. ("I was born at the age of twelve on the Metro-Goldwyn-Mayer lot," she once quipped.) She was only sixteen when she made *The Wizard of Oz*. After that, the pressure to keep producing hits was enormous, and she soon found herself, at an appallingly young age, on the Hollywood drug merry-go-round: sleeping pills at night to shake off the tension of shooting scenes all day, uppers in the morning to counteract the sleeping pills and to maintain that "bright-eyed" look for the cameras. (The drug-ravaged character Neelie O'Hara in Jacqueline Susann's *Valley of the Dolls* is modeled on Garland.) Despite her popularity, she was fired from MGM in 1950, due in part to her substance abuse—an irony given that the relentlessness of the studio system had perhaps nudged her into it. The latter half of her career was marked by both extraordinary successes—two Oscar nominations (for *A Star Is Born* and *Judgment at Nuremberg*), as well as a nineteen-week record-breaking concert engagement at New York's Palace Theater—and stunning disappointments and failures, such as her short-lived TV variety show on CBS. The final years of her life were a wasteland of legal difficulties, severe emotional problems, and suicide attempts. Although the drug overdose that finally killed her was deemed "accidental," many of her colleagues felt it had been inevitable. Said Ray Bolger, who danced down the Yellow Brick Road with her as Scarecrow in *The Wizard of Oz*, "She just plain wore out."

F. Lee Bailey *(b. 1933), U.S. attorney*

Controversial defense attorney, part of the so-called Dream Team that defended O. J. Simpson on murder charges in 1995; Bailey first rose to prominence in the 1960s, defending such high-profile clients as Sam Sheppard (the real-life model for *The Fugitive*) and Albert De-Salvo ("the Boston Strangler"), and, later, Patty Hearst.

Today is King Kamehameha Day in Hawaii. On this day in 1982, Steven Spielberg's *E.T. The Extra-Terrestrial* had its world premiere.

Joshua Jackson *(b. 1978), Canadian actor*

When he was eleven, his mother took him to an audition for a potato chip commercial, hoping that the harsh and rancorously competitive atmosphere of the "cattle call" would discourage him from wanting to become an actor. Instead, the left-handed young actor got the part. He has since appeared in numerous films—including *The*

Mighty Ducks and *Scream 2*—as well as on the television series *Dawson's Creek*.

12

Today is Independence Day in the Philippines. On this day, in 1939, the National Baseball Hall of Fame and Museum was dedicated.

George Bush (b. *1924*),
U.S. president

Whatever his other accomplishments or shortcomings as a political leader, Bush was the modern master of the malapropism, the verbal misstep: *lapsus linguae*, as the ancient Romans deemed it. Running for president in the spring of 1988, he spoke passionately of his four years as vice president under Ronald Reagan: "We have had triumphs," he proclaimed, "we have made mistakes, we have had sex. . . ." He meant, of course, to say "setbacks." At another rally four months later, he announced to hundreds of his supporters, "I hope I stand for antibigotry, anti-Semitism, antiracism." At a 1988 Memorial Day parade in Kennebunkport, Maine, he repeatedly welcomed everyone to a celebration of "Veterans Day," and at a rally on September 7, 1988, he mistook the day for December 7 and went on, at length, about the anniversary of the bombing of Pearl Harbor. Sometimes it wasn't so much a verbal stumble as a dazedly memorable comment. Visiting the Dead Sea on a tour of the Middle East in 1986, he turned to an Israeli general and inquired, "Tell me, General, how dead is it?" And on a tour of the concentration camp Auschwitz in 1987, he remarked, "Boy, they were big on crematoriums, weren't they?" Of the twelve initial candidates for president in 1988, three—all Republicans—were left-handed: Pat Robertson, Robert Dole, and George Bush. Bush, of course, was the winner. His presidency, joked fellow left-hander Dave Barry, raised "a troublesome constitutional issue, because every time he signs a bill into law he drags his hand through the signature and messes it up."

On this day, in 1894, W. E. B. Du Bois became the first African-American to receive a Ph.D. from Harvard.

Tim Allen (b. 1953), U.S. actor

Left-handed star of the megahit TV sitcom *Home Improvement*, and reportedly—at a salary of $1.25 million per episode—one of the highest-paid performers in prime-time television history. His television costar Richard Karn is also left-handed. (See February 17.)

Mary-Kate Olsen (b. 1986), U.S. actress

One of the Olsen twins (the other is right-hander Ashley), who appeared on the hit TV series *Full House*, beginning in 1987. She has also appeared in several feature films, including *The Little Rascals* in 1994 and *It Takes Two* in 1995.

Today is Flag Day in the United States. On this day, in 1873, the ruins of the ancient city of Troy were discovered by archaeologist Heinrich Schliemann. In 1973, the stage musical *The Rocky Horror Show* opened in London.

Richard Starnes (b. 1948), U.S. writer

The left-handed author of *The Flypaper War* faced unexpected difficulties over his handedness at an early age. "I can still remember the crisis I created in third grade," he wrote, "when I insisted on saluting the flag with my left hand. I've no doubt some whey-faced sleuth opened a dossier on me at that very time, one that must now occupy several filing cabinets and contain all manner of damning information about my persistent portsidedness. If you think I exaggerate the bias against us left-handers, trying raising your *left* hand the next time you bear witness in a court of law."

On this day, in 1867, the first successful gallstone operation was performed. In 1924, J. Edgar Hoover was named director of the FBI.

Brett Butler *(b. 1957), U.S. baseball player*

"Apparently I was a hyper kid," left-hander Butler acknowledged in his 1997 autobiography, *Field of Hope*. "I don't remember this, but my mother used to tell me that I was so full of energy, my early grade teachers used my belt to anchor me to my desk. One told my mother that it didn't matter if I was just an average student. 'He'll get by on personality alone,' she said." One of the best-liked players in modern baseball, Butler played for the Atlanta Braves, the Cleveland Indians, the San Francisco Giants, the New York Mets, and the Los Angeles Dodgers from 1981 until his retirement in 1997. Despite an early sterling career in college baseball, he was initially judged too small for the major leagues; he was finally drafted by the Atlanta Braves, in the *twenty-third* round—as a favor to his coach. A consistently strong player, his career batting average was .290, with a .314 peak in 1994. In 1996, he was diagnosed with cancer. Despite surgery and radiation—and the accompanying severe weight loss—he made a comeback later that year and astonished teammates by continuing his usual, reliable performance at bat. (He also received a standing ovation from Dodgers fans.) However, in 1997, at the age of forty, he decided to retire once and for all to devote his energy to his family. Butler—who both batted and threw left-handed—plays every other sport, except one, left-handed: "I learned to play golf right-handed and still do. It's the only sport I play right-handed."

Erroll Garner (1921–1977), U.S. jazz musician

Left-handed composer of the song "Misty," Garner first rose to prominence in the 1940s and developed an international following as one of the great jazz pianists.

On this day, in 1959, George Reeves, television's first Superman, committed suicide at his home in Beverly Hills. In 1961, Soviet ballet dancer Rudolf Nureyev defected to the West.

Phil Mickelson (b. 1970), U.S. golf pro

In 1990, Mickelson became the first left-hander to win the U.S. Amateur. Since turning pro in 1992, he has accumulated twelve PGA Tour victories, including the Bay Hill Invitational and the Sprint International in 1997. In 1998, he won the Mercedes Championship by one shot over Tiger Woods and Mark O'Meara.

On this day, in 1775, the Battle of Bunker Hill was fought. In 1963, Soviet cosmonaut Valentina Tereshkova became the first woman in space, orbiting the earth in the *Vostok 6* space capsule.

M. C. Escher (1898–1972), Dutch artist

The famous left-handed artist—renowned for his uncanny and visually provocative creations—attributed his decision to become a graphic artist rather than a painter to his left-handedness; he claimed that left-handers were more acute than right-handers as abstract thinkers and were more likely to be interested in shapes than in colors. One of his most famous lithographs, *Drawing Hands*, portrays a left hand holding a pencil and sketching a right hand; the right hand, in turn, is holding a pencil and sketching the left hand.

Greg Kinnear *(b. 1963), U.S. actor and talk show host*

Handsome star of the E! channel's enormously popular *Talk Soup* and the films *Sabrina* and *As Good As It Gets* (for which he was nominated for an Academy Award as Best Supporting Actor in 1998). "When I was growing up," the left-handed actor once confessed, "I had a sense of displacement, of being the odd man out. . . . I had a hard time in school. I never excelled scholastically. I was never good at anything."

Joe Piscopo *(b. 1951), U.S. comedian*

Bodybuilding comic, member of the cast of *Saturday Night Live* from 1980 to 1984, he has also appeared in numerous films, including *Johnny Dangerously* (1984) and *Dead Heat* (1988).

18 On this day, in 1815, the Battle of Waterloo was fought. In 1983, Sally Ride became the first U.S. woman in space, aboard the space shuttle *Challenger*.

Paul McCartney
(b. 1942), British singer and songwriter

McCartney, though hardly at odds with the world in the way that fellow left-handed rock musicians Kurt Cobain and Jimi Hendrix were, has still had some adapting to do. "When I was a kid," he once said, "I seemed to do everything back to front. I used to write backwards, and every time the masters at my school looked at my book, they used to throw little fits. I had difficulties outside school, too. I couldn't learn to ride a bike because I would insist on pedaling backwards and was quite convinced that mine was the right way, and everybody else's was wrong. I do everything with my left hand, and no matter how hard I try I can't alter the habit. A doctor once told me I shouldn't try to, because being left-handed is something to do with the brain."

Lou Brock *(b. 1939), U.S. baseball player*

"Everything moves wrong," teammate Bob Gibson once said of Lou Brock's style on the dance floor. "You never saw anybody so clumsy." Graceless or not, Brock had more than 3,000 hits playing for the Cardinals between 1961 and 1979. However, his greatest accomplishment was breaking Ty Cobb's long-standing career stolen-base record. A total of 938 stolen bases wasn't bad for a left-handed outfielder who couldn't dance.

On this day, in 1941, Cheerios were invented. In 1953, convicted spies Ethel and Julius Rosenberg were executed in the electric chair, in New York.

Lou Gehrig *(1903–1941), U.S. baseball player*

To this day, Gehrig remains one of the most compelling figures in baseball, not only because of his achievements (or because of his tragic death) but because he cut such an unlikely figure in the sport he excelled at. An alumnus of Columbia University, he was a quiet, thoughtful man, so modest and so openly devoted to his mother that sportswriters hardly knew how to classify him, especially in contrast to the rough-hewn earthiness of Babe Ruth or the abrasive "winning is everything" arrogance of Ty Cobb. Nicknamed "the Iron Horse" and "the Pride of the Yankees," Gehrig achieved one of the most extraordinary records in baseball history: between 1925 and 1939, he played 2,130 *consecutive* games, often despite various physical ailments (in 1934, he had to be carried off the field after pulling the muscles in his back, a problem he struggled with during much of his career). His other achievements, one after the other, contributed to the legend. In

1932, he hit four consecutive home runs in one game. During seven seasons, he had 150 or more RBIs, including 184 in 1931. In 1934, and again in 1936, he hit 49 home runs. In thirty-four games in seven World Series, he hit 10 home runs, drove in 35 runs, and batted .361. Gehrig finished his career with 1,990 RBIs, 493 home runs, and a .340 batting average. It was in 1939, at the age of thirty-five, that he felt compelled to pull himself out of the game. For a long time, he'd been having difficulties with a wide variety of perplexing symptoms: muscles that refused to function, chronic fatigue, vision problems. A series of tests at the Mayo Clinic brought the verdict: he had amyotrophic lateral sclerosis, a mysterious and usually fatal disease in which the body's muscles relentlessly atrophy. "Today I consider myself the luckiest man on the face of the earth," he told tens of thousands of fans assembled at Yankee Stadium for Lou Gehrig Day on July 14, 1939. Two years later, he was dead, and the illness that killed him (and which later struck such notables as David Niven and Stephen Hawking) became universally known as Lou Gehrig's disease.

20

On this day, in **1948**, *The Ed Sullivan Show* premiered on television.

Siobhan Fallon (b. 1967), U.S. actress

A regular on *Saturday Night Live* from 1991 to 1993, Fallon quickly emerged as an up-and-coming actress in feature films, including *Forrest Gump* (1994), *Men in Black* (1997), and *Krippendorf's Tribe* (1998). She has also been seen on the TV series *Seinfeld* and *The Golden Girls*.

On this day, in 1963, Cardinal Montini was elected Pope Paul VI. In 1975, the film *Jaws* opened in U.S. theaters.

Prince William *(b. 1982), British royal*

The son of Princess Diana and Prince Charles is left-handed, like his father, grandmother, great-grandmother, great-grandfather, great-great-great-grandfather, and great-great-great-great-grandmother, Queen Victoria.

Nicole Kidman *(b. 1967), Australian actress*

Statuesque left-handed wife of left-hander Tom Cruise and star of *Dead Calm, Days of Thunder, Batman Forever, To Die For, The Portrait of a Lady*, and *Eyes Wide Shut*: "You can live life terrified of doing everything, or you can choose some things that you really want and do them so that, when you're eighty years old, you won't regret having missed out. I don't want to have any regrets."

Today marks the beginning of the astrological sign Cancer. On this day, in 1847, the doughnut was invented. In 1941, Adolf Hitler ordered the German invasion of the Soviet Union.

John Dillinger *(1902–1934), U.S. bank robber*

Everyone knows the story of how left-handed outlaw John Dillinger—"public enemy number one"—was lured by brothel madam Anna Sage (the infamous "lady in red") to Chicago's Biograph Theater on the night of July 22, 1934, where, after viewing the film *Manhattan Melodrama*, he was gunned down by waiting FBI agents. The only problem is, the story probably isn't true. Increasing evidence over the last six decades indicates that it may not have been Dillinger at all who was shot that night, but an unsuspecting petty hoodlum, Jimmy

Lawrence, unwittingly used as part of a plot to help Dillinger escape the law. The evidence is persuasive. The man killed that night had brown eyes; Dillinger's were blue. The dead man was stocky and short; Dillinger was taller and leaner. The corpse was also missing all of Dillinger's birthmarks and scars. The FBI, in response to criticism at the time that the man they had killed didn't look anything like John Dillinger, offered up the admittedly plausible theory that Dillinger had had plastic surgery to alter his looks; unfortunately, according to autopsy results, there was no sign of plastic surgery ever having been performed on the body in the morgue. What, then, happened to the real John Dillinger? No one knows—which, if the theory is correct, is exactly what Dillinger wanted.

Carl Hubbell (1903–1988), U.S. baseball player

The master of the screwball (and known affectionately to his teammates as "the Meal Ticket"), Hubbell pitched for the New York Giants from 1928 to 1943 and established a 253–154 career record. However, he regularly discharged the ball with such a powerful clockwise snap of the wrist that eventually his entire left arm was disfigured: his left hand became permanently twisted with the palm facing out.

Bruce Campbell (b. 1958), U.S. actor

Chameleon-like, popular, left-handed actor known for his long association with director Sam Raimi and for his uncanny ability to dramatically alter his appearance for different roles. Campbell is best known for his film work in *The Evil Dead* (which he also produced) and *Evil Dead II*, as well as *Escape from L.A.* (1996), *Congo* (1995), and *The Hudsucker Proxy* (1994), but he has also been featured on the TV series *Ellen* (as Ed Billik) in 1996 and 1997, and starred in the syndicated series *The Adventures of Brisco County, Jr.* in 1993.

On this day, in 1868, the typewriter was patented by inventor Christopher Sholes. In 1993, Lorena Bobbitt and her husband, John Wayne Bobbitt, got into a, uh, really messy disagreement.

Josephine (1763–1814), consort of Napoleon

Both Napoleon and his bride Josephine were left-handed, which raises certain indelicate questions of bedroom logistics. Lying in bed together, face-to-face, one of them would have to—you see, one arm would be squished and—oh, never mind. It probably didn't make a whit of difference to their love life. According to Josephine herself, every time Napoleon tried to make love to her, her dog, Fortune, attacked him. Thrown out of the boudoir, the dog howled, barked, and scratched at the door. Two days after their wedding, in March 1796, Napoleon had had enough: he made his excuses and fled to Italy, leaving his new bride all alone. Well, not entirely alone. Josephine—beautiful, strong-willed, and very independent—wasn't known for her faithfulness. A contemporary described her as "paying her bills below her navel," and one of her numerous lovers rapturously characterized her as possessing "the prettiest little . . ."—but, no, that belongs to another book on an entirely different subject.

On this day, in 1779, a rare total eclipse of the sun was visible from the entire United States. In 1932, the monarchy in Thailand ended with a bloodless coup against the king.

Wayne Cashman (b. 1945), U.S. hockey player

Perhaps one of the most unusual advantages of being left-handed was described by hockey player Wayne Cashman, who played for the Boston Bruins. Cashman claimed that left-handedness gave him an advantage in the frequent fights that broke out on the ice. "The key to a hockey fight," he once remarked to an interviewer, "is the first punch. When you're a lefty and they're looking for your right fist, it helps."

Jack Carter (b. 1923), U.S. comedian

Popular comic, host of his own TV show in the 1950s, later a character actor in dozens of films, including *Viva Las Vegas* (1964), *The Amazing Dobermans* (1976), *History of the World: Part I* (1981), as well as a frequent guest star on TV, including the series *Caroline in the City*.

25

On this day, in 1876, the Battle of Little Big Horn—"Custer's Last Stand"—was fought. In 1997, Jacques Cousteau died.

Carly Simon (b. 1945), U.S. singer

The left-handed singer is known for such perennial favorites as "That's the Way I Always Heard It Should Be" (which catapulted her to fame in 1971) and "You're So Vain." In 1989, she won an Oscar for Best Song for "Let the River Run," from the film *Working Girl*.

Billy Wagner (b. 1971), U.S. baseball player

Named Houston Astros Rookie of the Year in 1996, pitcher Wagner has been called "the hardest-throwing left-hander in the National League." His fastball consistently approaches 100 miles per hour. "On most occasions," said one sportswriter, "he simply overpowers opposing batters."

26

On this day, in 1896, a 110-foot tidal wave crushed cities along Japan's east coast, killing almost thirty thousand people.

Chris Isaak (b. 1956),
U.S. singer

Chris Isaak is renowned for all kinds of physical attributes: his thick dark hair and his photogenic eyes (the brooding, seductive eyes at least partly explain why the video for his smash hit "Wicked World" was deemed MTV's all-time sexiest music video in 1998, ten years after it was first released); his voice (smooth, high, and even, in the tradition of Roy Orbison, but sultrier and more blatantly sexual); his handedness (he's left-handed, of course); and something else, which can only be acknowledged here by referring to a list Isaak recently appeared on, titled, aptly, "Endowment of the Arts."

George Michael (b. 1963), British pop star

The British pop idol was, in his youth, not only nearsighted and color-blind (as well as left-handed) but overweight, extremely awkward, and introverted—all of which left him with a deep sense of inferiority and confusion. Later, he acknowledged, "The whole idea of being a physically attractive personality never really occurred to me"—an amazing confession from a singer who for years was consistently ranked as one of the sexiest men in rock and roll.

Robert Davi *(b. 1956), U.S. actor*

A veteran of dozens of films, Davi has been at his cold-blooded, snarling best in *The Goonies*, *Die Hard*, *License to Kill*, and *Predator 2*. His most current role is on the NBC series *Profiler*.

27 On this day, in 1787, Edward Gibbon finished his *History of the Decline and Fall of the Roman Empire*, begun fifteen years earlier.

H. Ross Perot *(b. 1930), U.S. businessman and presidential candidate*

Left-handed Texas billionaire who twice ran, unsuccessfully, for President of the United States—in 1992 and 1996—on a populist platform of giving the government back to the people. "If you want the system to work again," he said, "you have to go back and make it work, with the people of the country being the owners and the elected officials being the servants. *Asleep* I can do a better job than they're doin' up there now." Perot's distinctive way of speaking, his frequent use of graphs and other visual aids, and his habit of sometimes speaking impulsively on political issues (and personal matters) provided fodder for impersonators and satirists—most notably Dana Carvey on *Saturday Night Live*—during both campaigns. He is also, incidentally, an expert windsurfer.

Helen Keller *(1880–1968), U.S. writer, lecturer, and advocate for people with disabilities*

In the summer of 1893, thirteen-year-old Helen Keller—accompanied by her teacher, Anne Sullivan, and their friend Alexander Graham Bell—visited the World's Fair in New York. The president of the fair, Mr. Higinbotham, had given Keller a special dispensation to touch all of the exhibits. She later wrote, "I recall with unmixed delight those days when a thousand childish fancies became beautiful realities. Every day in imagination I made a trip round the world, and I saw many wonders from the uttermost parts of the earth—marvels of invention, treasuries of industry and skill and all the activities of human life actually passed under my fingertips." She touched French bronzes, gold from Peru, the Hope Diamond, phonographs, telegraphs, and other recent inventions, relics from ancient Mexico, silks from the Middle East, statues from India, Venetian glass, industrial machinery, Egyptian artifacts—and faces. She touched the face of almost everyone she met, reading with her fingertips features and wrinkles and emotional expression. "In the three weeks I spent at the Fair," she wrote in her 1902 autobiography, *The Story of My Life*, "I took a long leap from the little child's interest in fairy tales and toys to the appreciation of the real and the earnest in the workaday world." Six years earlier, Keller—rendered blind and deaf by a severe fever at the age of a year and a half—had been a frustrated, violent animal, able to communicate her basic needs to her parents, but little more. It was Anne Sullivan, hired as a tutor when Keller was seven, who subdued the angry demons in the girl and brought her back into the human race. Their phenomenally close relationship—they were virtually inseparable for fifty years—was more like a marriage than most marriages: together they toured the country, lectured, and became activists not only in the fight for acceptance for the disabled but in the suffragette and labor movements as well. That Keller should turn out to be the object of one of the longest-running, most profligate series of jokes in modern times is, if nothing else, testament to how little the majority of people have come to terms with the essential truth of Martin Luther King, Jr.'s dramatic statement, "The salvation of mankind lies in the hands of the creatively maladjusted." Despite the staggering vicissitudes of her circumstances, Keller never stopped being earnestly humbled by life and grateful for any moment of happiness or freedom she could find within its fluctuations and cruelties—an attitude any individual, left- or right-handed, would do well to acquire.

28

On this day, in 1838, Victoria was crowned Queen of England. In 1914, World War I began, with the assassination of Archduke Ferdinand in Sarajevo.

Bruce Davison (b. *1946*), U.S. actor

Is it possible that left-hander Bruce Davison has never entirely lived down his early role in the 1971 thriller *Willard*, about a boy and his killer rats? How else to explain the fact that this wonderful actor, a veteran of over sixty films (including the 1977 critically acclaimed, powerhouse prison drama *Short Eyes*), is still largely underused and underrated? He garnered an Academy Award nomination for his performance in the wrenching 1990 AIDS drama *Longtime Companion*. But still, nine years and twenty-five films after that, he's almost always in the background. Pity. If a hallmark of left-handers is soul—that indefinable quality embracing heart, quiet passion, and artistry—then Davison certainly has it.

Mary Stuart Masterson (b. *1966*), U.S. actress

Mary Stuart Masterson has established a career playing roles that were once described as "scrappy" or "tomboyish." Today we would call them "empowered," reflecting Hollywood's uneasy attempt to maintain its tradition of glamour while paying homage to the current social mood. Empowered *or* scrappy, she's appeared in over two dozen films, most notably *Gardens of Stone* (1987), *Fried Green Tomatoes* (1991), and *Benny & Joon* (1993).

29

Today is the Feast of Saints Peter and Paul in Spain, Chile, Costa Rica, Peru, Italy, and other countries. On this day, in 1971, three Soviet astronauts died in space, on the *Soyuz 11* mission, when a leak in their space capsule caused decompression.

Stanley Ralph Ross *(b. 1939), U.S. writer, actor, and producer*

Left-hander Ross wrote for the television shows *Batman*, *The Man from U.N.C.L.E.*, *Columbo*, *Banacek*, and *All in the Family*, and developed such popular series as *Wonder Woman* and *Where in the World Is Carmen San Diego?* A producer, director, and entertainment software developer, he has also acted, appearing in the TV shows *Falcon Crest* and *Family Medical Center*.

30

On this day, in 1908, the mysterious Tunguska Fireball exploded over Siberia. In 1936, *Gone with the Wind* was published.

Robert D. Ballard *(b. 1942), U.S. oceanographer*

In future generations, Robert Ballard will be remembered as one of the great scientist-explorers of the twentieth century, the Alexander Humboldt of his era. He not only discovered the wreckage of the *Titanic* under the icy waters of the Atlantic, he subsequently located and explored the remains of the *Lusitania*, the *Andrea Doria*, and the *Bismarck* as well. It wasn't simply a matter of finding pretty pictures to spice up *National Geographic* specials. The perfection of technology, the melding of oceanography and computer science, the discovery of answers to specific, haunting questions of maritime history—all have added enormously to the length and breadth of understanding in a dozen different fields. Often overlooked is the fact that he also discovered volcanic vents on the ocean floor off the Galápagos Islands and was the first to discover the existence of chemosynthetic marine life—plants that synthesize food chemically, rather than from sunlight—a discovery with extraordinary implications for modern agriculture, as well as for the search for life on other planets. A man of enormous integrity and honesty, Ballard refused to establish salvage rights, as was his option, to the *Titanic* after finding her in 1985: he believed no one should have any rights to the wreckage, that the ravaged ocean liner should be allowed to lie in peace on the ocean floor. Some tragedies, he believed, are too great to pick over for profit or sensationalism.

Left-handers Born in
July

July: *Seventh month of the year, called Quintilis until 44
B.C., when it was renamed in honor of Julius Caesar*

Today is International Joke Day. On this day, in
1979, the U.S. Mint unveiled the Susan B. Anthony
dollar. In 1997, China took control of Hong Kong
after 156 years of British rule.

Dan Aykroyd *(b. 1952), Canadian actor*

Watching the various alumni of *Saturday Night Live* try to keep
their careers intact after leaving the show, it's difficult not to think of
that early *Star Trek* episode in which a dazzling electromagnetic creature, having fallen in love with a humanoid, reveals she can never
leave her home planet, not even for love. "If I leave this place even for
a tiny march of days," she plaintively announces, "I will cease to exist." The ranks of *SNL* veterans who have "ceased to exist"—just
in terms of career misfires, not self-destructive drug use, illness, or
violence—is staggering. What thrives on the small screen late at
night, when so many viewers are half asleep, stoned, or reaching for
the next beer, soon dies on the big screen, where people pay half a
week's wages to be entertained. One very successful exception is left-
hander Dan Aykroyd. Aykroyd's extraordinary twisted mimicry became an icon of the seventies, as he lampooned everyone from Julia
Child to Richard Nixon and participated in one immortal piece of
comic inventiveness after another: Bass-o-Matic, Killer Bees, Coneheads, the Blues Brothers. The metamorphic genius was, more than a

decade after his departure from *SNL*, nominated for a Best Supporting Actor Oscar for his serious (though good-natured) role as Jessica Tandy's son in *Driving Miss Daisy*. Although his presence in the Bruce Beresford racial melodrama may have caused some audience members to do a double take ("Is that who I *think* it is?"), no one questioned the right of the remarkably talented performer to be there.

Roger Connor *(1857–1931), U.S. baseball player*

The left-handed first baseman—nicknamed "Dear Old Roger" for his quiet, unprepossessing manner—was so well liked (and underpaid) that fans once spontaneously took up a collection for him in the bleachers and, having accumulated more than $500, bought him a gold watch to show their appreciation. Connor held the major-league lifetime record for home runs, 138, until Babe Ruth shattered it in 1921.

2

On this day, in 1777, Vermont became the first state to abolish slavery. In 1937, Amelia Earhart's plane disappeared over the South Pacific.

Joe Magrane *(b. 1964), U.S. baseball player*

The left-handed pitcher played major-league ball for nine years, starting in 1987, when he was signed by St. Louis. He retired in 1996 with a 57–67 record and a 3.81 ERA. Although he pitched left-handed, he batted right-handed.

3

On this day, in 1863, the Battle of Gettysburg was fought.

Tom Cruise (b. 1962), U.S. actor

The actor's dyslexia—at times so profound he was virtually unable to read—played a role in charting his destiny: he took refuge in sports as a way of dealing with the alienation his dyslexia caused. From sports he moved to acting, after injuring his knee in a wrestling tournament in high school. "I would pick up a new sport as a way to make friends," he said later. "Acting provided me with a way to express myself."

Dave Barry (b. 1947), U.S. writer

In 1991, Canadian psychologist Dr. Stanley Coren and a colleague, Dr. Diane Halpern, made headlines when they announced the results of a study alleging that left-handers live an average of *nine years less* than right-handers. Using death statistics from Southern California and following them up with questionnaires to determine whether the deceased were left- or right-handed, they concluded that, due to serious accidents and other problems, left-handers have a lower life expectancy than right-handers: sixty-six years, as compared with seventy-five for right-handed individuals. Their findings were controversial. "When I first saw the newspaper article about lefties dying sooner," humorist Dave Barry wrote in his national column, "I thought maybe the cause would be ink absorption. Because of the way we write, most of us lefties go through life with big ink smears on the edges of our left hands." Barry continued: "According to the researchers ... left-handers have a lot more accidents than right-handers. I know why this is: We read books backwards. Really. When left-handers pick up books, they tend to start reading from the last page. This saves us a lot of time with murder mysteries, but it's a bad habit when we're reading, say, the instructions for operating a barbecue grill, and we begin with 'STEP 147: IGNITE GAS.' " The Pulitzer Prize–winning journalist concluded with a dyslexic warning to the right-handed majority: "Planet foolish this over take will we day one."

(Incidentally, a nine-year British study released in 1998 showed *no* difference in life expectancy between left-handers and right-handers.)

Montel Williams *(b. 1956), U.S. talk show host*

The left-handed, Emmy Award–winning former naval intelligence officer became host of the syndicated daytime talk show *The Montel Williams Show* in 1992.

Robert Haag *(b. 1956), "Meteorite Man"*

Left-hander Haag has been obsessed by meteorites ever since childhood, when he and his parents watched an exploding meteor fill the sky over a beach in Mexico. In the years since, he has led an Indiana Jones existence traveling to Australia, Hong Kong, Mexico, the Florida Keys, Nigeria, Poland, and other locations in search of the beautiful—and highly valuable—rocks that fall from the sky. Although several tons of meteorites—ranging from the innocuously small to the headline-generating twenty-five-pound rock that landed on a car in Peekskill, New York, in 1992—fall to earth every day, the overwhelming majority disappear into the obscurity of deserts, inaccessible mountains, vast jungles, and remote areas like Antarctica and the inhospitable Nullarbor Plain of Australia; they're never found. The ones that are found can fetch anywhere from several hundred dollars to several million, depending on their origin and rarity. Haag's obsession—his cheerful, unrelenting, and somehow *very* left-handed perseverance in tracking down meteorites from every corner of the world—has brought him a kind of offbeat fame, a healthy income, and enormous happiness.

Today is Independence Day in the United States. On this day, in 1776, Congress adopted the Declaration of Independence. In 1924, the first Caesar salad was made, at a restaurant, Caesar's Place, in Tijuana, Mexico.

Eva Marie Saint (b. *1924*), *U.S. actress*

Lovely Eva Marie Saint shocked moviegoers in 1959 when she aggressively seduced Cary Grant in the dining car in Alfred Hitchcock's *North by Northwest*. Another Hollywood bad girl was born: who would have guessed that beneath the soulful exterior that won her an Oscar five years earlier in *On the Waterfront*, there was a ruthless femme fatale capable of uttering the coldly calculating words, "I wouldn't order dessert if I were you"? If only audiences had known she was left-handed, they wouldn't have raised their eyebrows at all. A lack of inhibition, as everyone knows, comes naturally to left-handers, even Saintly ones.

On this day, in 1946, the first bikini was unveiled, at a fashion show in Paris. In 1954, Elvis Presley had his first recording session, in Memphis.

Dwight Davis (*1879–1945*), *founder of the* Davis Cup

In 1900, left-hander Davis founded the International Lawn Tennis Challenge Trophy, popularly known as the Davis Cup. It was the first truly international tennis event. The man behind the tournament was himself U.S. men's doubles champion (with teammate Holcombe Ward) for three consecutive years, from 1899 to 1901.

Katherine Helmond (b. 1934), U.S. actress

Describing the radiant, inimitable left-hander Katherine Helmond to anyone unfamiliar with her work is like trying to explain the experience of biting into fresh mango to someone who isn't even sure if it's a fruit or a tropical dance. Helmond—one of the most perversely underused actresses in Hollywood—is always a pleasure to watch, whether undergoing industrial-strength cosmetic surgery in Terry Gilliam's macabre satire *Brazil* (1985) or smothering amnesiac heiress Goldie Hawn with crass maternal love in *Overboard* (1987). She costarred for six years in the popular sitcom *Who's the Boss?*, with Tony Danza and Judith Light, beginning in 1984; but it was her earlier five-year stint as beleaguered, soulful Jessica Tate in the risqué but sweet-tempered series *Soap*, beginning in 1977, that made her, if not a full-fledged star, then at least a "name." The controversial series—many objected to its frivolous portrayal of adultery, satanic possession, murder, and other issues—drew thirty-two thousand letters of protest *before* it ever went on the air. One religious organization dramatically dubbed it "a deliberate effort . . . to tear down our moral values." No one need have worried. Despite its often flippant attitudes, the alternately hilarious and poignant series ultimately said more about real family values (and loyalty, and human frailty, and love) than a hundred routine family sitcoms kept afloat by bland characters and laugh tracks—just as the piquant and unclassifiable Helmond herself has said more about mesmerizing audiences than a hundred of the cookie-cutter actresses around her.

On this day, in 1535, Thomas More was beheaded by Henry VIII for refusing to support Henry's divorce from Catherine of Aragon. In 1919, the first dirigible crossed the Atlantic.

Sylvester Stallone (b. 1946), U.S. actor

In general, left-handers have been ostracized from the boxing ring, and even if they work their way up through the amateur ranks boxing left-handed, they often have to learn to fight right-handed to get the pro matches. The reasons for this aren't clear, except that most promoters seem to regard left-handed boxing as dangerous and inequitable, rather like allowing some people to drive on the left side of the road. Sylvester Stallone was obviously aware of the boxing world's contempt for left-handers when he invented the character Rocky Balboa. Rocky is a failed left-handed boxer who makes his living breaking arms for a loan shark. When the world champion, Apollo Creed, suddenly finds himself without an opponent for an important match, Rocky be-

comes the unlikely choice—despite the objection of Apollo Creed's manager, who protests, "I don't want you messin' around with no southpaw." Rocky himself blames his shabby career on his left-handedness and tells girlfriend Talia Shire, "Nobody wants to fight no southpaw. Ya know what I mean?" Rocky does not win the fight (victory is reserved for the film's sequels), but he comes so close to beating the champ that Creed must have rued the day he went "messin' around" with a left-handed prizefighter. By contrast, the question of actor Stallone's actual hand preference is sticky. Once he achieved fame, Stallone magically became right-handed and could be seen in his films writing (and, just as often, shooting) with his right hand. Revealingly, his watch is still almost always on the right wrist, usually a characteristic of left-handers. The unfortunate truth: Hollywood directors and publicists aren't especially thrilled by left-handedness, and not infrequently instruct their left-handed actors to portray themselves on-screen as right-handed. Left-handedness is still seen as a trait that may alienate some audience members.

Jennifer Saunders (b. 1958), British actress and writer

Rather than waste time trying to condense Saunders's career, or reciting a roster of her film and television credits, let's cut to the chase: as the comic genius behind the smash-hit comedy series *Absolutely Fabulous*, Saunders is perhaps the first British writer since Joe

Orton not only to make pure wickedness genuinely and screamingly funny (not to mention strangely poignant at times) but to have invented an entirely new language to depict it. Not one of the characters on the show—except perhaps for poor sack-clothed Saffron—speaks in anything approximating true conversational English; the dialogue—endlessly scathing and hilarious—goes beyond slang and resembles instead a barely coherent, stream-of-consciousness shorthand, a kind of verbal nervous breakdown: hardly linear, hardly proper, and often consisting of long repetitions of "Sweetie, darling, hmm?" The show is an acquired taste: people who loathe it on first viewing have been known to end up watching it again and again, hypnotized, and finally infatuated. If that other left-handed masterpiece *Alice in Wonderland* had been about two aging, Lacroix-loving, Bolliguzzling hipsters in pursuit of a different kind of white "rabbit," *Ab Fab* is what it would have looked like.

On this day, in 1981, President Reagan nominated Sandra Day O'Connor to be the first woman on the Supreme Court.

Ringo Starr *(b. 1940), British musician*

The legendary drummer—and least ostentatious member—of the Beatles is, like lead singer Paul McCartney (see June 18), left-handed.

Today is the feast day of St. Kilian. On this day, in 1835, the Liberty Bell cracked while tolling for the death of Supreme Court Chief Justice John Marshall.

Nelson Rockefeller *(1908–1979), U.S. vice president*

Rockefeller was governor of New York from 1958 to 1974 and served as U.S. vice president under Gerald Ford from 1974 to 1976. The grandson of Standard Oil founder John D. Rockefeller, he was, as a boy and young man, expected to live up to stringent family expectations of proper behavior and appearance. Left-handedness was just one of many unacceptable delinquencies in the rigid world of the Rockefeller millions. "My father didn't believe in people being left-handed," Nelson once recalled. To break Nelson of his left-handedness at an early age, his father devised an ingeniously humiliating contraption, elaborately constructed of string and elastic, to be used at the dinner table: whenever little Nelson tried to eat with his left hand, the father snapped the elastic and yanked on the string, conditioning Nelson (in a painful way) to become right-handed. The result was that Nelson grew up severely dyslexic: once he became a public figure, he had to rigorously memorize every word of his speeches so as not to flounder in front of cameras, reporters, and constituents. When Nelson was an adult and had a family of his own, his children often wondered why he never read aloud to them. "Daddy can't read" was the whispered reply from their mother.

Today is Independence Day in Argentina. On this day, in 1540, Henry VIII's fourth marriage, to Anne of Cleves, was annulled. In 1960, the U.S. nuclear-powered attack submarine *Thresher* was launched.

Nikola Tesla (1856–1943), *Croatian-U.S. inventor*

Tesla claimed, in the fall of 1899, to have received signals from an extraterrestrial intelligence at his electronics laboratory in the foothills of the Rockies near Colorado Springs. The assertion drew predictably derisive comments from his contemporaries, but still, a century later, it gives one pause to wonder. The man who, in essence, designed and developed alternating current, was an extraordinary genius whose notebooks to this day are still pored over by scientists and engineers looking for research leads and clues to the still unfolding secrets of electricity, so rich are Tesla's laboratory papers with raw ideas, brilliant speculations, and promising avenues of investigation. Although Tesla had a side to him that was undeniably, and sometimes distractingly, eccentric—modern psychiatry would label him obsessive-compulsive, with an almost overriding germ phobia—he discovered the rotating magnetic field, the foundation of virtually all alternating-current machinery, and—until he sold them to businessman George Westinghouse in 1885—he held the patent rights to most alternating-current dynamos, transformers, and motors. The son of an Orthodox priest and a brilliant though illiterate mother, he started inventing things at an early age, often relying more on intuition and passion than on strict understanding and application. While still in his teens, he broke several ribs and spent more than a month in the hospital after attempting to design and fly a reliable airplane on the family farm. In 1884, he left his native Croatia and sailed to the United States, where, with several dazzling letters of introduction in his pocket, he went to work for Thomas Edison. The contrast in temperament between the two inventors—Edison steely, ruthlessly analytical, always with an eye to profit; Tesla fervent, impractical, indifferent to financial success—precipitated a mutual loathing that climaxed with Tesla's defection to a laboratory of his own. Working alone over the next several decades, he made numerous discoveries that paved the way for radar, remote-control technology, television, radio, and the practical application of X rays. He also loved to astonish visitors by generating indoor bolts of lightning, some over a hundred feet long, and by discussing his work on a so-called death ray that he claimed could disintegrate thousands of airplanes with a single stroke of electricity from hundreds of miles away. Although he had few intimate relationships throughout his life—one of his only close friends was Mark Twain—his funeral at the Cathedral of St. John the Divine in New York City drew hundreds of mourners, including a roster of Nobel Prize winners who hailed his intellect. It should be noted that Tesla, who was ambidextrous, died peacefully, surrounded by his pet pigeons, in a third-class hotel room in Manhattan, while the tyrannical, right-handed Edison, plagued by gastric ulcers, died of acute uremia and was kvetching about his medical condition, and its treatment, almost to the end.

Elias Howe (1819–1867), U.S. inventor

Left-hander Howe invented the sewing machine in the 1840s and was granted a patent for it in 1846. When he realized there was little interest in his new invention, he moved to England and took a menial job. Several years later, he returned to the United States and discovered, to his consternation, that sewing machines were being manufactured and marketed all across the country, in violation of his patent.

He turned to the courts for compensation, and in 1854 he was recognized as the legal inventor of the machine, and thereafter received the appropriate royalties from its production and sale.

Today is the Feast of Fortune in Japan. On this day, in 1925, the Scopes "Monkey Trial" began in Dayton, Tennessee. In 1991, Boris Yeltsin was inaugurated as the first democratically elected president of Russia.

John Sholto Douglas *(1844–1900), British nobleman, ninth Marquess of Queensberry*

Some left-handers—not many—are just plain jerks. Left-hander John Sholto Douglas was responsible for devising the Marquess of Queensberry rules of boxing (the foundation of modern boxing rules) and was himself an amateur athlete and pugilist. He was also infamous in his time as a thoroughly disagreeable and bellicose man, having physically attacked numerous people—including one of his own sons, Percy—in public. His first wife divorced him because of his sexual infidelities; his second sought an annulment after he deserted her. He was obsessed with what he regarded as weakness or effeminacy of any sort, and when he learned that another son, Lord Alfred Douglas, was having a relationship with Oscar Wilde, he went into a frenzy, threatened to kill them both, and hired thugs to stalk the pair all over England. (Wilde was compelled to hire twenty armed guards to keep Queensberry and his henchmen from physically assaulting the cast, stage crew, and audience at the opening night of *The Importance of Being Earnest*.) It was Sholto Douglas's public accusation of Wilde's homosexuality that eventually led to the playwright's conviction and imprisonment for two years' hard labor on charges of "indecency"—an imprisonment that destroyed Wilde's physical health, ended his creativity, and left him a broken man.

Today is National Cheer Up the Sad and Lonely Day in the United States. On this day, in 1974, the remains of the *Skylab* space station fell back to earth.

Lisa Rinna (b. 1965), U.S. actress

The wife of actor Harry Hamlin, left-hander Rinna is best known as Billie Reed Brady (1992–1995) on the daytime soap opera *Days of Our Lives* and as Taylor McBride (since 1996) on *Melrose Place.*

Nicole d'Oresme (1325–1382), French mathematician

Much more than a mathematician, the ambidextrous Oresme was also a Roman Catholic bishop, an economist, a translator (primarily of Aristotle, from the contemporaneous Latin into French), a cosmologist (he presaged Copernicus by refuting the theory that the earth was stationary and stood at the center of the universe), and a social philosopher who openly savaged astrologers, clairvoyants, and occultists in his treatise *Book on Divinations.* Among his many contributions to the field of mathematics, he laid the foundations for the development of analytic geometry. Today, incidentally, is not the date of his birth, which is unknown, but the date of his death in 1382.

12

On this day, in 1961, residents of Shreveport, Louisiana, reported a violent, inexplicable rain of hundreds of unripe peaches from a cloudy sky. In 1976, the game show *Family Feud* debuted.

Richard Simmons

(b. 1948), U.S. exercise guru

The doyen of health and exercise—variously described as "the Pied Piper of Pounds," "the Clown Prince of Fitness," and "the Apostle of Adipose"—has a left-handed father as well as a left-handed brother, and is, in his own words, "a very strict left-hander." "About the only thing I can do with my right hand is wave," he once said.

13

On this day, in 1645, Czar Michael, founder of the Romanov dynasty, died. In 1793, French revolutionary Jean-Paul Marat was assassinated while taking a bath in his tub.

Paul Prudhomme *(b. 1940), Cajun chef*

The left-handed master chef has popularized the cooking of his native Louisiana through six best-selling cookbooks—including *Fiery Foods That I Love*—and his numerous appearances on television. He has also developed his own retail line of distinctive Cajun seasonings and sauces.

Nathan Bedford Forrest (1821–1877),
Confederate general

Forrest may have been a widely acclaimed tactical genius on the battlefields of the Civil War, but he is primarily remembered for his wholesale slaughter of more than three hundred blacks, including women and children, at Fort Pillow, Tennessee, in 1864. "Take no more Negro prisoners," he ordered his men. He was one of the founders of the Ku Klux Klan after the war, and became that organization's first Grand Lizard, er, Wizard.

14

Today is Bastille Day in France. On this day, in 1865, the Matterhorn was successfully scaled for the first time.

Gerald Ford (b. 1913), U.S. president

We used to say jokingly that he even thought left-handed.

—One of Gerald Ford's former high school friends

Leaving the White House for a skiing vacation one Christmas, President Ford became so entangled in his dogs' leashes that he nearly fell over. "Merry Christmas," he shouted to the press, "and a Merry—uh—a Happy New Year!" During his three-year stint as the country's chief executive, Ford was seen stumbling down ramps, hitting his head on the sides of swimming pools, and generally knocking things over, all of which led to his acquiring various pejorative nicknames in the press, including "President Klutz," "Mr. Ten Thumbs," and "Old Bungle Foot." (Ten years earlier, Lyndon Johnson had quipped, "Jerry Ford is a nice guy, but he played too much football in college with his helmet off.") His notorious clumsiness spawned a continuing series of satiric skits (featuring Chevy Chase) on *Saturday Night Live*, and one columnist mused that Ford might very well become "the first president to be laughed out of office." Said Ford philosophically, in his own defense, "You have to expect the bitter and sweet and take a little kidding and let the press and other people get in a few barbs and let it roll off your back like water off a duck's back."

Terry-Thomas *(1911–1990), British actor*

As a popular actor in the 1950s and 1960s, left-hander Terry-Thomas had two trademarks: his bushy mustache and the gap between his two upper front teeth. Renowned for a frantic, often angst-ridden form of physical comedy, he appeared in some four dozen films, including *The Mouse on the Moon* (1963), *It's a Mad Mad Mad Mad World* (1963), *Those Magnificent Men in Their Flying Machines* (1965), *Where Were You When the Lights Went Out?* (1968), and *The Bawdy Adventures of Tom Jones* (1977).

15

Today is St. Swithin's Day. On this day, in 1783, the first successful steamboat made its maiden voyage, in France. In 1997, fashion designer Gianni Versace was shot and killed outside his home in Miami Beach.

"Shoeless" Joe Jackson *(1889–1951), U.S. baseball player*

The story of the so-called Chicago Black Sox and the fix of the 1919 World Series has been told and retold so many times, from so many different perspectives, it scarcely needs repeating here; its appearance as a crucial (and sentimental) plot element in Kevin Costner's 1989 film *Field of Dreams* was a sure sign of its complete assimilation into the American cultural consciousness, as defining a point in American history as the stock-market crash of 1929 or the kidnapping of the Lindbergh baby. Jackson himself was one of the most powerful and revered left-handed hitters in the history of baseball, with a peak of .408 in 1911 and a career average (before he was banned from the game for life in 1920) of .356. He treated his bats lovingly: each one had a name—Black Betsy, Blond Betsy, Big Jim, Caroliny, et al.—and during the winter, when he fled Chicago for his home in South Carolina, he took his bats with him, explaining to a sportswriter, "Bats don't like to freeze no more than me." Incidentally, he got his nickname—

"Shoeless" Joe—after a 1908 game in which his new shoes (and the resulting blisters) were so painful that he removed them and played the remaining innings in his stocking feet.

On this day, in 1945, the first atomic bomb was exploded, in a test in New Mexico. In 1969, *Apollo 11* lifted off from Cape Canaveral on its eight-day mission to the moon.

Vincent Sherman (b. 1906), U.S. film director

The veteran director of more than thirty feature films—including *Old Acquaintance*, *Mr. Skeffington*, *Harriet Craig*, and *The Young Philadelphians*—was switched to right-handedness as a child. "My mother," he told an interviewer, "told me that very early in life I began using my left hand for everything. She thought that being left-handed could be a handicap, and since she and my father were right-handed, she felt it only proper to force me to use my right hand. For that reason, I tell people I became very mixed up for the rest of my life."

Today is Constitution Day in Korea. On this day, in 1955, Disneyland opened, in Anaheim, California. In 1989, the B-2 "stealth bomber" made its first test flight.

Anne Ramsay (b. 1959), U.S. actress

Ramsay had a recurring role on *Star Trek: The Next Generation* as Ensign Clancy, and she played Lisa Stemple on the hit series *Mad About You*, beginning in 1992. She was also seen as left-handed baseball player Helen Haley in the 1992 film *A League of Their Own* (costarring Geena Davis and Madonna).

On this day, in 1817, Jane Austen died. In 1995, the Montserrat volcano Soufrière Hills began erupting.

Jessamyn West *(1902–1984), U.S. writer*

"Writing is so difficult," West once said of her chosen profession, "that I often feel that writers, having had their hell on earth, will escape punishment hereafter." A devout Quaker, the left-handed author is best known for the popular novel *Friendly Persuasion*, later made into the classic 1956 film starring Gary Cooper and Anthony Perkins. She was also the author of the oft repeated aphorism, "A religious awakening which does not awaken the sleeper to love has roused him in vain."

Steve Forbes *(b. 1947), U.S. businessman and politician*

The CEO of Forbes Inc.—son of the late 'flamboyant millionaire Malcolm Forbes and an unsuccessful candidate for the Republican nomination for president in 1996—is left-handed.

On this day, in 1877, the first Wimbledon tennis championship began. In 1984, Geraldine Ferraro became the first woman vice presidential candidate of a mainstream party.

Vicki Carr *(b. 1941), U.S. singer*

The enormously popular, left-handed singer has been responsible for such hits as "It Must Be Him," "For Once in My Life," "She'll Be There," "Sunday Morning Coming Down," and "Can't Take My Eyes Off of You."

Today is National Ice Cream Day. On this day, in 1923, Mexican revolutionary Pancho Villa was assassinated. In 1976, the *Viking I* spacecraft made a safe landing on the Martian surface.

Neil Armstrong's left foot (1969)

At exactly 10:56 P.M. Eastern Daylight Time, on June 20, 1969, Neil Armstrong became the first human being to step foot on the lunar surface. It was Armstrong's *left* foot—wearing a size 9½B boot—that first made contact with the moon.

On this day, in 1970, Egypt's Aswan Dam began operation. In 1988, Massachusetts governor Michael Dukakis officially became the Democratic party candidate for president.

Marshall McLuhan (1911–1980), U.S. writer

The so-called Oracle of the Electronic Age became famous for advancing the concept of "the Global Village" and for writing extensively on the sociological impact of television, computers, and other electronic media in his popular books *Understanding Media* (1964) and *The Medium Is the Message* (1967).

Today is National Liberation Day in Poland. On this day, in 1934, bank robber John Dillinger was allegedly gunned down by FBI agents outside a Chicago movie theater. In 1994, the final fragments of Comet Shoemaker-Levy 9 crashed into Jupiter.

Albert Brooks (b. 1947), U.S. actor and director

Interviewed on America Online in 1997, Brooks was asked by a fan, "When did you know you wanted to go into comedy?" "I was the class clown in school," Brooks replied, "and I knew I wanted to go into comedy when I saw my first report card." Born in Beverly Hills (his real name is Albert Einstein), the left-hander landed his first acting job in 1970 on an episode of *Love, American Style* titled "Love and the Model." He appeared on *Saturday Night Live* during the 1974–75 season and had small parts in the movies *Taxi Driver* and *Private Benjamin*. But it wasn't until his feature-film debut as writer, director, and star of the critically acclaimed *Real Life* that his career began to soar. The comedy—about an opportunistic filmmaker who ruins the lives of an average American family while trying to make a documentary about them—was vintage Brooks: few belly laughs, lots to admire, lots to think about, and a refreshingly absurdist view of everyone's preoccupation with being "normal." Brooks has since gone on to write, direct, and star in *Lost in America* (1985), *Defending Your Life* (with Meryl Streep, in 1991), and *Mother* (with Debbie Reynolds, in 1996). He also won an Academy Award nomination for his role as the sweating—and sweating, and sweating—news anchor in *Broadcast News* in 1987.

Robert Dole *(b. 1923)*, *U.S. senator and presidental candidate*

Although born right-handed, Dole became left-handed in 1945 after a combat injury in Italy permanently crippled his right hand.

Terence Stamp *(b. 1939)*, *British actor*

Endowed with extraordinary, striking good looks, Stamp made a spectacular—and Oscar-nominated—film debut in 1962 as Herman Melville's otherworldly and naïve Billy Budd in the Peter Ustinov–directed film of the classic novella. Over the next ten years, he alternated between offbeat and mainstream roles: as the deranged kidnapper in *The Collector* (1965), as the swashbuckling but faithless lover in *Far from the Madding Crowd* (1967), as the pansexual young stranger in Pier Paolo Pasolini's avant-garde *Teorema* (1968). He also appeared in the Federico Fellini segment of the omnibus horror film *Spirits of the Dead* and in Alan Cooke's *Mind of Mr. Soames*, about a man who, having been in a coma since birth, wakes up at the age of thirty and must learn, from scratch, to be a human being. It's almost a truism of Stamp's career that the films he's in are excoriated or ignored by critics when they come out, only to be lavished with praise years later. *Far from the Madding Crowd*—a lush, romantic epic—was greeted tepidly when it was first released in the late 1960s (critics were too busy praising more "relevant" fare—like *Billy Jack*), but has since acquired a reputation as a masterpiece of sorts. And *Spirits of the Dead*—having no scenes of Vietnam protesters rioting or dropout lawyers smoking pot—was dismissed as irrelevant and decadent by many critics who twenty years later hailed it as an exquisite gem. In all of this, Stamp's reputation suffered, though his craft never did, not for a moment. During the 1980s, he showed up in a dozen or so films—*Superman II, Wall Street, Young Guns*—but it was in 1994 that he gave perhaps the most remarkable and mesmerizing performance of his long career. In the otherwise pleasant but sophomoric film *The Adventures of Priscilla, Queen of the Desert*, Stamp eclipsed everything around him as the world-weary, indomitable transsexual Bernadette ("Bernie"): as in most of his films, every time he was on-screen, it was simply impossible to take one's eyes off him.

23

Today marks the beginning of the astrological sign Leo. On this day, in 1846, Henry David Thoreau was arrested and thrown in jail for a night for refusing to pay a one-dollar poll tax.

Anthony Kennedy (b. 1936), *U.S. Supreme Court justice*

The left-handed jurist—a graduate of Stanford and Harvard—practiced law from 1962 to 1975, when he was nominated to the federal judiciary by Gerald Ford. In 1988, he became an associate justice of the U.S. Supreme Court.

24

Today is Simón Bolívar Day in Ecuador and Venezuela. On this day, in 1938, instant coffee was invented.

Barry Bonds *(b. 1964), U.S. baseball player*

The controversial left-handed outfielder—paid a record $43.75 million for a six-year contract with the San Francisco Giants in 1993—might not have grown up left-handed at all if his father—retired major-league ballplayer Bobby Bonds—had had his way. Father Bonds wanted his son to be right-handed. "I wouldn't let him take his baby bottle with his left hand," the elder Bonds once told an interviewer. "I'd pull it away and get him to take it with his right. But then he'd just switch it over, so I lost." As a child, Barry himself seemed an unlikely candidate to become one of the most formidable and famous sports figures in the world. "I was a mama's boy," he acknowledged to *Playboy* magazine in 1993. "I'd rather watch my mom put her makeup on. Or put on a wig and dance with her; we would both pretend we were Janet Jackson." Bonds's athletic prowess quickly manifested itself in high school, when, playing for the school baseball team, he batted .467. He continued awe-inspiring performances at bat throughout college in Arizona. In 1986, he joined the Pittsburgh Pirates. By 1990, he was an All-Star, having hit 33 home runs (his average that season was .301), with 114 RBIs and 52 stolen bases. Twice named MVP (in 1990 and again in 1992), Bonds hit 46 home runs in 1993, 42 in 1996, and 40 in 1997. He left the Pirates to sign with San Francisco in 1993. Often criticized for his flamboyant playing style and his conspicuous lifestyle outside the ballpark (even his gold and diamond jewelry has aroused controversy), Bonds acknowledges, "I can be arrogant on the field. I'm doing my job, giving the people what they paid for. Entertainment."

Pat Oliphant *(b. 1935), Australian-U.S. political cartoonist*

The Pulitzer Prize–winning, left-handed cartoonist got his start drawing weather maps for a newspaper in Adelaide, Australia, while still in his teens. When the newspaper's regular political cartoonist left to take another job, Oliphant was offered the chance to fill in and soon became one of the newspaper's star attractions. In the 1960s, he came to the United States, working first for the *Denver Post* and then the *Washington Star*. He won a Pulitzer Prize in 1966 for his widely acclaimed political cartoons, regularly skewering figures from both the left and the right, and is today the most widely syndicated editorial cartoonist in the world. Oliphant is also a sculptor, specializing in depictions of U.S. presidents—including Nixon, Ford, Carter, Reagan, and Bush—and is the founder of the BGA: the Bad Golfers Association. He readily acknowledges he is "one of the worst golfers in America."

Dan Hedaya *(b. 1940), U.S. actor*

One of the busiest character actors in modern-day Hollywood, left-hander Hedaya has appeared in dozens of films, as Alicia Silverstone's workaholic father in *Clueless* (1995), as Bette Midler's ex-husband, Mortie, in *The First Wives Club* (1996), as General Perez in *Alien Resurrection* (1997). His other film credits include *Blood Simple* (1984), *In & Out* (1997), *Ransom* (1996), *Nixon* (1995), *The Usual Suspects* (1995), *Maverick* (1994), and *The Addams Family* (1991).

Simón Bolívar *(1783–1830), Venezuelan soldier-statesman*

When you want to enslave a country, to reduce it to economic or physical rubble or merely suffocate it through dictatorship, it's always best to call a right-hander—say, someone in the mold of Lenin or Adolf Hitler. But when you're looking to liberate a nation, no one but a left-hander will do. "Simón Bolívar . . . is regarded by many as the greatest genius the Hispanic-American world has produced," one historian has written. Ungovernable as a child, influenced by Voltaire and Rousseau as a young man, stimulated by the glory and exploits of Napoleon (while despising the French emperor's betrayal of republican ideals), Bolívar returned to his native Venezuela after his long years of education in Europe, when he was twenty-four, and soon embarked on his lifelong crusade to liberate the Spanish-dominated colonies of Latin America. Venezuela fell out of Spain's clutches first, thanks to Bolívar's skillful negotiating, inspired writings, and fearless exploits on the battlefield. Venezuela was inevitably eventually followed by Ecuador, Columbia, Peru, and Bolivia. That the consistently brazen and adventurous Bolívar was dubbed, even by some of his own supporters, "a dangerous man" seems oddly redundant; after all, an "un-dangerous" man would've been content to stay at home and goose-step along with everyone else.

Today is St. James Day in Spain. On this day, in 1956, the transatlantic ocean liner *Andrea Doria* collided with another ship off Nantucket and began to sink. In 1978, the first "test-tube" baby was born, in England.

Jerry Doyle (b. 1960), U.S. actor

The left-handed actor—formerly a corporate jet pilot and a stockbroker—is best known to television audiences as security chief Michael Garibaldi on the science fiction series *Babylon 5*.

On this day, in 1775, the U.S. Post Office was established, with Benjamin Franklin as its first postmaster general. In 1952, Evita Perón died.

Dorothy Hamill (b. 1956), U.S. ice-skating champion

In the late 1970s, it seemed as if every woman in America wanted to look like Dorothy Hamill: the famous "wedge cut" hairdo worn by the Olympic figure skater was as pervasive as the Supremes' "beehive" fifteen years earlier. Left-hander Hamill—one of the most popular competitors in American figure skating—won her first championship, the U.S. Ladies Novice, when she was twelve. In 1975, she won the freestyle world championship, and a year later took the gold medal in women's figure skating at the Winter Olympics. The epitome of the

bright, energetic, and gracious all-American competitor, she joined the Ice Capades shortly after her Olympic victory. "I don't mind the celebrity status," she once said, "and I don't mind signing autographs either. When I was a little girl, I missed getting Peggy Fleming's autograph, and I never forgot that."

27

On this day, in 1921, insulin was discovered. In 1953, the Korean War ended. In 1990, Zsa Zsa Gabor began serving jail time in Los Angeles for having slapped a Beverly Hills policeman.

Keenan Wynn (1916–1986), U.S. actor

A ubiquitous presence in three decades of Hollywood films, starting with his first role in the 1942 Busby Berkeley musical *For Me and My Gal*, Wynn played supporting roles and character parts—frequently as thugs or members of the military—in almost ninety movies. He particularly distinguished himself as Bat Guano, the rifle-toting colonel who torments Peter Sellers over exact change for a pay phone in Stanley Kubrick's *Dr. Strangelove* (1964), and as the disoriented, grieving man at the emotional center of Robert Altman's *Nashville* (1975).

Sasha Mitchell (b. 1967), U.S. actor

Left-hander Mitchell got his start modeling Calvin Klein jeans in the late 1980s and working for noted fashion photographer Bruce Weber. From 1989 to 1991, he starred as James Richard Beaumont on *Dallas*, and later developed a cult following for his role in three of the *Kickboxer* movies, starting in 1991. As anyone who has seen the *Kickboxer* films can attest, he sports an enormous tattoo of a dragon over his entire left shoulder.

 **28** On this day, in 1945, a U.S. Army bomber crashed into the Empire State Building at the seventy-ninth floor, killing thirteen people. In 2061, Halley's comet will make its return to the vicinity of earth.

Robert Hughes (b. 1938), Australian art critic

Hughes became the art critic for *Time* magazine in 1970, and has authored numerous books, including *Heaven and Hell in Western Art* (1968); *The Fatal Shore*, a history of Australia (1987); and *The Culture of Complaint* (1993). He was switched from left-handedness as a boy.

Rudy Vallee (1901–1986), U.S. entertainer

Rudy Vallee is proof of how dramatically ideas of what's sexually attractive change from generation to generation. Looking at pictures of him now, it's hard to understand what all the fuss was about. Vallee was one of the heartthrobs of American nightclubs and motion pictures in the 1920s and 1930s. That the left-handed actor-singer was himself completely swayed and transformed—not for the better—by all the swooning and attention is the stuff of Hollywood legends: he once suggested that the city fathers of Los Angeles change the name of Sunset Boulevard to Rue de Vallee. He was serious, but they declined. During his heyday, his most popular films were *The Vagabond Lover* (1929), *George White's Scandals* (1934), and *Sweet Music* (1935). As he aged, he turned into a successful character actor, appearing in *How to Succeed in Business Without Really Trying* (1967) and *Won Ton*

Ton, the Dog Who Saved Hollywood (1976), and as the villainous Lord Phogg on TV's *Batman*.

Vida Blue *(b. 1949), U.S. baseball player*

Blue has been credited with single-handedly reviving a national interest in baseball in the early 1970s. During his first full year pitching for the Oakland A's in 1971, home-game attendance *quadrupled* from the previous year. His stylish left-handed delivery (he added an unusual snap of the wrist as the ball left his hand), his good looks, and his stunning accuracy (his first season, he was 24–8), all contributed to his enormous appeal. He turned down a $2,000 offer from A's manager Chuck Finley to have his name legally changed to "True Blue."

Garfield Sobers *(b. 1936), West Indian cricketer*

A native of Barbados, left-hander Sobers began playing championship cricket at the age of sixteen and quickly distinguished himself as one of the most talented players of all time. Between 1953 and 1974, he batted 8,032 runs, and established a long-standing record of 365 not-outs in 1957. A published author as well—he wrote the novel *Bonaventure and the Flashing Blade* (1967) and several books on cricket—he was knighted in 1975.

 29 On this day, in 1958, NASA was established. In 1981, Prince Charles and Lady Diana Spencer were married in Westminster Abbey.

Melvin Belli *(b. 1907), U.S. attorney*

Flamboyant lawyer nicknamed "the King of Torts" for his often dramatic participation in malpractice and negligence lawsuits and for his courtroom defense of Jack Ruby on charges of murdering Lee Harvey Oswald. Also a sometime actor, he is remembered by television audiences of the sixties as Gorgan, the epitome of corruption and evil, in an episode—"And the Children Shall Lead"—of the original *Star Trek.*

Wil Wheaton *(b. 1972), U.S. actor*

Left-handed actor best known for his role as River Phoenix's best buddy in the 1986 film *Stand by Me,* and as boy-genius-bound-for-interdimensional-glory Wesley Crusher on *Star Trek: The Next Generation.*

Ted Lindsay *(b. 1925), Canadian hockey Hall of Famer*

Nicknamed "Terrible Tempered Ted" for his fights on the ice—and his outspoken public views on hockey and the National Hockey League—left-hander Lindsay played for the Detroit Red Wings and the Chicago Blackhawks in a seventeen-year career beginning in 1944. He was named eight times to the league's first All-Star team, and in 1960 received the Art Ross Trophy as the league's top scorer.

 **On this day, in 1898, corn flakes were invented. In 1975, Teamsters president Jimmy Hoffa disappeared.**

Lisa Kudrow *(b. 1963), U.S. actress*

You often have to be awfully smart to play a ditsy blond successfully. Kudrow graduated from Vassar with a bachelor's degree in biology and intended to pursue a career in pure research. Fate intervened in the unlikely form of *Saturday Night Live* cast member Jon Lovitz, a friend of Kudrow's brother; Lovitz persuaded the would-be researcher to pursue a career in comedy. She landed parts on various TV series—including *Mad About You, Coach, Cheers,* and *Newhart*—but it wasn't until 1994 that she became an Emmy-nominated star in her own right, as the vulnerable, scatterbrained, awful-folk-song-singing Phoebe on the smash-hit series *Friends*. The sixties had Goldie Hawn, the seventies had Diane Keaton, and the nineties have Lisa Kudrow. In her spare time, she's a renowned left-hand pool shark. As anyone who's ever watched a Marilyn Monroe or Judy Holliday film knows, only a fool messes with a ditsy blond.

Casey Stengel (1890–1975), U.S. baseball manager

I was not successful as a ballplayer, as it was a game of skill.

—Casey Stengel

From 1949 to 1960, Stengel led the New York Yankees to ten pennant victories and seven world championships. Never one to walk away from a challenge, he became the first manager of the newly formed New York Mets in 1962, when he was seventy-one. The Mets soon established themselves as so hopelessly bad that everyone loved them. "Can't anyone here play this game?" Stengel once hollered in disgust at his players. During another game, one of his players asked him sarcastically, "Have *you* ever played baseball?" "Sure, I played," Stengel snapped back. "Did you think I was born at the age of seventy sitting in a dugout trying to manage guys like you?" (In fact, Stengel had played major-league ball from 1912 to 1925 for Brooklyn, Pittsburgh, and other franchises.) The team, and Stengel, provided fodder for good-natured jokes across the country, becoming, among other things, a staple of *The Tonight Show*'s opening monologue for several years running. And Stengel's antics in the ballpark became legendary. Once he furtively captured a bird in the dugout and quickly hid it under his cap; later, when he got into a dispute with an umpire, he doffed his cap in the umpire's direction and, to the delight of fans, the bird fluttered out. His Gracie Allen logic produced several oft quoted non sequiturs. "The team," he once boasted to a sportswriter, "has come along slow, but fast." On another occasion, he announced, "There comes a time in every man's life—and I've had many of them." Stengel had, in his youth, originally intended to become a dentist. However, when he started wielding dental tools left-handed in school, one of his professors cried out in horror, "You're a left-hander, a left-hander!" Stengel soon abandoned the pursuit of dentistry in favor of baseball. He later liked to joke, "I was a left-handed dentist who made people cry." Still, he was content to be a southpaw. "Left-handers," he often said, "have more enthusiasm for life."

Laurence Fishburne (b. 1961), U.S. actor

The Tony and Emmy Award–winning left-handed performer got his start as a child actor in the daytime soap opera *One Life to Live*, landed a role at the age of fourteen in Francis Ford Coppola's *Apocalypse Now* (he lied about his age to secure the part of an unhinged Vietnam soldier), and went on to critical acclaim in major roles in *Boyz n the Hood* (1991), *What's Love Got to Do with It* (as Ike Turner, in 1993), *Searching for Bobby Fischer* (1993), and *Othello* (1995). His outspoken disdain for divisiveness or separatism of any sort is often reflected in his choice of roles. "One day we're all going to wake up and realize," he told an interviewer, "that this is not about black America and white America and red America and yellow America and brown America. Why? Look at television. The most popular thing isn't *60 Minutes*. It's MTV. That's what the little ones are looking at. And they see everybody. Chinese, Jewish, black, white—the kids see themselves. It's great. Reality is not what we've been told it is—everything separate. Never has been."

William Atherton (b. 1947), U.S. actor

The left-handed actor turned in stunning lead performances early in his career in Steven Spielberg's *Sugarland Express* (1974) and John Schlesinger's *Day of the Locust* (1975), but was all too quickly marginalized into repetitive villainy as the obnoxious, priggish bureaucrat in *Ghostbusters* (1984), the obnoxious, corrupt college professor in *Real Genius* (1985), the obnoxious, cold-blooded reporter in *Die Hard* (1988), the obnoxious, cold-blooded reporter traveling by plane in *Die Hard 2*, et cetera.

Henry Ford (1863–1947), U.S. industrialist

The 1974 edition of the esteemed *Encyclopaedia Britannica* mentions only in passing that Henry Ford "subsidized a newspaper that specialized in anti-Jewish articles." Well, that's one way of putting it. Why not just come out with it? Ford *owned* the notorious *Dearborn*

Independent, dictated much of its anti-Jewish editorial content, and was an ardent admirer of Adolf Hitler, just as Hitler swooned over the efficiency and anti-Semitism of Henry Ford. "The Jews are the conscious enemies of all that Anglo-Saxons mean by civilization," the *Independent* once proclaimed. (The curious can go to Web site www.hfmgv.org/histories/hf/D.1218.jpg—part of the Henry Ford Museum archives—to see one of the newspaper's *milder* front pages.) The automobile manufacturer's ferocity in financing anti-Jewish propaganda was so well known that the early Nazi government publicly praised him as "a great anti-Semite," and he rates a unique, favorable mention in Hitler's *Mein Kampf,* surely the one book most people would have preferred to have been left out of. "At least Germany keeps its people at work," Ford once asserted. One can only imagine his pride when, on his seventy-fifth birthday in 1938, he became the first American to receive Hitler's Supreme Order of the German Eagle. Yes, the first American. True, he perfected the assembly-line process of automobile manufacturing (contrary to popular myth, the actual idea for the assembly line came from Ransom E. Olds, of Oldsmobile fame), and he achieved his stated ambition—"When I'm through, everybody will be able to afford an automobile and about everybody will have one"—and revolutionized the landscape of the country (and eventually the world) in the process. Still, the American love affair with the car notwithstanding, his status as a folk hero seems, well, more than a little off-target, and as with other early Hitler apologists—Charles Lindbergh and George Bernard Shaw, for example—one can admire the achievements without particularly falling victim to the PR. After the war, Ford claimed—as did almost the entire population of Germany—to have had no idea what was *really* going on in Hitler's concentration-camp-strewn empire. He also became famous for his oft repeated assertion, "History is bunk." As the Church Lady used to say, "How con-*veee*-nient."

31

On this day, in 1954, the second-highest peak in the world, K2, was successfully scaled for the first time.

Barry Van Dyke (b. 1951), U.S. actor

The left-handed son of left-handed entertainer Dick Van Dyke got his show-business start on his father's celebrated sitcom, *The Dick Van Dyke Show*, in 1961, playing a ten-year-old boy named Florian. Some fifteen years later, he began his acting career in earnest, with guest shots on such popular shows as *The Love Boat* and *The Dukes of Hazzard*, as well as in various made-for-TV movies. He reached an even wider audience in the 1990s, when he joined the cast of his father's TV mystery drama, *Diagnosis Murder*.

Edward Herrmann (b. 1943), U.S. actor

Herrmann made his screen debut in 1971 in the peculiar Italian film *Lady Liberty*, starring Sophia Loren as an Italian woman trying to get—no, we are not making this up—a huge sausage through U.S. Customs. The bizarre comedy also featured an appearance by the twenty-three-year-old transvestite Candy Darling. Herrmann's film work since then has been distinctly conventional. He is most famous for his stunning portrayal of Franklin Delano Roosevelt in the Emmy Award–winning television movies *Eleanor and Franklin* in 1976 and *Eleanor and Franklin: The White House Years* in 1977.

Left-handers Born in
August

August: Eighth month of the year, named after Augustus,
Julius Caesar's successor as Emperor of Rome

Today is Lughnasadh, the Wiccan celebration of first harvest. On this day, in 1873, the first cable car began operation in San Francisco. In 1981, MTV premiered.

Allen Ludden (1922–1981), U.S. game show host

Given that left-handers are so frequently associated with nonverbal forms of communication, it's perhaps surprising that a left-hander became virtually synonymous with *the* classic word-oriented game show of 1960s television, *Password*. Ludden didn't create *Password* (TV game show impresarios Mark Goodson and Bill Todman did), but he became, as host, its face to the world; and though he had also hosted the tremendously popular *College Bowl* on television—and had done stage work and professional singing—hosting *Password* remained, to his death, his signature career achievement. More important for Ludden, it introduced him to actress Betty White, who began appearing on the show as a regular contestant shortly after its inception. The two—destined to become one of Hollywood's longest-lasting couples—were married in 1963.

2

On this day, in 1498, Christopher Columbus discovered the islands of Trinidad and Tobago. In 1990, the Iraqi army began its invasion of Kuwait.

James Baldwin

(1924–1987), U.S. author

"It is a great shock at the age of five or six," Baldwin reflected in a 1965 speech, "to find that in a world of Gary Coopers you are the Indian." For Baldwin, discovering that he was "the Indian" meant being African-American, left-handed, and homosexual—as well as bursting with a moral indignation that put him at odds with an often hypocritical and complacent world. Baldwin was an *angry* man, and was not—even slightly—content to suffer his rage in silence. "My life, my *real* life, was in danger, and not from anything other people might do," he wrote in an essay in 1955, "but from the hatred I carried in my own heart." Baldwin's essential message—the urgency of resolving racial, religious, and other differences to avert the self-destruction of society—is as urgent today as when he first began delivering it in such acclaimed novels as Go *Tell It on the Mountain* and *Giovanni's Room* in the 1950s.

3

Today is the beginning of the Festival of Hungry Ghosts in China. On this day, in 1933, the Mickey Mouse watch went on sale for the first time.

Carol Leifer *(b. 1956), U.S. comedienne and writer*

Leifer—a former stand-up comic familiar to viewers of *The Tonight Show* and *Late Night with David Letterman*—became a writer for

Seinfeld in 1993 and one of the show's coproducers in 1995. She's also written for *Saturday Night Live* and *The Larry Saunders Show*.

Today is Coast Guard Day in the United States. On this day, in 1944, Anne Frank and her family were arrested by police in their attic hideaway in Amsterdam.

Maurice "Rocket" Richard *(b. 1921), Canadian hockey Hall of Famer*

Richard—nicknamed "Rocket" for his unparalleled swiftness and intensity on the ice—played professional ice hockey for eighteen years, beginning in 1942. The first NHL player to score 50 goals in a season, he was legendary for his defeat-dealing, left-handed slap shot, which one sportswriter compared to the lethal strike of a cobra.

On this day, in 1914, the first traffic lights in the U.S. were installed, at an intersection in Cleveland, Ohio. In 1962, Marilyn Monroe committed suicide.

Joseph Merrick *(1862–1890), "the Elephant Man"*

Merrick was a seemingly healthy child until the age of five. Then he abruptly began to manifest symptoms of a peculiar and frightening disease: his head became enormous, almost three feet in circumference; his right arm grew grotesquely attenuated, so that it eventually ended in a twelve-inch-long wrist and a finlike hand; his hip began to buckle and bulge outward—normal walking became impossible. "From the brow projected a huge bony mass, like a loaf, almost covering one eye," said one eyewitness, "while from the back of the head hung a bag of spongy, fungous-looking skin. . . . The lower limbs were grossly deformed." The disease that consumed his body—neurofibromatosis—was a rare genetic disorder characterized by extreme skeletal deformities and the growth of benign tumors over the surface of the body. By the time Merrick was in his teens, he was so severely disfigured he was exhibited in a London freak show. He was billed as "the Elephant Man." The exhibit—which often drove spectators to flee weeping—was closed down several times by the police. Eventually, his case came to the attention of medical authorities, and under the auspices of London Hospital (where he became a permanent resident in 1886), he found refuge. Word of his unique condition spread in the London newspapers; people were astonished to discover that he was an enormously sensitive, sympathetic, well-read, and gracious individual. Queen Victoria visited him several times at his permanent apartments in the hospital, as did a host of other distinguished figures in politics and the arts. He died at the hospital at the age of twenty-eight: because of the weight of his deformed skull, he was forced to sleep sitting up; on the night of his death he apparently tried to sleep lying down, "like other people." He choked to death in his sleep. Whether Merrick was born naturally left- or right-handed is unknown; but like much of his body, his right arm and hand were severely disfigured by neurofibromatosis. By contrast, his left hand remained virtually untouched by the condition, and was in fact quite delicate in size and shape. He often sketched with his left hand, and was facile enough with it to construct numerous paper replicas of churches and other public buildings in London, a hobby that kept him occupied during many of his hours in his hospital rooms.

6 Today is Independence Day in Jamaica. On this day, in 1926, Gertrude Ederle became the first woman to swim the English Channel. In 1945, the atomic bomb was dropped on Hiroshima.

Sir Alexander Fleming (1881–1955), *Scottish bacteriologist*

The ambidextrous Fleming accidentally discovered penicillin in 1928 but didn't quite grasp what to do with it once he'd found it. Returning from a brief vacation, he noticed that petri dishes in which he'd been running bacteriology experiments had been contaminated by mold: the mold—*Penicillium*—killed the bacteria wherever it came into contact with it. Fleming dutifully wrote a brief paper on the matter—and then moved on to something else. His serendipitous discovery languished for almost a dozen years, until two brilliant biochemists, Howard Florey and Ernst Chain, stumbled on Fleming's monograph and began their own in-depth experiments with *Penicillium*. It was only then that the first antibiotic was actually isolated, purified, tested, and, finally, mass-produced. When the Nobel Prizes were handed out in 1945, Fleming shared the Prize for Medicine with Florey and Chain.

Today is Independence Day in the Ivory Coast. On this day, in 1942, the Battle of Guadalcanal was fought. In 1970, black activist Angela Davis was put on the FBI's "Most Wanted" list.

Jack the Ripper (1888), *British serial killer*

Today, of course, isn't Jack the Ripper's birthday—no one knows when that is—but it is the date of his first known killing. On August 7, 1888, thirty-five-year-old London prostitute Martha Turner was murdered on the streets of the city's notorious East End. She was stabbed thirty-nine times, and her throat was slit. Her wounds indicated either a left-handed or ambidextrous assailant. Twenty-four days later, on the morning of August 31, 1888, forty-two-year-old prostitute Mary Ann Nicholls was murdered and gruesomely disemboweled: her throat was cut from ear to ear, her body mutilated, and various organs were partially excised. A short time afterward, a letter (in red ink) arrived at London's Central News Agency: "I am down on whores and I shant quit ripping them. . . . I love my work and want to start again. . . . Yours Truly, Jack the Ripper." Less than a week later, two more East End prostitutes—forty-five-year-old Elizabeth Stride and forty-three-year-old Catherine Eddowes—were also dead. From the results of an autopsy on Nicholls's body, officials concluded that the Ripper was left-handed and had probably used a razor-sharp surgical knife to eviscerate her. Those suppositions were later corroborated by the killings of Stride and Eddowes. In the case of Eddowes, the face and body were savagely, if somewhat flamboyantly, mutilated, as if the killer had spent a great deal of time at his "work." Her left kidney, as well as several other organs (including her uterus), had been removed with surgical precision. (Part of her missing kidney was later mailed to London businessman George Lusk, who headed a vigilante group formed to solve the Ripper murders. "The other piece," wrote the killer in an accompanying note, "I fried and ate. . . . Was very nice.") Despite their revulsion, investigators were overwhelmed by the expertise with which Eddowes's organs had been extracted; from that alone, many of them concluded that the killer must be a seasoned surgeon or physician. In all, over a period of several months, as many as fourteen women were brutally murdered by the Ripper, though some criminologists set the official figure at only six. Twenty-four-year-old Mary Jane Kelly was murdered in November: parts of her body were neatly cut off and then carefully reassembled by the killer into bizarre "sculptures" at the scene of the crime. (According to witnesses, Kelly had been seen walking the streets singing "Sweet Violets" just before her death.) Forty-seven-year-old Annie Chapman was, like the others, grotesquely mutilated. Although the Ripper's identity was never established, persistent rumors suggested that the killer might be Queen Victoria's own grandson, the Duke of Clarence, who was, like many members of the British royal family, left-handed (see January 8), and who was known, even to his contemporaries, as a deeply disturbed and sadistic man who frequented (and often physically abused) street prostitutes. Adding controversy to the case is the fact that many of the papers pertaining to the initial Ripper investigation are still sealed under the Official Secrets Act. Other individuals long suspected of having been the Ripper include Dr. Thomas Cream, a left-handed Scottish surgeon who was hanged in 1892 for having murdered five prostitutes with strychnine; John Montague, a brilliant but mentally unstable lawyer who drowned himself shortly after the murders stopped; James Kenneth Stephen, a poet of light verse (and a cousin of Virginia Woolf) whose handwriting was said to match the Ripper letters sent to newspapers; George Chapman, a barber turned pub keeper who was later hanged for killing several barmaids; and Francis Tumbloty, a sadistic, left-handed American surgeon who frequented London prostitutes and who was, at the time of his death in 1903, widely regarded to have been the Ripper. Ironically, some good came of the notorious murders: their appalling viciousness illuminated the plight of East End slum dwellers and helped initiate a reform movement to improve conditions for the area's orphans, prostitutes, and homeless people. Once regarded as "scum" and "trash," East Enders soon found themselves sympathetically referred to in the press as "those poor unfortunates."

On this day, in 1899, the refrigerator was patented. In 1974, President Richard Nixon resigned from office.

Keith Carradine (b. 1949), U.S. actor

Left-hander Carradine—son of Hollywood horror-film icon John Carradine—has appeared in an array of offbeat, memorable film roles working with some of the world's best directors: Ridley Scott in *The Duellists* (1977), Alan Rudolph in *Welcome to L.A.* (1977) and *Choose Me* (1984), and Louis Malle in *Pretty Baby* (1978), among others. His daughter is the equally talented and charismatic actress Martha Plimpton.

On this day, in 1975, the Superdome was opened in New Orleans. In 1984, synchronized swimming became an official competitive event at the Summer Olympics.

Brett Hull (b. 1964), Canadian hockey player

Son of National Hockey League Hall of Famer Bobby Hull (see January 3), "Golden Brett," as his fans call him, won the league's Most Valuable Player award in 1991; in 1996, playing for the St. Louis Blues, he topped the 500-goal milestone, becoming the twenty-fourth player in league history to do so.

Rod Laver *(b. 1938), Australian tennis player*

In 1962, Australian left-hander Rod "the Rocket" Laver became the second man ever to win the Grand Slam of tennis: the Australian, English, French, and U.S. championships in the same year.

On this day, in 1792, King Louis XVI and Marie Antoinette were overthrown by the suspension of the limited constitutional monarchy, which had been in effect for the previous ten months. In 1821, Missouri was admitted to the Union.

Larry Corcoran *(1859–1919), U.S. baseball player*

Corcoran, who usually pitched right-handed but batted left-handed, played for Chicago, New York, and other teams between 1880 and 1887. He was the second major-league player (after Tony Mullane—see January 30) to switch-pitch—that is, alternate pitching left-handed and right-handed—in a single game. Corcoran accomplished the feat, to the delight of baseball fans, in 1884, playing for the Chicago White Stockings.

On this day, in 1952, Ibn Talal Hussein became King of Jordan. In 1965, the Watts race riots began in Los Angeles, resulting in thirty-four deaths and $50 million in property damage.

Rupert Frazer *(b. 1958), British actor*

Left-hander Frazer appeared as Wigram Battye in the TV miniseries *The Far Pavilions* in 1984, and as Lieutenant Werner von Haetten in another successful miniseries, *War and Remembrance*, in 1989. He also appeared in the films *Gandhi*, *The Shooting Party*, and Steven Spielberg's *Empire of the Sun*.

12

Tonight, the annual Perseid meteor shower traditionally reaches its peak. On this day, in 1918, Air Mail service was introduced by the U.S. Post Office.

Mary Roberts Rinehart *(1876–1958), U.S. writer*

Mary Roberts Rinehart eschewed the romantic companionship of men all her life, and instead slept with her pen—literally. Loathing typewriters, she wrote her numerous books, plays, and magazine articles in longhand, but for years had problems finding a pen that was comfortable for her. Kenneth Parker, of the Parker Company, learned of her dilemma and sent her, as a gift, a special snub-nosed model: she loved it so much she took it with her everywhere and locked it away in a special box by her bedside at the end of each working day. Servants were forbidden to touch it, or even the box, when they were cleaning. It's small wonder that handwriting was so aggravating to the prolific novelist. Born naturally left-handed, she was switched to right-handedness as a child. (Her left hand was tied behind her back to make certain she didn't use it.) From then on, penmanship became a physically unnatural, awkward experience, though she apparently made up for it, in part, by employing a very large, bold script. Originally trained as a nurse, Roberts turned to writing in her late twenties. Over the next fifty years, she turned out more than fifty books, most of them mysteries, many of them best-sellers, including *The Circular Staircase*, *The Yellow Room*, and *The Red Lamp*. She is often called "the American Daphne du Maurier."

13

On this day, in 1942, the film *Bambi* had its world premiere. In 1961, the East Germans began erecting the Berlin Wall.

Today is International Left-handers' Day!

Fidel Castro (b. *1926*),
Cuban dictator

The world would have been a different place if only Fidel Castro had thrown a meaner fastball. In 1946, Castro—then a twenty-year-old left-handed baseball pitcher from the University of Havana—flew to the United States to try out for a place on the Washington Senators baseball team. Castro excelled at a wide variety of sports and had previously been voted his country's best all-around school athlete. Unfortunately, the Senators turned him down—one complaint was that his fastball wasn't good enough—and he returned to Havana, where he pursued his law degree and subsequently devoted himself—with the help of good friend and fellow revolutionary Che Guevara—to the overthrow of Cuban president Fulgencio Batista.

Ben Hogan (*1912–1997*), *U.S. golfer*

A natural left-hander, Hogan switched to golfing right-handed after he was repeatedly told that left-handers could never be good golfers. Years after he achieved renown, he regreted the conversion. "At that age," he once wrote, "I was gullible enough to believe people and make the change, but I wouldn't now." Hogan was named PGA Player of the Year four times during his career, and was one of only four players to win all four Grand Slam titles.

14

Today is Independence Day in Pakistan. On this day, in 1935, the Social Security system was established.

Graham Walker (b. 1953), Australian production designer

Open your notebooks, please, and take out your pencils; today's lecture is on motion-picture production design, otherwise known as "art direction." No, you may *not* be excused, and anyone caught jumping forward to August 15 will have to stay after class and sit through the complete films of Joan Crawford. There, you see—I *knew* you wanted to stick around. Production design is, simply put, virtually *everything* you see on the screen during a motion picture—except, of course, for the actors, the costumes, and the clouds in the sky. The brightly colored, surreal poppy fields and Munchkin homes of *The Wizard of Oz*—production design. The harrowing, convoluted steel entrails of the mother ship in *Alien*—production design. The impeccably precise re-creation of dining rooms and staterooms in *Titanic*—production design. Production designers are, in fact, generally responsible for the entire mood and atmosphere of a film, and without them everything in movies would pretty much look like everyday life—that is to say, *Batman* and *Gone With the Wind* might as well have been filmed in front of the local convenience store or Laundromat. Now that you know all of this—or perhaps your memory's simply been refreshed—you're ready to fully appreciate the artistry and ingenuity of left-handed production designer Graham Walker. Although, early in his career, he lent his talents—as a set dresser—to such films as Peter Weir's eerily miraculous *Picnic at Hanging Rock*, his first major film as production designer was the stunning and influential *Road Warrior*, the Mel Gibson classic that taught the world how to wear chrome-studded leather without embarrassment. Walker went even further with the same striking, primitive-futuristic look four years later, when he was production designer for *Mad Max Beyond Thunderdome*. It obviously took a left-hander to fully understand the meaning of "post-Apocalyptic anarchy" and create something visually glorious from it. Among Walker's other achievements are his production designs for

"Crocodile" Dundee, Dead Calm (with its chilling look of emptiness and utter abandonment), *The Sum of Us,* and *The Island of Dr. Moreau.* Now you know. Class dismissed.

15

On this day, in 1947, India and Pakistan became two separate countries, with Jawaharlal Nehru as the first prime minister of India.

William Rushton (1937–1996), British actor

The left-handed comedian and actor was one of the original cast members of David Frost's groundbreaking political satire series, *That Was the Week That Was,* first on British television, then imported to NBC. Rushton was also seen in a variety of small character roles in such films as *Those Magnificent Men in Their Flying Machines* and *The Bliss of Mrs. Blossom,* in the 1960s. He was one of the founders of the British satirical magazine *Private Eye.*

16

On this day, in 1985, Madonna married Sean Penn. In 1988, Republican presidential candidate George Bush announced that Dan Quayle would be his running mate.

Napoleon (1769–1821), French dictator

The ambitious French emperor could vanquish almost anything—except for the Duke of Wellington and his own handwriting. As a vain, temperamental—and left-handed—young Corsican, he entered the military college at Brienne, France, in 1779, and soon distinguished himself with, among other things, his utterly illegible penmanship and his to-tal inability to spell any word correctly. "His teachers couldn't deci-pher his compositions," one of his schoolmates later recalled, "and he himself had trouble rereading what he had written." Years later, after Napoleon became emperor, his former penmanship instructor applied to him for a government pension. "Ah, so you're the one!" Napoleon reportedly told the old man. "Well, you don't have much to brag about!" Nonetheless, he granted his former teacher a generous pen-sion of 1,200 francs.

James Cameron *(b. 1954), Canadian film director*

Just as the cosmic pairing of left-handers Queen Victoria and Bob Dylan on the same birthday—May 24—gives one pause, so, in an en-tirely different way, does the synchronicity of southpaws Napoleon and James Cameron sharing a natal day. "I am king of the world!" Cameron shouted in 1998 after accepting his Oscar for Best Picture of the Year, *Titanic*; it's the kind of thing Napoleon probably liked to re-peat to himself in front of his mirror after a shower. When Cameron was a boy, he rallied his young playmates to help him build a fully functional medieval catapult that heaved large boulders and made siz-able impact craters in the neighbors' lawns. As an adult, he rallied his colleagues in Hollywood to help him build—and then sink—the most famous luxury liner in history. Often criticized in the press (and not so privately among his show-business brethren) for megalomaniac ten-dencies, Cameron doesn't like to think of himself as a perfectionist; he calls himself a "greatist," "I only want to do it until it's great," he once explained to actor Tom Arnold. *Titanic*, of course, became the highest-grossing film of all time, the apex of a film career full of blockbusters, including *The Terminator*, *Terminator 2*, *Aliens*, and *True Lies*. Anyone who has already sampled a number of entries in this book will quickly realize that Cameron's obsessiveness—and his scope of vision—is en-tirely in keeping with his left-handedness.

17

Today is Independence Day in Indonesia. On this day, in 1939, the film *The Wizard of Oz* had its gala premiere in Hollywood. In 1969, Hurricane Camille struck the coasts of Louisiana, Mississippi, and Alabama.

Robert De Niro *(b. 1943), U.S. actor*

Two-time Oscar-winning actor—for *The Godfather Part II* (1974) and *Raging Bull* (1980)—known for his incredible obsessiveness and his ability to "morph" into any role: he gained forty pounds to play the post-championship, out-of-shape Jake La Motta for only a few minutes of on-screen time in *Raging Bull*. "I can never recognize him from one movie to the next," author Truman Capote once remarked. His numerous film credits include *Taxi Driver* (1976), *The Last Tycoon* (1976), *1900* (1976), *New York, New York* (1977), *The Deer Hunter* (1978), *Once Upon a Time in America* (1984), *The Mission* (1986), *Goodfellas* (1990), *Awakenings* (1990), *Cape Fear* (1991), *Casino* (1995), and *Heat* (1995).

Guillermo Vilas *(b. 1952), Argentinian tennis player*

Renowned for his precision play and invincible backhand, left-hander Vilas was ranked number one in the world in 1977 after winning ten tournaments, including the U.S. Open, and fifty consecutive matches.

18

On this day, in 1587, the first English child born in the Americas—Virginia Dale—was born in Roanoke, Virginia. In 1997, the largest U.S. labor strike in history—of 185,000 UPS workers—came to an end.

Robert Redford *(b. 1937), U.S. actor and director*

"People have been so busy relating to how I look," Redford confessed to an interviewer, "it's a miracle I didn't become a self-conscious blob of protoplasm." It's equally miraculous he didn't become a professional baseball player: the left-hander was a naturally gifted athlete who attended the University of Colorado on a baseball scholarship, with dreams of one day joining the major leagues (hence his choice to play the title role in Barry Levinson's 1984 mood-drenched hymn to baseball, *The Natural*). He dropped out of college in 1957 and traveled to Europe, having decided to become a painter. However, it was acting lessons at the American Academy of Dramatic Arts soon afterward that finally won out: after making his debut on Broadway in 1959, he secured small roles on television, in *The Twilight Zone* and *Alfred Hitchcock Presents*, among other shows, and went on to feature films with the now all-but-impossible-to-find *War Hunt*, about the Korean War, in 1962. Though nominated, Redford has never won an Academy Award for his acting; he did, however, win an Oscar as Best Director, for his extraordinary 1980 directorial debut, *Ordinary People*.

19

Today is National Aviation Day in the United States. On this day, in 1856, condensed milk was patented. In 1989, Malcolm Forbes celebrated his seventieth birthday with a lavish, celebrity-studded party in Tangier.

Bill Clinton (b. *1946*),
U.S. president

Clinton's hands (left or right) have played a significant role in his presidency, perhaps more of a role—for better or worse—than those of any other president in history. His hands have at least one ardent fan, fellow left-hander Sarah Jessica Parker. "Bill Clinton has the most beautiful hands," she once said in an interview after meeting him. "They're exquisite, truly beautiful. He has really long fingers, and his hands are enormous. He has really clean nails. They're almost like an artist's hands. They don't belong on a politician's body. . . . Once you notice his hands, you never forget."

Christian Slater *(b. 1969), U.S. actor*

By the time Slater was twenty-five, he had been through at least four well-publicized romances—with Winona Ryder, Chilean actress Valentina Vargas (his costar on *The Name of the Rose*), Patricia Arquette (his costar on *True Romance*), and model Christy Turlington—had done liberal amounts of cocaine and ecstasy, as well as hallucinogenic mushrooms and a variety of other substances, had been arrested twice (once spending ten days in jail for kicking the arresting policeman in the head), had been through drug rehab once, had made nineteen motion pictures—including *Heathers, Pump Up the Volume, Robin Hood: Prince of Thieves,* and *Interview with the Vampire*—had been a presenter at the Academy Awards, and had been named "Most Desirable Male" at the MTV movie awards. That he went on to see twenty-six, twenty-seven, and twenty-eight, etc., makes his comment—"I'm the luckiest man on the face of the planet"—something of an understatement.

20 On this day, in 1882, Tchaikovsky's *1812 Overture* had its premiere, in Moscow.

Robert Plant *(b. 1948), British singer*

Left-handed lead singer of the rock group Led Zeppelin and main lyricist for many of the group's hit songs, including the blockbuster "Stairway to Heaven."

H. P. Lovecraft *(1890–1937), U.S. writer*

Lovecraft's works—which are often cited for their elegant and poetic use of language—include the brilliant short stories "The Case of Charles Dexter Ward," "The Shadow over Innsmouth," and "At the Mountains of Madness." Stephen King has often named Lovecraft as his favorite author and as a major influence on his own work.

Isaac Hayes (b. 1942), U.S. musician

Left-handed singer and composer perhaps best known for his title song for the 1973 movie *Shaft*. Hayes has also done considerable acting—he appeared as "the Duke of New York" in John Carpenter's *Escape from New York*—and most recently was the voice of the school cafeteria chef on the hit series *South Park*.

On this day, in 1911, the *Mona Lisa* was stolen from the Louvre in Paris. (It was recovered two years later.) In 1959, Hawaii became the fiftieth state.

Angelina Jolie (b. 1975), U.S. actress

The daughter of actor Jon Voight, Jolie won a Golden Globe Award in 1998 for her performance in the TV movie *George Wallace*, as Wallace's second wife, Cornelia. She also starred in the title role of the controversial HBO movie *Gia*, about supermodel (and heroin addict) Gia Carangi, who died of AIDS.

On this day, in 1762, Ann Franklin became the first woman editor of a U.S. newspaper, the Newport, Rhode Island, *Mercury*.

Norman Schwarzkopf (b. 1934), U.S. military leader

As leader of U.S. forces during the Persian Gulf War in 1991, Schwarzkopf was invited to dine with Saudi tribesmen one night. At the banquet, large communal platters of food were set out. The only problem was, Muslim custom regards it as a severe breach of etiquette to eat with the left hand. "You only eat with your right hand," Schwarzkopf later explained. "The left hand is polluted. It's a Muslim custom." Left-hander Schwarzkopf had no difficulty as long as he paid close attention to what he was doing. However, every so often, distracted by conversation, he automatically started to reach for food with his left hand. "It was so awkward," he said, "that I literally sat on my left hand. I just stuck my left hand under my rear." Schwarzkopf's mother, incidentally, was ambidextrous, and insisted he not be switched to right-handedness as a child.

Today marks the beginning of the astrological sign Virgo. On this day, in 1926, silent-screen idol Rudolph Valentino died, at the age of thirty-one.

Louis XVI (1754–1793), King of France

Poor Louis. While arguments can be made that history has unjustly maligned his wife, Marie Antoinette (she never said, "Let them eat cake," and when the French Revolution finally materialized, she showed more courage than her husband), it's difficult to find anything nice to say about Louis, even if he was left-handed. On the day (July 14, 1789) that the detested Bastille was stormed by a mob of twenty thousand angry Parisians—the mob also killed the mayor of Paris that day and established a new municipal government—Louis wrote only one word in his personal diary: "*Rien*"—"Nothing," meaning that nothing of any interest or significance had occurred that day. As the Revolution progressed, the king—weak-willed and incapable of action—increasingly indulged his fondness for stag hunting as a way of relieving his boredom with it all. He was finally arrested in the fall of 1791 (he had dismissed Marie Antoinette's earlier pleas to flee to the safety of her brother Leopold's Austrian empire); he was eventually put on trial for crimes against the people and guillotined on January 21, 1793. When the executioner held up his severed head for all to see, the crowd cried out, "Long live the Republic!" His wife suffered a similar fate ten months later, except that on her way to the guillotine she was pelted with rocks and excrement. According to observers, she didn't even so much as flinch.

On this day, in A.D. 79, Mount Vesuvius erupted, destroying the cities of Pompeii and Herculaneum.

Marlee Matlin (b. *1965*), U.S. *actress*

In 1987, Marlin won an Oscar as Best Actress for her volcanic film debut, the lead in *Children of a Lesser God*. Although she's had few major film roles since, she has kept busy, and visible, with guest-starring roles on various TV shows, notably in a hilariously memorable episode of *Seinfeld*. She is also known for her outspoken fund-raising work on behalf of the deaf and people with AIDS.

On this day, in 1904, the only son—the hemophiliac boy Alexis—of Czar Nicholas II and his wife, Alexandra, was born.

Andy Varipapa (*1891–1984*), U.S. *champion bowler*

Varipapa started out as a right-handed bowler, and was twice winner of the BPAA All-Star Tournament, in 1946 and 1947. An expert trick-shot artist, he made nationwide tours and thrilled fans with his exhibitions. At the age of seventy-eight, he suddenly developed a debilitating wrist ailment in his right hand; he then taught himself to bowl left-handed, and within less than two years was averaging 180 on the lanes. (Varipapa's birthday is also listed in some sources as March 31.)

26 Today is Women's Equality Day. On this day, in 1920, the Nineteenth Amendment to the U.S. Constitution, giving women the right to vote, was ratified.

Peggy Guggenheim *(1898–1979), U.S. art collector*

If ever there was a black sheep in the family, it was left-hander Peggy Guggenheim. Born into the Guggenheim millions—her father was Benjamin Guggenheim, who went down with the *Titanic* as he and his cabaret singer mistress were returning home from Europe—she has sometimes been referred to as "the wayward Guggenheim." She scandalized her wealthy and prominent family with her numerous affairs (including at least one with another woman) and with her "ill-suited" marriage to the irrepressible Parisian bon vivant Laurence Vail, nicknamed "the King of Bohemia." ("I had a collection of photographs of frescoes I had seen at Pompeii," Peggy later wrote. "They depicted people making love in various positions, and of course I was very curious and wanted to try them all out myself. It soon occurred to me that I could make use of Laurence for this purpose. . . . I think Laurence had a pretty tough time because I demanded everything I had seen depicted in the frescoes.") It was through Vail that Peggy first met and socialized with such artistic luminaries as Pablo Picasso, Gertrude Stein, and Marcel Duchamp. Blessed with a nearly infallible eye for the best in modern art—and with the defiance to act on her convictions, despite the pronouncement of her relatives that she was collecting "trash" and "junk"—she opened a number of galleries where she championed the early work of such masters as Kandinsky, Miró, Klee, Mark Rothko, and Jackson Pollock. In fact, she gave Pollock his first one-man show and financially supported him in exchange for many of his paintings. "I think I'm rather stupid," she once said of herself. "Yes, I do. I have no memory, I don't remember anything. That's very bad for an intellectual." The Peggy Guggenheim Collection—the most important assemblage of modern art in Italy—is still on display in the palazzo in Venice where she spent her final years and draws tens of thousands of visitors a year.

27 On this day, in 1883, the volcanic South Pacific island of Krakatoa exploded, sending plumes of ash fifty miles into the atmosphere and triggering tidal waves throughout the Pacific Basin.

Joe Cunningham (b. 1931), U.S. baseball player

The left-handed first baseman played for St. Louis, Chicago, and Washington from 1954 to 1966, with a peak batting average of .345 in 1959. He also batted over .300 in 1957 and 1958.

28 On this day, in 1963, Martin Luther King, Jr., delivered his speech "I Have a Dream" in front of the Lincoln Memorial in Washington, D.C.

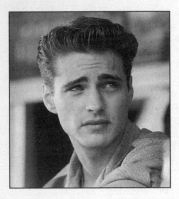

Jason Priestley (b. 1969), Canadian actor

Priestley achieved teen heartthrob status as one of the stars of the hit TV show *Beverly Hills 90210*, beginning in 1990, and went on to appear in the feature films *Calendar Girl* (1993), *Tombstone* (1993), and *Love and Death on Long Island* (1997).

On this day, in 1896, chop suey was invented by a chef in New York City. In 1966, the Beatles performed together in concert for the last time.

Conni Marie Brazelton *(b. 1955), U.S. actress*

Although she's appeared in the films *Hollywood Shuffle* (1987) and Wes Craven's *People Under the Stairs* (1992), Brazelton is most recognizable to TV viewers as RN Conni Oligario on the hit series *ER*.

On this day, in 1983, Guion Bluford, Jr., became the first black U.S. astronaut in space, aboard the space shuttle *Challenger 3*.

Ted Williams *(b. 1918), U.S. baseball player*

Able to spot when home plate was even a fraction of an inch out of line—and reputed to be able to read the label of a 78 rpm as it was spinning on a turntable—Williams possessed such unnaturally sensitive vision that ophthalmologists once estimated it occurred in only one out of every hundred thousand individuals. With that advantage, he might have wound up hitting more home runs than Babe Ruth during his career—if it hadn't been for two wars. He lost five of his best ball-playing years to military service, first as a navy pilot during World War II, then during the Korean War. As it was, Williams—known as "the Splendid Splinter" for his tall, lean frame—hit 521 home runs and had a lifetime batting average of .344 in a career spanning two decades with the Boston Red Sox. His batting action was so fast—and so precise—he usually waited until the very last moment to swing at a pitch. Widely regarded as the greatest hitter of his time, Williams was the last major-league player to bat over .400. His peak was .406 in 1941.

31 Today is Independence Day in Trinidad and Tobago. On this day, in 1997, Princess Diana was killed in a car crash in Paris.

Marsha Clark (b. 1953), U.S. attorney

One of the prosecuting attorneys in the O. J. Simpson murder trial, Clark, like numerous other high-profile lawyers—Clarence Darrow (see April 18), Melvin Belli (see July 29), Louis Nizer (see February 6), and others—is left-handed. One of her opposing attorneys in the Simpson trial, F. Lee Bailey (see June 10), was also left-handed.

Eddie Plank (1875–1926), U.S. baseball player

A left-handed pitcher for the Phillies from 1901 to 1914, and St. Louis from 1915 to 1917, Plank often drove batters to distraction with his strange behavior on the mound: he frequently delivered long, inspirational monologues to the ball before pitching it, and sometimes spent endless minutes obsessively fussing with every detail of his uniform. Apparently the ball was listening to him—he was the first pitcher of the modern era to win 300 games. He ended his career with a 326–194 record.

Left-handers Born in
September

September: Ninth month of the year, originally the seventh month on the ancient Roman calendar; hence its name, from the Latin septem, meaning "seven."

1

On this day, in 1914, the last known passenger pigeon died, at the Cincinnati Zoo. In 1985, the remains of the *Titanic* were located on the floor of the Atlantic Ocean.

Jim Corbett (1866–1933), U.S. boxing champion

On September 7, 1892, twenty-six-year-old left-handed boxing challenger Jim Corbett stunned the sports world by defeating reigning heavyweight champion (and right-hander) John Sullivan in a twenty-one-round bout at the Olympic Club in New Orleans. A knockout won Corbett the world heavyweight boxing title—and elicited boos and sneers from spectators, none of whom had ever seen a boxer dance, dodge, and zigzag around the ring the way Corbett did. Corbett—who had previously earned his living as a bank teller—spent weeks in advance choreographing his footwork for the match with Sullivan. (He was later remembered as one of the most scientific boxers in the history of the sport.) The initial boos and hisses of that first night (he was snidely nicknamed "the Dancer") eventually turned to widespread admiration among boxing fans: known for his impeccable dress and gracious manners, Corbett, a handsome man, soon became a popular national celebrity, nicknamed "Gentleman Jim" by the press. He held on to the championship title for five years, until 1897, when he finally lost it to a twenty-four-year-old right-handed challenger, Bob Fitzsimmons, in a bout in Carson City, Nevada. Corbett went on to establish a successful career as an actor; among his numerous stage credits was the title role in George Bernard Shaw's *Cashel Byron's Profession*, about—of course—a prizefighter.

On this day, in 31 B.C., the Battle of Actium was fought, between the naval forces of Octavian and those of Antony and Cleopatra. In 1898, the machine gun was first used in battle, at the Battle of Omdurman in the Sudan.

Keanu Reeves (b. 1964), U.S. actor

Reeves was named Most Valuable Player on his high school hockey team in 1981. Ten years later, he was named Most Desirable Male at the MTV movie awards. The left-handed star—handsome, earnest, with a perennial air of restless energy and impatience about him—has only one real problem: he rarely laughs, on-screen or off. He loves ballroom dancing, motorcycles, surfing, horseback riding, and his bass guitar. His name is Hawaiian for "cool breeze over the mountains." He's evasive about his personal live, so it's impossible to say what he's looking for in a prospective life partner, but he once said of himself, "I'm a meathead, man. You've got smart people, and you've got dumb people. I just happen to be dumb." He has also said, "When I don't feel free and can't do what I want I just react. I go against it." If all of this sounds like the superficial dish one usually reads in a teen-oriented fanzine, it's because Reeves himself is strangely elusive and cursory about his life, even when he's the object of a major celebrity profile in *Vanity Fair* or *People*. No problem. He's almost always a pleasure to watch, whether giving a performance without a false note, as in the megahit *Speed* (1994), or struggling with a role (and an accent) not entirely suited to his talents, as in Francis Ford Coppola's *Bram Stoker's Dracula* (1992). After all, no one expected—or especially wanted—Rita Hayworth or Steve McQueen to be profound.

Jimmy Connors (b. 1952),
U.S. tennis champion

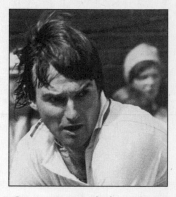

"No one's ever given me anything on the court," Jimmy Connors once told an interviewer. "Maybe that's one reason I prefer singles. It's just me and you. When I win, I don't have to congratulate anyone. When I lose, I don't have to blame anyone." He first learned to play from his mother and grandmother, both tournament players themselves, who taught him "to be a tiger on the court." Connors started playing professional tennis in 1972, and two years later, with the help of a powerful double-fisted backhand, won the Australian, Wimbledon, and U.S. Open championships. In 1976, he won twelve tournaments, including the U.S. Open, and defeated more than 90 percent of his opponents. He was ranked number one in the world. By the early 1980s, with fewer and fewer victories to his credit, Connors was starting to be written off by sportswriters. Then he won at Wimbledon in 1982 and at the U.S. Open in both 1982 and 1983. Almost a decade later, in 1991—when he was approaching forty—he amazed the tennis world by going to the quarterfinals of the U.S. Open. "The secret of Jimmy's big comeback," said his manager, Ray Benton, "is that he never really went away." As a left-hander, Connors seems to have had few problems. In fact, he regards left-handedness as a distinct advantage in tennis. He does admit to one difficulty: "When I'm shaking hands, sometimes I put my left hand out. It's tough for me to shake right-handed."

Martha Mitchell (1918–1976), wife of U.S. Attorney
General John Mitchell

Despite Martha Mitchell's intelligence and extraordinary memory as a child, her parents refused to leave well enough alone: they employed rigorous measures to break her of her left-handedness. Her left hand was tied behind her back at the dinner table; if she refused to eat with her right hand, she went hungry. Similar measures were enforced at school. "Here I was, just a child," she said later. "It made me feel like an outcast; I developed a horrible sense of insecurity and an inferiority complex." The insecurity lasted throughout her adult life: she was dyslexic, and lapsed into stuttering whenever she felt overwhelmed by emotional situations. In the late 1960s and early 1970s, she achieved a not-entirely-flattering prominence as the wife of President Nixon's controversial attorney general John Mitchell. She was known for her outspoken, often reactionary views on hippies, environmentalists, and Vietnam War protesters (whom she labeled "Bolsheviks"). Her frequent verbal gaffes—she tended to say "embellished" instead of "abolished," and "alleviate" instead of "eliminate," often lending bizarre, unintended meanings to her public remarks— were widely, and sometimes gleefully, reported by the beltway press. Her penchant for mixing up telephone numbers also became legendary in Washington, and it wasn't uncommon for total strangers to suddenly find themselves talking at length with the wife of the U.S. attorney general: having dialed a wrong number, Martha was so flustered and embarrassed she'd stay on the line and chat nervously for hours, sometimes well into the night, with whomever she'd called.

Nate Archibald (b. 1948), U.S. basketball player

Left-hander "Nate the Skate" played in the NBA for fourteen years, beginning with the Cincinnati Royals in 1970. A three-time All-NBA First Team selection, he competed in 876 games and scored 16,481 points. Named to the Basketball Hall of Fame in 1991, he was legendary for his lightning speed and frequently airborne grace on the court. He was also nicknamed "Tiny" because of his relatively small height: six foot one.

3

On this day, in 1189, Richard the Lion-Hearted was crowned King of England. In 1783, a treaty ended the Revolutionary War between Britain and the United States. In 1954, *The Lone Ranger* was heard for the last time on radio, after twenty-one years on the air.

Albert De Salvo *(1931–1973), "the Boston Strangler"*

De Salvo achieved grim notoriety in 1965 when he confessed to being the notorious Boston Strangler. A former U.S. Army middleweight boxing champion, the left-handed De Salvo (who prided himself on being a nonsmoker and a teetotaler) murdered thirteen Boston women between June 1962 and January 1964; he raped and then strangled his victims, tying a ludicrous bow—known as "the Strangler's knot"—under their chin. His youngest victim was nineteen, the oldest was eighty-five; most were in their fifties or sixties. De Salvo claimed to have sexually assaulted nearly a thousand other women as well. Because there was little physical evidence connecting him to the murders, De Salvo was never officially charged as the Boston Strangler. Instead, he was sentenced to life imprisonment on multiple counts of sex offenses and robbery. Ironically, he acquired a bizarre coterie of adoring female fans: he was fond of sending them a copy of a book about him with the inscription, "Can't wait to get my hands around your throat." "Hey," he cheerfully told the press, "they even know me in the Soviet Union!" He was stabbed to death by a fellow inmate in 1973.

4

On this day, in 1682, English astronomer Edmond Halley first saw the brilliant comet that would eventually bear his name. In 1893, author Beatrix Potter first conceived the character Peter Rabbit.

Henry Ford II *(1917–1987), U.S. automobile manufacturer*

The powerful industrialist, who ran Ford Motor Company between 1945 and 1979, was—like his grandfather, Henry Ford—left-handed.

During his tenure at the company, Ford introduced the popular Mustang and Thunderbird, and also the ill-fated Edsel.

5

On this day, in 1958, Boris Pasternak's novel *Doctor Zhivago* was first published in the United States. In 1997, Mother Teresa died.

John Cage *(1912–1992), U.S. composer*

Among twentieth-century composers, Cage has the unique ability, long after his reputation peaked in the 1960s, to start incendiary arguments that wreak havoc on friendships, marriages, and academic relationships. On the one side are those who see him as a visionary, revolutionary, and musical prophet; on the other side are those who see him as a flake and something of a sham. Cage's most notorious composition, titled 4'33", was exactly four minutes and thirty-three seconds of silence: a performer walked onto the stage, sat at a piano (or in front of any instrument, or combination of instruments), and did—nothing. He also pioneered the use of unorthodox sounds in the creation of music: his introduction in the 1930s of the "prepared piano," in which various objects are placed on or into the strings to substantially alter the sound, radically influenced subsequent generations of avant-garde composers—whether for better or for worse depends on your taste. He also composed electronic music and incorporated noise from radios, tape recorders, and electronic devices into his compositions. The result was not exactly the kind of thing apt to open the pocketbooks of fur-swathed patrons of the local symphony, and performances of his work were usually restricted to the halls of academia, where, afterward, theorists and professors could sometimes be heard shouting at one another over its relative merits. The mutinous quality of Cage's thinking, the almost compulsive anarchy of his musical compositions, the obsessive focus on abstraction—all are trademarks of the left-hander. The big question, of course, is: Will anyone still be listening a hundred years from now?

Cathy Guisewite *(b. 1950), U.S. comics artist*

On November 22, 1976, *Cathy*—a comic strip written by left-handed cartoonist Cathy Guisewite—premiered in sixty newspapers across the country and quickly established itself as one of the most popular comic strips in the nation. The strip featured a single working woman named Cathy, who was—like her talented creator—left-handed. More than twenty years later, *Cathy* appears in fourteen hundred newspapers worldwide, is featured in over thirty books, and has been immortalized on everything from greeting cards to pajamas. Guisewite—who worked in advertising for five years before her mother strong-armed her into sending "humiliating drawings of my miserable love life to Universal Press Syndicate"—lives in Los Angeles with her "one true love," a dog named Trolley. She claims to do her best work while listening to depressing music and eating M&M's.

Kristian Alfonso *(b. 1964), U.S. actress*

The ravishingly beautiful left-handed actress, named one of the most beautiful women on television by *Soap Opera Digest*, originally wanted to become a professional figure skater. She won a gold medal at the Junior Olympics when she was thirteen. An injury two years later, while she was bobsledding, forced her to abandon the sport, and she turned to modeling instead. By her mid-teens, she had already appeared on more than thirty magazine covers, including *Vogue* and *Harper's Bazaar*. At the age of nineteen, she joined the cast of the daytime soap opera *Days of Our Lives*. She went on to recurring roles on the prime-time dramas *Falcon Crest* and *Melrose Place*.

On this day, in 1988, a pair of Elton John's sunglasses sold at auction for $16,830. In 1995, baseball player Cal Ripken, Jr., broke Lou Gehrig's old record of having played in 2,130 consecutive games.

Henri de Tonty *(1650–1704), Italian explorer*

Tonty accompanied the French explorer La Salle on his explorations of the Great Lakes and the Mississippi River in the late 1600s.

He also oversaw construction of the *Griffon*, the first ship to sail the Great Lakes. Tonty explored, and helped establish fur-trading settlements, in what is now Illinois. In 1700, four years before his death, he chose to make Louisiana his final home. Tonty came by his left-handedness accidentally: as a young man in his mid-twenties, he had joined the French army and lost his right hand in combat.

Today is National Grandparents Day in the United States. On this day, in 1921, the first Miss America pageant was held.

Daniel Inouye *(b. 1924), U.S. senator*

Inouye lost his right arm to a German rifle grenade while fighting in Italy in World War II. He was awarded the Distinguished Service Cross, the Bronze Star, and the Purple Heart. In 1959, Inouye was elected the first congressman from the newly admitted state of Hawaii; he was also the first Japanese-American member of Congress. Three years later, Inouye was elected to the U.S. Senate, a job to which his Hawaiian constituency returned him for more than thirty years.

Today is National Literacy Day. On this day, in 1892, the Pledge of Allegiance was first published, in *The Youth's Companion*.

Peter Sellers *(1925–1980), British actor*

"If you ask me to play myself," left-hander Sellers once remarked, "I will not know what to do. I do not know who or what I am." The talented and tormented actor—twice nominated for Academy Awards, in Stanley Kubrick's *Dr. Strangelove* (1964) and Hal Ashby's *Being There* (1979)—became known for an uncanny ability to become instantly *absorbed* into any character that flitted across his imagination. The results, while memorable to fans of his biggest hits—*The Lady-*

killers (1955), *The Mouse That Roared* (1959), *Lolita* (1962), *The Pink Panther* (1964), *The Party* (1968)—left the *real* people around him uneasy and off-balance. "I think his mother had gained such an incredible influence over him," said comedian Spike Milligan, "that he virtually abdicated his own rights to any individual personality. Finally, he had to invade other bodies to register at all. He was like a ghoul, he had to feast off somebody else. But he did it so well, it became an art. He was not a genius. Sellers—he was a freak." A difficult man—high-strung, demanding, sometimes cruel (and an often insufferable skirt chaser)—he aroused antipathy from a long list of show-business colleagues. "Nobody here believes that there's a man alive who can control that asshole," said Hollywood producer Mike Frankovich, who worked with Sellers in the 1970 comedy *There's a Girl in My Soup.* Yet the extraordinary gift for "antiself" was inestimably valuable to those who criticized him. Sellers's talents were so stunning he was frequently called upon, in postproduction, to anonymously redub other actors' lines when the actors themselves were not available: in the 1954 John Huston comedy *Beat the Devil,* for example, many of the lines audiences heard uttered by Humphrey Bogart are, in fact, Sellers—imitating Bogart—and were redubbed in an editing room after shooting was completed since Bogart himself was unavailable to do it. Sellers died of a heart attack, the last of several, at the age of fifty-four.

Sid Caesar *(b. 1922), U.S. comedian*

A veteran of some three dozen films and numerous stage appearances, Caesar became a cultural icon in the 1950s with his hit television comedy series *Your Show of Shows.* In his 1982 autobiography, *Where Have I Been?,* he wrote movingly of his various personal demons including his battle with alcoholism.

Today is Chrysanthemum Day in Japan. On this day, in 1850, California was admitted to the Union. In 1895, the American Bowling Congress was founded.

Julia Sawalha *(b. 1968), British actress*

The beautiful young actress donned sackcloth clothes and heavy glasses and affected a morbidly conservative bent of mind to play Saffron Monsoon—tsk-tsking daughter of Edina Monsoon (Jennifer Saunders)—on the smash-hit comedy burlesque *Absolutely Fabulous*.

Henry Thomas *(b. 1971), U.S. actor*

Best known as Elliott in *E.T. The Extra-Terrestrial* (1982), left-hander Thomas has also been seen in *Cloak and Dagger* (1984), *Psycho IV: The Beginning* (1991), *Legends of the Fall* (1994), and as Raymond Buckey in the TV movie *Indictment: The McMartin Trial* in 1995.

On this day, in 1953, the first Swanson's TV dinners went on sale. In 1977, convicted killer Hamida Djandoubi became the last person to be executed by guillotine in France.

Randy Johnson *(b. 1963), U.S. baseball player*

Randy Johnson is hard on his fellow left-handed ballplayers: he hasn't allowed a home run to a left-handed batter since 1992. Johnson—nicknamed "the Big Unit" for his six-foot-ten height—played for Montreal in 1988 and was traded to the Seattle Mariners halfway through the 1989 season. The four-time All-Star won the Cy Young Award in 1995, led the major leagues in strike-outs from 1994 to 1997, and had the best strike-out-per-nine-innings ratio in major-league history.

On this day, in 1609, the island of Manhattan was discovered by Henry Hudson. In 1789, Alexander Hamilton became the first U.S. secretary of the treasury.

Kristy McNichol *(b. 1962), U.S. actress*

Emmy Award–winning actress who first gained notice at the age of fifteen as Buddy in the TV drama *Family*, which ran from 1976 to 1980, and was later cast as policewoman Barbara Weston in the NBC comedy *Empty Nest*, from 1988 to 1992.

On this day, in 1851, *Moby-Dick* was published.

Angie Harmon *(b. 1972), U.S. model and actress*

After her appearance on the cover of *Seventeen*, Harmon quickly became a highly successful model, appearing in *Vogue*, *Cosmopolitan*, *Harper's Bazaar*, and other magazines. In 1995, a chance meeting with *Baywatch* star and producer David Hasselhoff on a cross-country flight led to her being cast in the series *Baywatch Nights*.

On this day, in 1857, Milton Hershey, creator of the Hershey bar, was born.

Ron Rifkin *(b. 1950), U.S. actor*

Rifkin portrayed District Attorney Ellis Loew in the critically acclaimed *L.A. Confidential* in 1997, and Dr. Carl Vucelich on the hit

TV series *ER*, from 1995 to 1996. He has also appeared in the films *Wolf* (1994), *Manhattan Murder Mystery* (1993), *The Sting II* (1983), and *Silent Running* (1971).

 On this day, in 1981, *Entertainment Tonight* premiered. In 1982, Princess Grace of Monaco was killed in a car accident.

Joey Heatherton *(b. 1944), U.S. actress*

Heatherton appeared in the late 1960s with Dean Martin on the TV variety show *Dean Martin Presents the Golddiggers*. Best known as a slim, sexy singer and dancer, she had a sporadic film career, starring as Xavier Hollander in the 1977 film *The Happy Hooker Goes to Washington*, and was later cast as a shrieking religious fanatic by director John Waters in the offbeat 1990 musical *Cry-Baby*.

 Today is Respect for the Aged Day in Japan. On this day, in 1971, the international environmental organization Greenpeace was founded.

Don Amendolia *(birthday unknown), U.S. actor*

Look for Amendolia in *Wayne's World* as the hilariously "new, improved" announcer that cagey producers bring in to soup up Wayne and Garth's cable-access basement show. Look for him also as a bank worker in *Boogie Nights* and as a salesman in *Ed Wood*. He's had roles in *Without a Trace* (1983) and *The Secret of My Success* (1987) as well, and appeared as Emory Battis on the TV series *Twin Peaks*.

On this day, in 1908, General Motors was founded. In 1977, Maria Callas died.

Mickey Rourke (b. *1953*),
U.S. actor

Mickey Rourke's birthday is alternately listed in reference books as July 16, and the year of his birth is variously given as 1950, 1953, 1955, 1956, and 1960. His real name is inconsistently cited as Philip Andre Rourke, Jr., and Mickey Stavros. His height and weight—even on studio fact sheets—vary. There's even disagreement over how many tattoos he has (the generally accepted number is six). All of this vagueness and ambiguity may be part of the Rourke mystique: he has spent much of his career, since his first film role in Steven Spielberg's *1941* in 1979, cultivating an outlaw image, disdainful of convention and boundaries. That's part of what made him so mesmerizing to fans in two of his most popular roles: the arsonist in *Body Heat* (1981) and the arbitrageur-bondage-fetishist in *9½ Weeks* (1986). His apparently purposeful obfuscation in doling out facts about himself is entirely congruous with a left-handed impulse to anarchy: what could be more anarchistic in Hollywood—a community that panics over the slightest deviation in personal image—than to have *no* precise outline to one's image at all? Rourke is generally reported to be left-handed, but—who knows? He may actually have three hands, or none at all.

Allen Funt (b. *1914*), *producer of* Candid Camera

The concept was simply brilliant: put ordinary people in impossible or bizarre situations, and then install a hidden camera to record their often stunned and hilarious reactions. For some twenty years, *Candid Camera* subjected unsuspecting restaurant diners to microscopic dinner portions; hopeful job applicants to strange voices coming from filing cabinets; mystified gas-station attendants to cars without engines ("Would you look under the hood for me, please? I think something's wrong with my car . . ."). Even before *Candid Camera* premiered on television in 1948, prankster Funt had made a name for himself on radio with the popular *Candid Microphone*: same principle, but with a microphone instead of a camera. In 1970, Funt took advantage of the escalating liberality in motion pictures to do on the big screen what was forbidden on television: *What Do You Say to a Naked Lady?*—X-rated at the time of its release—featured a generously beautiful, stark naked woman eliciting often priceless reactions from sleepy subway commuters, polite supermarket clerks, and office workers on an elevator.

Ed Begley, Jr. *(b. 1949), U.S. actor*

The former stand-up comic has appeared in films—*Cat People, Eating Raoul, The Accidental Tourist, She-Devil*—and was twice nominated for an Emmy for his role on the TV hospital drama *St. Elsewhere* in the 1980s.

On this day, in 1983, Vanessa Williams was crowned the first African-American Miss America.

Marc Brunell *(b. 1970), U.S. football player*

Known for his spontaneity, agility, and power, left-handed quarterback Brunell played his first two NFL seasons with the Green Bay Packers before joining the Jacksonville Jaguars in 1995. In 1995 and 1996, he led the NFL in rushing, and by 1997 had become one of the rising superstars of the game. "Guys like Brunell," said former NFL coach Rick Kotie, "drive defenses nuts with their ability to improvise."

18

Today is Independence Day in Chile. On this day, in 1851, *The New York Times* began publication. In 1981, the film *Mommie Dearest* had its world premiere.

Phyllis Kirk *(b. 1926), U.S. actress*

Kirk appeared in only a handful of films during her brief Hollywood career from 1950 to 1957, but she achieved horror-film immortality as the pretty but too-curious-for-her-own-good visitor to the House of Wax, who can't believe how *lifelike* Vincent Price's waxworks are.

Robert Blake *(b. 1933), U.S. actor*

Perennial "bad boy" of TV and films, Blake gave perhaps his best performance as killer Perry Smith in the 1967 film adaptation of Truman Capote's *In Cold Blood.* A decade later, he won an Emmy as the star of the popular TV series *Baretta*—as a jeans-and-T-shirt, nothing-by-the-rules kind of cop—which ran from 1975 to 1978.

Jack Warden *(b. 1920), U.S. actor*

Winning, often gruff, no-nonsense star (always with an undercurrent of decency and open-mindedness): he was perfect as the doctor who chucks convention to lead an honest but unconstrained life on a South Seas island in *Donovan's Reef* (1963). Warden was twice nominated for Academy Awards, for his performances in *Shampoo* (1975) and *Heaven Can Wait* (as Coach, in 1978), but was as much of a standout in *Twelve Angry Men* (1957), *And Justice for All* (1979), and *Being There* (1979). In 1972, he won an Emmy for his role as football coach George Halas in the made-for-TV movie *Brian's Song.*

On this day, in 1964, *Flipper* debuted on television.

Paul Williams (b. 1940), U.S. songwriter

The left-handed actor, singer, and songwriter has written such hit songs as "We've Only Just Begun," "Rainy Days and Mondays," "Old-Fashioned Love Song," and "Out in the Country." An occasional actor known for his diminutive stature and elfish looks, he's appeared in films as diverse as *Battle for the Planet of the Apes* (1973), *Phantom of the Paradise* (for which he also composed the music, in 1974), and Oliver Stone's *Doors* (1991).

On this day, in 1519, Ferdinand Magellan's ships left Spain to begin their circumnavigation of the world. In 1955, Argentina president Juan Perón was overthrown by a military coup.

Anne Meara (b. 1929), U.S. comedian

The left-handed actress—part of famed comedy team Stiller and Meara, with husband Jerry Stiller—is a veteran of numerous TV series, including *Rhoda*, *Archie Bunker's Place*, *ALF*, and the daytime soap opera *All My Children*. Perhaps her best performance was as one of the comatose hospital patients returned to life in Penny Marshall's moving 1990 drama, *Awakenings*. Meara's son, comic Ben Stiller, is also left-handed.

Alexander the Great (356–323 B.C.), Macedonian conqueror

As history has shown time and again, left-handers rarely like to do things in small ways. When Alexander's closest general and boyhood companion Hephaestion (some biographers have suggested that he was the Macedonian conqueror's lover) died near Babylon in 324 B.C., an inconsolable Alexander not only had the body cremated atop an awesome two-hundred-foot pyre constructed of tiers of sculpted ships, centaurs, bulls, lions, and wreaths, all in combustible softwood, but he also made plans for one of the most spectacular and lasting memorials one human being has ever contemplated for another: he planned to carve Mount Athos, the *entire* mountain, into a huge likeness of Hephaestion, so large that a small town of ten thousand people could fit, appropriately, in the palm of the statue's left hand. Likewise, that same year, when Alexander decided it was time for the known world to formally acknowledge his years of exploration, battle, and conquest, he chose divinity as his proper reward and decreed that every city in his vast empire make the appropriate declaration that he was now a god. Every city complied, though one—Sparta—obeyed only in form, not in spirit. Their official decree announced, "Since Alexander wishes to be a god, let him be a god." It should be noted that Sparta was an austerely militaristic and conformist community, full of right-handers presumed to have had no sense of drama (or humor) at all.

On this day, in 1973, Henry Kissinger became U.S. secretary of state. In 1996, John F. Kennedy, Jr., married Carolyn Bessette.

Ricki Lake *(b. 1968), U.S. actress and talk show host*

When shown Jean Cocteau's spellbinding 1946 masterpiece *Beauty and the Beast*, Greta Garbo is alleged to have exclaimed, at the Beast's inevitable transformation into handsome actor Jean Marais, "Give me back my Beast!" More than fifty years later, many of Ricki Lake's fans can empathize. Personal transformations are very much a dangerous, double-edged sword: Maria Callas—much of her life an overweight workhorse on the operatic stage—became a swanlike icon of glamour and jet-set freedom when she slimmed down and fell in love (unhappily, as it turned out) with billionaire Aristotle Onassis; but she also derailed her career and discovered that being the belle of everyone's ball has its empty, unsatisfying, and horribly cruel side. Not every transformation winds up as neat and cheery as Charlotte Vale's in *Now Voyager*. For many of us, then, there are two Ricki Lakes: the one soulful, vulnerable, feisty, utterly charismatic—and fat (a more politically correct term would be appropriate only if it was meant as a criticism); the other slim, assimilated into the great homogeneous body of mainstream American culture, and quite perky and sexy in the bright-eyed, shiny brunette way of any of a thousand other TV personalities. In an odd way, the old Ricki Lake was much more true to her left-handedness; the other has become strangely right-handed. The one *knew* how stupid and callous the world can be in its demands for conformity and physical perfection; the other seems to have bought into everything she previously disdained. Of course, only Lake can decide what's right for her. Still, go rent John Waters's *Hairspray*, the endearing 1988 classic in which Lake portrays an unyielding, overweight, and deeply passionate outcast who triumphs over the beautiful people of the world; then turn on her daytime talk-fest, *The Ricki Lake Show*, and compare the two very different individuals. See what we mean?

22 Today is Mabon, a Wiccan celebration of the coming of winter. On this day, in 1776, Nathan Hale was hanged. In 1964, *Fiddler on the Roof* opened on Broadway.

Tommy Lasorda *(b. 1927), U.S. baseball manager*

The feisty and highly successful left-handed manager of the Los Angeles Dodgers piloted the team to world championships in 1981 and 1988. Renowned at one time for his insatiable appetite, he also holds an unofficial record for pregame gluttony when he consumed one hundred raw oysters—with several jars of horseradish—before a game with Houston in 1986. Now considerably slimmed down and in his seventies, he swims one hundred laps at a time. He has said that he would like his epitaph to read, "Dodger Stadium was his address, but every ballpark was his home."

23 Today marks the beginning of the astrological sign Libra. It is also Unification of the Kingdom Day in Saudi Arabia. On this day, in 1846, the planet Neptune was discovered.

Jason Alexander (b. 1959), U.S. actor

Left-handed sidekick to left-handed comic Jerry Seinfeld on *Seinfeld*, but also Tony Award-winning Broadway musical actor in *The Rink, Merrily We Roll Along,* and *Jerome Robbins' Broadway*; TV commercial spokesman for Mercedes-Benz, Hershey's chocolate, Dr Pepper, McDonalds, and Rold Gold pretzels; voice-over artist for various characters on the TV cartoon series *Dinosaurs* (1990–91); character actor who roughed up and tried to rape Julia Roberts in the final reel of *Pretty Woman* (1990) and has appeared in more than three dozen other films, including *The Mosquito Coast* (1986), *Brighton Beach Memoirs* (1986), *Jacob's Ladder* (1990), *Coneheads* (1993), *North* (1994), and *Love! Valour! Compassion!* (1997), in which he played a Broadway musical–obsessed gay man named Buzz. But never, not now, not ever, not in any way, shape, or form, the *real* George Constanza: "People are always coming up to me and saying they are just like me, meaning George. I pity those people and put a lot of distance between us quickly."

24 On this day, in 1934, Babe Ruth played his first game with the New York Yankees. In 1968, *60 Minutes* premiered. In 1991, Theodor Geisel—"Dr. Seuss"—died.

Jim Henson (1936–1990), U.S. puppeteer

Henson achieved wealth and fame in the 1970s and 1980s with his enormously popular Muppet characters, which started out on *Sesame Street* and went on to star in their own wildly successful, syndicated half-hour show, complete with guests like Julie Andrews, Peter Sellers, Elton John, Steve Martin, and Rudolf Nureyev. Ironically, Henson had never intended to become a professional puppeteer. "I mean, it

didn't seem to be the sort of thing a grown man works at for a living," he once told an interviewer. One of the earliest and most popular Muppets was the lovelorn, banjo-strumming amphibian Kermit the Frog, who eventually became a kind of alter ego for the low-key and essentially intro-verted Henson. Kermit was, like his creator, left-handed. Other fabri-cated creatures from the blissfully whimsical Henson menagerie in-cluded Big Bird, Cookie Monster, Oscar the Grouch, Zoot, and, of course, Miss Piggy. (Originally a minor character on the show, Miss Piggy quickly skyrocketed to superstardom and found herself dancing a pas de deux from "Swine Lake" with Nureyev and singing a duet, from "Pigaletto," with Beverly Sills.) "When you do puppets," Henson told the *New York Post*, "you can create the whole show yourself—write it, perform it, direct it, design it. Everything. It's a whole thing, a mood. It's a way of saying something, I guess, but I don't start out to say things. I try to keep it, first of all, entertaining, and then humor-ous. Also, puppetry is a good way of hiding."

Anthony Newley *(b. 1931), British entertainer*

Often eccentric and unpredictable, with a distinctive singing style, Newley coauthored and cocomposed the hit London and Broadway musical *Stop the World—I Want to Get Off* and wrote the music for *Willy Wonka and the Chocolate Factory*. He also appeared in the films *Oliver Twist* (1948), *How to Murder a Rich Uncle* (1957), and *Doctor Dolittle* (1967). He startled many of his fans with the X-rated erotic extravaganza *Can Hieronymus Merkin Ever Forget Mercy Humppe and Find True Happiness?*—costarring his then wife, Joan Collins, as well as a bevy of *Playboy* models—in 1969.

25 On this day, in 1513, Spanish explorer Vasco Balboa became the first European to see the Pacific Ocean. In 1979, *Evita* opened on Broadway.

Billy Ray Cyrus *(b. 1961), U.S. country singer*

Left-hander Cyrus skyrocketed to fame in 1992 with his hit single "Achy Breaky Heart," named the Country Music Association's Single of the Year. His first album, *Some Gave All*, was nominated for five Grammy Awards and was one of the biggest-selling debut albums in recording history.

Mark Hamill *(b. 1951), U.S. actor*

Hamill is one of the most successful actors in Hollywood history: his nineteen feature films have grossed over $1.1 *billion*. His film debut came in the 1977 megahit *Star Wars*, in which he originated the role of Luke Skywalker, a performance that, like Anthony Perkins's in *Psycho*, became a straitjacket (albeit a cushy one) for the rest of his career. Aside from his encore bows as Skywalker in *The Empire Strikes Back* (1980) and *Return of the Jedi* (1983), he has appeared in almost two dozen other feature films, some—like *The Big Red One*, in 1980— critically praised, some—like *Village of the Damned*, in 1995—mediocre but watchable, and some—like *Time Runner*, in 1993—just plain and simply bombs.

Glenn Gould *(1932–1982), Canadian pianist*

"Don't go outside in the fresh air," Glenn Gould's mother told him when he was a small boy, "you might catch a germ." Gould—a highly suggestible child prodigy, unduly influenced by every word that his mother spoke—took her literally for the next forty years of his life, and her advice probably killed him. As an internationally acclaimed pianist in adulthood—perhaps the greatest twentieth-century inter- preter of Bach's keyboard works—he often appeared onstage eccentri- cally bundled in heavy coats and scarves, sweaters and caps; he once stopped in the middle of a performance in San Francisco to complain about a draft coming from an open door somewhere up in the balconies—he refused to resume play until the door was shut. Throughout his adult life, he was besieged by constant, often bizarre (and usually groundless) physical ailments—constant shivers, diverse spasms in his limbs, pain in his prostate, palpitations, severe dizziness, spastic stomach, tightness in the throat—as well as by a succession of unfortunate mental lapses: he complained to friends that the furniture in his apartment was staring at him, and he once called a friend in the middle of the night to accuse his Toronto neighbors of climbing on his roof, spying on him, and blinking secret messages to him with their flashlights. Before a concert in New York, a piano technician good-naturedly slapped Gould on the back: outraged and terrified, Gould sued him, claiming that the innocent gesture had caused him severe physical injury and had ruined his career. (It hadn't and it didn't.) By 1964, when Gould was thirty-two, he had become so terrified of germs and so unable to cope with the outside world that he withdrew from the concert world entirely and devoted himself to performing only in recording studios: "It's a terrible distraction," he once said of his increasingly eccentric behavior. "I would stop it if I could, but I can't." And yet, through all of it, there was the undeniable, and internationally acclaimed, musical genius. As the undisputed keyboard master of contrapuntal music, especially Bach and Beethoven, he garnered universal accolades, and in 1957 was the first Western classical musician invited to perform behind the Iron Curtain, in Moscow and Leningrad. On a morning in 1982, just after his fiftieth birthday, Gould complained to friends of numbness and weakness along the left side of his body; he suspected he had suffered a major stroke. He was taken to the hospital, and within days lay comatose in the respiratory intensive care unit. Barely a week later, he was dead. An autopsy revealed that while virtually every organ in his body was healthy, untouched by disease of any sort, the arteries, especially in his brain, were fatally clogged and weak. A little fresh air and exercise now and then, contrary to his mother's early advice, might have saved his life. Gould was left-handed—when he made a brief foray into conducting, he even conducted with his left hand—which may in part explain his dynamic brilliance as an interpreter of contrapuntal music, since the force of the counterpoint rests with the pianist's left hand. Gould himself rarely mentioned his left-handedness in interviews or essays, though he sometimes remarked in bafflement that he could never understand why so many of the great composers had ignored the canonic opportunities for the left hand.

On this day, in 1985, Shamu, the first killer whale born in captivity, was born at Sea World in Orlando.

Dave Martinez *(b. 1964), U.S. baseball player*

Martinez joined the major leagues in 1986 and has played for Montreal, San Francisco, and the Chicago White Sox, among others. Known for his discipline and skill as a defensive first baseman—and as a versatile "details" man, one who's meticulous about doing even the small things right—he had his best year at bat so far in 1996, when he batted .318 for Chicago.

On this day, in 1980, Marvin Hagler became world middleweight champion after defeating opponent Alan Minter with a third-round knockout.

Kiel Martin *(1944–1990), U.S. actor*

The left-handed actor got his start on the daytime soap opera *The Edge of Night* in the 1960s, but was most familiar to TV audiences as Detective J. D. LaRue on the hit series *Hill Street Blues*, beginning in 1981.

Today is Confucius's birthday. On this day, in 1066, the Norman Conquest began. In 1978, Pope John Paul I died.

William Windom (b. 1923), U.S. actor

Popular left-handed actor best known in the 1960s as Congressman Glen Morley (alternately wooing and chiding beautiful governess Inger Stevens) on *The Farmer's Daughter*, and in the 1980s as Dr. Seth Hazlitt (Angela Lansbury's chess partner, among other things) on *Murder, She Wrote*.

On this day, in 1950, the first telephone answering machine was invented.

Lord Nelson (1758–1805), British naval commander

Nelson's right elbow was shattered by gunfire during a sea skirmish in the Canary Islands in 1797. The entire arm had to be amputated (without anesthetic) shortly after the accident. "A left-handed Admiral will never again be considered as useful," Nelson wrote plaintively of his future, "therefore the sooner I get to a very humble cottage the better." As it turned out, Nelson was still *very* useful to the British navy: he commanded the British fleet in the war with Napoleonic France six years later, and continued to lead ships into battle until he was killed by French forces at the Battle of Trafalgar in 1805—a battle, incidentally, that Nelson won for the British.

30

On this day, in 1455, the first Gutenberg Bible was printed. In 1955, film star James Dean was killed in an automobile collision near Paso Robles, California.

Fran Drescher *(b. 1957), U.S. actress*

When left-handers decide to pursue their own obsessive vision of personal style, the results can be traditionally elegant—as in the case of Celine Dion or Kristian Alfonso—or they can be, well, Fran Drescher. Described by one critic as looking like "a giant party favor that exploded prematurely," and by another as "the Creature from the Tacky Lagoon," left-hander Drescher debuted in the TV series *The Nanny* in 1993 and has enjoyed fashion-driven stardom ever since. Her autobiography is titled *Enter Whining*.

Left-handers Born in
October

October: Tenth month of the year, originally the eighth month of the ancient Roman calendar; hence its name, from the Latin octem, *meaning "eight"*

Today is World Vegetarian Day. On this day, in 1888, the first *National Geographic* was published.

Rod Carew *(b. 1945), U.S. baseball player*

"Trying to sneak a pitch past him," said pitcher Catfish Hunter, "is like trying to sneak the sunrise past a rooster." During his eighteen-year career with the Minnesota Twins, left-handed batter Carew had 3,053 hits and was the American League batting champion seven times. His lifetime batting average was .328. Carew attributed his success to one thing: the loving attention he lavished on his bats. He rubbed them down with alcohol after every game and kept them safely segregated, in a locked closet, away from the other players'. He also sometimes put them in a special "hot box" to "bake out the bad wood." That he felt a deep, almost spiritual connection with the tooled, three-foot lengths of wood was evident to everyone around him. "I can't stand a dirty bat," he once said with disdain. "Some guys leave pine tar on their bats and never clean them off. I can't understand that. How can they get a feel for the wood?" On another occasion, he told a sportswriter, "I see guys bang their bats against the dugout steps after they make an out. That bruises them, makes them weaker. I couldn't do that. I baby my bats, treat them like my kids, because using a bat is how I make my living."

Randy Quaid *(b. 1950), U.S. actor*

The left-handed older brother of Dennis Quaid (see April 9), Randy Quaid was first discovered by director Peter Bogdanovich, who cast him in *The Last Picture Show* in 1971, and subsequently in *What's Up Doc?* and *Paper Moon*. Since then, he's built a career portraying good-hearted but lumbering average guys—as in *The Last Detail*, for which he was nominated for an Academy Award in 1973—or good-hearted but lumbering not-so-average guys, as in his inspired performance as President Lyndon Johnson in the TV movie *LBJ: The Early Years* in 1987, or, plain and simply, boors, as in the extremely popular *National Lampoon Vacation* series.

James Whitmore *(b. 1921), U.S. actor*

The twice-Oscar-nominated left-hander has had roles in over fifty films, ranging from science fiction blockbusters (*Them!* and *Planet of the Apes*) to wartime melodramas (*Battle Cry* and *Tora! Tora! Tora!*) to musicals (*Kiss Me Kate* and *Oklahoma!*). His first Oscar nomination was for the World War II drama *Battleground*, in 1949; his second was for his stunning impersonation of Harry S Truman in *Give 'Em Hell, Harry!* in 1975.

2

On this day, in 1967, Thurgood Marshall became the first African-American on the U.S. Supreme Court. In 1985, Rock Hudson died of AIDS.

Maury Wills *(b. 1932), U.S. baseball player*

As a shortstop with various farm clubs for seven years, the right-handed Wills had little prospect of ever playing major-league baseball—until his manager suggested he start batting left-handed against right-handed pitchers. Wills was, if nothing else, determined: he made the unusual mid-career conversion with barely a hitch. He still wasn't a power hitter, but he was able to bunt and bounce the ball around the infield and get safely to first base often enough to do what he truly excelled at: stealing bases. In 1960, a year after he joined the Dodgers, he stole 50 bases—the most recorded in the National League since 1923. In 1962, he stole 104 bases, besting Ty Cobb's previous single-season record of 96. Wills' exploits on the diamond thrilled fans and inspired other players (notably, Lou Brock and Ricky Henderson). He was nicknamed, by fans and teammates, "the Artful Dodger."

On this day, in 1970, singer Janis Joplin died of a heroin overdose. In 1990, East and West Germany were reunited into a single country.

Jack Wagner (b. 1959), U.S. actor

Best known as Dr. Peter Burns on *Melrose Place*, left-hander Wagner originally intended to become a professional golfer but succumbed instead to acting after winning a drama scholarship to the University of Arizona. "I decided that I have much more control over what I do on stage," he told an interviewer, "than whether or not my golf ball goes out-of-bounds when it hits a tree." He has also appeared on the daytime soap operas *Santa Barbara* and *General Hospital*.

On this day, in 1957, the first man-made satellite, *Sputnik*, was launched. Also in 1957, the first episode of *Leave It to Beaver* was aired.

Charlie Leibrandt (b. 1956), U.S. baseball player

The famous left-handed pitcher played for Cincinnati, Kansas City, and Atlanta in a fourteen-year major-league career, beginning in 1979. When he retired in 1993, he had accumulated a 140–119 record and a 3.71 ERA.

On this day, in 1969, *Monty Python's Flying Circus* debuted on British television.

Larry Fine (1902–1975), U.S. comic actor

So much has been written about the Three Stooges—in J. Forrester's fine 1981 book *The Stooges Chronicles*, and elsewhere—that it seems redundant to try and rephrase or condense any of it here. Besides, the Stooges simply *are*—and either you love them or you hate them. And if you love them, you're certain to prefer watching them to reading about them. And if you hate them, nothing anyone can say will impress or interest you very much. The only real surprise is that—with all of their subversive craziness—only one of them, Larry, was left-handed.

On this day, in 1927, the first talking motion picture, *The Jazz Singer,* was given its world premiere, in New York City. In 1989, actress Bette Davis died at the age of eighty-one.

Fred Travalena (b. 1942), U.S. comic

The left-handed comedian and actor is especially known for his impersonations of U.S. presidents, as well as other characters including Elvis Presley, Michael Jackson, and Robert De Niro. President Bush was so impressed with Travalena's impression of him that he rewarded the comedian with an official hosting slot at Bush's 1989 inaugural. Travalena has also appeared in films (*The Buddy Holly Story*) and on television (*Murphy Brown*), and was a frequent guest on the popular game show *Hollywood Squares*.

7

On this day, in 1737, a cyclone over the Bay of Bengal, India, sent forty-foot waves over coastal towns, killing more than three hundred thousand people. In 1950, the Korean War began.

June Allyson (b. *1917*), U.S. *actress*

Despite having become in recent years the butt of interminable jokes as a result of her television appearances as spokeswoman for a certain less-than-glamorous, antimicturitional undergarment, left-hander Allyson was the very epitome of perky girl-next-doorness during the 1940s. Though never a star of the caliber of Betty Grable or Judy Garland, she was extremely popular, always reliable, and an important component of the glossy, carefree MGM musicals. Among her best-known films were *Girl Crazy* (1943), *Two Girls and a Sailor* (1944), *Two Sisters from Boston* (1946)—you get the idea. In the 1950s, she turned to dramatic roles, in such films as *The Glenn Miller Story* (with James Stewart, in 1954), and *Strategic Air Command* (1955). To anyone who's ever seen a June Allyson film, there's no mystery at all why she was chosen to represent that certain less-than-glamorous, antimicturitional undergarment: for her entire thirty-year career, she exemplified all-American nothing-can-ever-get-me-down optimism.

Oliver North (b. *1943*), U.S. *conservative activist*

We were going to write a several-page entry about the controversial, left-handed former deputy director of the National Security Council—who, in the mid-1980s, became the central figure in the arms-for-hostages Iran-Contra scandal—but (1) most of our original reference material got inadvertently shredded, and (2) our beautiful, leggy secretary—we think her name was Fawn something—smuggled our rough draft out of the house in her panties and we haven't seen her since.

Henry A. Wallace *(1888–1965), U.S. vice president*

Left-hander Wallace was vice president under Franklin Delano Roosevelt, from 1941 to 1945.

On this day, in 1906, the first hair permanent was demonstrated, in London.

Walter Lord *(1917–1996), British author*

Lord authored what many regard as the definitive book on the sinking of the *Titanic—A Night to Remember—*which became a best-seller in 1955. He followed it with a sequel, *The Night Lives On,* several years later.

Stephanie Zimbalist *(b. 1956), U.S. actress*

The left-handed actress starred in the popular series *Remington Steele,* with Pierce Brosnan, from 1982 to 1987.

Today is Alphabet Day in Korea. On this day, in 1967, Che Guevara died.

Sir Thomas Urquhart *(1611–1660), Scottish linguist and translator*

More than three hundred years after his death, the birthday of this eccentric left-handed poet, scholar, and linguist is lost to history; it seems appropriate to celebrate his life and work today, which is, after all, Alphabet Day. Urquhart was obsessed with trying to develop what he regarded as the ideal universal language, in which each word, instead of being read from left to right, would be read the same either backwards or forward. (Think of words like "bob," "dad," "wow," and "ere.") He even wrote about the subject in a passionate 1653 book titled *Logopandecteision: An Introduction to the Universal Language.* Urquhart is best known to modern readers for his racy and largely unsurpassed English translations of the French satirist Rabelais. He was also an able soldier, a mathematician, a historian, a memoirist, and, according to everyone who knew him, a walking encyclopedia of arcane knowledge and titillating gossip about everyone who was anyone in Europe. He was, all in all, the spiritual great-grandfather of another eccentric left-handed poet, mathematician, and linguist, Lewis Carroll. He died, so the story goes, of apoplexy during a fit of uncontrollable laughter one night, after being told a particularly amusing story. He was a cheerful forty-nine.

10 Today is Independence Day in Fiji. On this day, in 1913, the Panama Canal opened. In 1935, *Porgy and Bess* opened on Broadway.

Lisa Blount *(b. 1957), U.S. actress*

Blount was nominated for a Golden Globe as Best New Female Star of the Year for her role as Lynette Pomeroy in the 1983 film *An Officer and a Gentleman.* She has subsequently appeared in the films *Great Balls of Fire!* (1989), *Femme Fatale* (1991), and *Needful Things* (1993), as well as in the made-for-TV movie *Get to the Heart: The Barbara Mandrell Story* in 1997.

11

Today is General Pułaski Memorial Day in the United States. On this day, in 1975, Bill Clinton married Hillary Rodham. In 1983, First Lady Nancy Reagan introduced the antidrug slogan, "Just say no."

Luke Perry *(b. 1966), U.S. Actor*

Born Coy Luther Perry, the left-handed actor took the nickname "Luke" when he was five years old and saw Paul Newman in *Cool Hand Luke*. After leaving home at the age of seventeen, he got his first major role in 1987, as Ned Bates on the daytime soap opera *Loving*. Three years later, he won the part of brooding Dylan McKay on the hit show *Beverly Hills 90210*. At the peak of his popularity—which some observers partly attributed to his sideburns—he was regularly mobbed by adoring women at every public appearance: in August 1991, his appearance at a shopping mall drew ten thousand fans who, unable to control themselves, suddenly rushed the stage, causing numerous bystanders to be seriously injured. Perry left *Beverly Hill 90210* in 1995. He has since appeared in the films *The Fifth Element* (1997) and *The Florentine* (1998), as well as in the TV miniseries *Robin Cook's Invasion*.

Steve Young *(b. 1961), U.S. football player*

The left-handed Salt Lake City native played for Tampa Bay before replacing legendary quarterback Joe Montana on the San Francisco 49ers. Deemed *Sports Illustrated*'s Player of the Year in 1992 and 1994, and twice named NFL Most Valuable Player, he led the 49ers to victory at Super Bowl XXIX, over San Diego, in 1994.

On this day, in 1911, the state of California gave women the right to vote.

Sid Fernandez *(b. 1962), U.S. baseball player*

Before severe problems with his left elbow caused his game to falter in the early 1990s, Fernandez was a consistently winning pitcher for the New York Mets. In 1989, he had a 2.83 ERA; in 1992, 2.73. Although he attempted a comeback in 1997, he was only able to pitch (and win) one game in the first week of the season; his arm gave out on him again, and he was forced, after fifteen years in the major leagues, to retire once and for all.

On this day, in 1792, the cornerstone of the White House was laid in Washington, D.C. In 1983, the first cellular phone system was introduced, in Chicago.

George "Rube" Waddell *(1876–1914), U.S. baseball player*

Waddell, who pitched for the Philadelphia Athletics before World War I, is rated by some authorities as the fastest left-handed pitcher of all time. However, he never drew a regular salary for his work: instead, whenever he needed a little money, he went to the team's manager for five or ten dollars. His frequently odd behavior—obsessed with firemen, he sometimes missed a game to watch them put out fires—and his occasional drunkenness while pitching contributed to the notion that all left-handed pitchers are flaky and crazy. Waddell retired from major-league ball in 1910 with a 193–143 career record and a 2.16 ERA.

On this day, in 1947, Chuck Yeager became the first human being to break the sound barrier. In 1964, Martin Luther King, Jr., was awarded the Nobel Peace Prize.

Harry Anderson (b. *1949*), U.S. *actor*

The left-handed magician-turned-actor was a semiregular on *Cheers* in 1982—as Harry "the Hat" Gittes—before landing his own series, the enormously popular *Night Court* in 1984. After *Night Court* left the air, Anderson moved on to another hit sitcom, *Dave's World*, in which he played, appropriately, nationally known, left-handed humor columnist Dave Barry (see July 3).

Gary Graffman (b. *1928*), U.S. *pianist*

A natural right-hander, Graffman began experiencing problems with his right hand after he sprained it during a 1967 concert in Berlin. By 1979, it had become so severely disabled he was no longer able to use it. He kept his concert career going with performances of Ravel's *Concerto in D Major for the Left Hand* and other works for the left hand alone.

Today is National Poetry Day in the United States. On this day, in 1917, Mata Hari was executed by a French firing squad. In 1951, *I Love Lucy* premiered on television.

Alexander Dreyschock (*1818–1869*), *Bohemian composer and pianist*

Whether or not Dreyschock was born left-handed—he was probably ambidextrous, but music-history books are mum on the subject—it was his left hand that generated his fame as a brilliant and formidable pianist in the nineteenth century. To the amazement of critics and audiences alike, Dreyschock often played lengthy and labyrinthine piano solos (usually of his own composition) with his left hand—material that would have quickly exhausted the left hands of lesser performers. His virtuosity was so extraordinary that English composer J. B. Cramer once exclaimed, "My God, the man has no left hand! He has two *right* hands!"

Today is World Food Day at the United Nations. On this day, in 1793, Marie Antoinette was guillotined. In 1846, anesthetic was used for the first time in major surgery.

Leon "Goose" Goslin (1900–1971), *U.S. baseball player*

The Washington Senators may have been the worst team in the league ("First in war, first in peace, last in the American League"), but that didn't stop their star outfielder, Leon Goslin, from batting in 100 or more runs in each of eleven seasons. Goslin's regular play, however, was nothing compared with his performance in World Series competition. In the 1924 series, he had six consecutive hits (a record), and he belted in 3 home runs each in both the 1924 and 1925 series. After the 1933 season, he was traded to Detroit, where his hitting propelled the team to pennant victories in 1934 and 1935. His ninth-inning single in the sixth game of the 1935 series gave Detroit the championship.

Today is the International Day for the Eradication of Poverty. On this day, in 1777, the Battle of Saratoga was fought. In 1919, RCA was formed.

Howard Rollins, Jr. (1950–1996), *U.S. actor*

The accomplished but deeply troubled actor made a huge impact with his starring role in the 1981 hit film *Ragtime*, then costarred in the popular TV series *In the Heat of the Night.* Drugs and other personal problems ended his career. He died of AIDS in 1996.

On this day, in 1974, Benjamin Britten's opera *Death in Venice* had its U.S. premiere at the Metropolitan Opera. In 1989, the Jupiter explorer *Galileo* was launched.

Martina Navratilova *(b. 1956), Czech-U.S. tennis champion*

One of the most celebrated ambidextrous individuals in modern sports, Navratilova started out writing left-handed—just like her mother—but because she kept getting ink smears all over her writing hand, a teacher suggested she try writing with her right hand instead. She did—and found, to her surprise, that it came as naturally as writing left-handed. She has told interviewers that much of the time, and while she is engaged in a wide variety of activities, it doesn't occur to her to favor one hand over the other. However, she prefers to play tennis left-handed. Born and raised in Czechoslovakia, the young Navratilova played in her first tournament when she was eight years old, despite the objections of some officials that she was too small for the tennis court. By the time she started competing in international tournaments, she was a muscular five feet eight and weighed 140 pounds. She soon made a name for herself with an aggressive net-charging style and a 90-mile-per-hour serve. Her punishing volleys overpowered most of her opponents. In 1978, she won her first Wimbledon singles title, and for a time she seemed unbeatable, winning six major world championships in a row and setting an all-time record for consecutive match victories (74). She was also the first tennis player to earn $10 million. All in all, she has won more than 1,300 singles matches, including 9 Wimbledon titles. In 1975, Navratilova moved from the sports page to the front page when she announced her intention to defect to the United States. She became an American citizen six years later. In the late 1980s, her personal life made headlines, culminating in a much publicized "palimony" suit by former lover Judy Nelson in 1991. (The suit was settled out of court.) In recent years,

Navratilova has become an outspoken activist for animal rights, environmental issues, and AIDS.

19

Today is Ascension of Muhammad Day in Indonesia. On this day, in 1812, Napoleon began his retreat from Moscow.

Divine *(1946–1988), U.S. entertainer*

The aptly named Divine was not much of an actress. But then, let's be honest, neither was Joan Crawford. What Divine had—like Crawford and other divas of the silver screen—was that amorphous quality called "presence." Whether she was competing for the title "Filthiest Person Alive" in *Pink Flamingos* (Divine's final scene, a *cause terrible* in cult circles, easily won the title), or trying to hang herself from the kitchen refrigerator in *Polyester*, or getting a makeover with daughter Ricki Lake in *Hairspray*, there was something mesmerizing about the three-hundred-pound man in a dress: not just the bizarre spectacle of such unlikely drag but a compelling mixture of damn-the-world courage with honest-to-God compassion and gentleness. Director John Waters—von Sternberg to Divine's Dietrich—first noticed his star-to-be when the two were growing up in Baltimore: Divine was the only junior high schooler who required a special police escort to and from school every day because he was constantly being beaten senseless by his schoolmates. ("One day I had to go to the school nurse for something else and she made me take off my shirt, and I didn't want to because she'd see the bruises. She was horrified . . .") Divine's death, at the age of forty-two—on the heels (no pun intended) of his first mainstream success, in *Hairspray*—was sad indeed. He was all about nonconformity—which is something every left-hander can identify with. (Well, *almost* every left-hander: see March 22.)

20 On this day, in 1805, Napoleon's troops were victorious over the Austrian army at the Battle of Ulm. In 1968, Jackie Kennedy married Aristotle Onassis.

Keith Hernandez *(b. 1953), U.S. baseball player*

When left-hander Hernandez was a boy, he dribbled a basketball—with his right hand—to and from school every day. "I wanted to be as good with my right hand as I was with my left," he said many years later, "and it worked. I became a very good ball handler." The first baseman played major-league ball from 1974 to 1990, first with St. Louis, then with the New York Mets, and, finally, with Cleveland. In 1979, his best year at bat, he won the National League's MVP award and batted .344, with 105 RBIs. He almost repeated the performance the following year, with a .321 average and 99 RBIs. (He led the league in runs scored that year.) In 1983, he was unexpectedly traded to the New York Mets; unknown to fans and the press, the cause was cocaine use. "When I started using it," he later acknowledged, "the biggest fuckin' lie about cocaine was that it's not addictive. . . . Anybody who does it recreationally is taking a tremendous risk. Cocaine will grab you by the throat, and the next thing you know you're in trouble." He cleaned up his drug use ("The urges stayed with me for the rest of the '83 season, and I had those urges during all of '84 and '85 as well") and played for seven more years, retiring in 1990 with a .296 career average. "I will miss the guys much more than the games," he said in a *Playboy* interview, "and I think that's true for most ex-ballplayers. I won't miss having to drive in the clutch run with two outs in the ninth inning. But I will miss the three a.m. bus rides from the airport into Cincinnati, where there's music going and everybody's singing and laughing. Those are the great times."

Eric Scott *(b. 1958), U.S. actor*

Left-hander Scott is best known for his role as redheaded Ben on *The Waltons*, from 1972 to 1981. He has also appeared in six made-for-TV *Waltons* movies, and in the 1981 feature film *The Loch Ness Horror*. (See also June 3.)

On this day, in 1789, the political terms "left" (liberal) and "right" (conservative) were first introduced, during the French Revolution. In 1965, the comet Ikeya-Seki was so brilliant it was visible to the naked eye in daylight.

Benjamin Netanyahu *(b. 1949)*, *Israeli prime minister*

Known as "Bibi" to his friends, left-hander Netanyahu became the youngest prime minister in Israeli history when he was elected on May 29, 1996, by a slim 29,457-vote majority out of more than 3 million votes cast. Although born in Tel Aviv, he was raised in the U.S. and attended high school in Philadelphia after his father, a prominent right-wing Zionist, moved the family to the United States. Netanyahu attended Harvard and the Massachusetts Institute of Technology. Regarded as one of the first Israeli politicians to employ American-inspired campaign tactics—with an emphasis on smooth appearance and carefully polished pronouncements—he was elected on a largely conservative agenda, including outspoken opposition to further compromise with the Palestinians. He later began to somewhat soften many of his initially hard-line approaches to his country's dilemmas.

Whitey Ford *(b. 1928)*, *U.S. baseball player*

Nicknamed the Yankees' "Chairman of the Board" (and also christened "Slick" by Yankees manager Casey Stengel for his smooth-talking abilities in any situation), Ford was long rumored to have finessed his way onto the team by calling Stengel one afternoon and offering the suggestion, in a disguised voice, "If you ever want to win the pennant, you'd better call up that kid Ford from Kansas City." Widely regarded as the best pitcher in Yankees history, Ford had a career record of 236–106 and helped catapult the team to eleven pennant victories in the 1950s and 1960s. He received the Cy Young Award in 1961, retired in 1967, and was elected to the Baseball Hall of Fame in 1974.

On this day, in 1978, Cardinal Karol Wojtyla became Pope John Paul II.

Roger E. Mosley *(b. 1944), U.S. actor*

Left-hander Mosley is best known for playing Tom Selleck's side-kick T.C. on the popular TV series *Magnum P.I.* in the 1980s, although he's also appeared in a variety of action films including *The New Centurions, Stay Hungry, Semi-Tough,* and *The Jericho Mile.* In recent years, he's primarily been visible as a close friend of O. J. Simpson, and has often been sighted on the golf course with him.

Today marks the beginning of the astrological sign Scorpio. On this day, in 1989, Hungary declared itself an independent republic after forty years of Communist dictatorship.

Pelé *(b. 1940), Brazilian soccer player*

I was born to soccer just as Beethoven was born for music.

—Pelé

At one time, Edson Arantes do Nascimento—better known as "Pelé"—was arguably the world's most famous left-handed (and left-footed) athlete. As the undisputed superstar of the world's most popular sport, he garnered the adoration of millions (especially in his native Brazil) and took home what was once reputed to be the highest salary in sports history. Over a twenty-one-year career, he scored 1,282 goals in 1,364 games and helped the Brazilian national team capture the World Cup three times, in 1958, 1962, and 1970. A 1964 article on his uncanny abilities observed, "Loping or sprinting, he could drag the ball from one foot to the other as if it were a yo-yo on the end of an invisible string. . . . [I]ntuitively, at any instant, he seemed to know the position of all other players on the field, and to sense just what each man was going to do next." Unfortunately, as his fame increased, so did the enmity of his opponents. Physical attacks against him became commonplace during a game. "Nobody in the game had more fun than I did when I first became a professional," he told one journalist. "This honeymoon came to an abrupt end." After a brief stint playing for the New York Cosmos (for a reported $4.7 million), Pelé retired in 1977.

John Holliman (1948–1998), U.S. television journalist

Left-hander Holliman started working for CNN in 1980—he was, in fact, one of their first correspondents—and although he rose to public prominence as part of the CNN team (including Bernard Shaw and Peter Arnett) that broadcasted live during the U.S. bombardment of Baghdad at the beginning of the Gulf War in January 1991, it was primarily as a science correspondent that he repeatedly distinguished himself. Compare, for example, his coverage of the 1997 Mars *Pathfinder* mission to any other news agency's: in a television era when au pair murder trials and celebrity funerals gobble up endless hours of live "news" coverage, CNN—and Holliman—relentlessly carved out large chunks of airtime for space-shuttle missions and planetary exploration, as well as detailed analyses of critical environmental issues and controversial scientific breakthroughs such as cloning. Some of the credit goes to Ted Turner—who is an enthusiastic champion of space-science issues—but in Holliman, CNN found the perfect voice for its agenda of balancing the sensational with the scientifically profound. Holliman's intelligence and eagerness were a breath of fresh air in a career field where correspondents so often reserve their passion for their hair and speak with *Vanity Fair*–like smugness about significant issues (the smirk having replaced the thoughtful question); his name became virtually synonymous with articulate, meaningful television journalism. He was, not surprisingly, almost as avid about his left-handedness. "I've always kind of enjoyed it," he told *Lefthander* magazine in 1991. "Nobody tried to discourage me, of course. Everybody said, 'It's just great.' So I was highly encouraged to be the best I could be with whatever I was given. And it certainly was what I had been given. Nobody else in our family, even back a couple of generations, is a lefty."

Lee "Lefty" Grissom *(1907–1983), U.S. baseball player*

Left-hander Grissom was among the most superstitious ballplayers in major-league history. He started pitching for Cincinnati in 1934. By 1938, he was having severe arm trouble; no remedy seemed to work. Finally, a teammate told him that pitching legend Lefty Grove had relieved *his* arm problems by having two of his teeth pulled. The superstitious Grissom went to the dentist soon afterward and had not just two good teeth extracted but *four*. When he returned to the mound after the surgery, he quickly discovered that he still had severe arm trouble. "It seemed like a good idea when I heard about it," Grissom said later. "I figured if I could win some games, it was worth it. The teeth-pulling didn't hurt me. But it damn sure didn't help my arm." Grissom retired in 1941 with a career record of 29–48.

On this day, in 1931, Al Capone was sentenced to eleven years in prison for tax evasion. In 1945, the United Nations was officially chartered as an international peacekeeping organization.

Jackie Coogan *(1914–1984), U.S. actor*

It's simply impossible to explain the hold that seven-year-old left-hander Jackie Coogan had on America in the 1920s. Of all the famous child actors in American films, Coogan was the *most* famous, the *most* beloved, and (adjusted for inflation) the most highly paid. Before he even reached puberty, he received $1.5 million for a two-year contract at MGM. He made his feature-length film debut, opposite Charlie Chaplin, in the wrenching 1921 melodrama *The Kid*, a film that still, nearly eighty years later, has the power to bring tears to the eyes of stouthearted men who otherwise weep only when their favorite team flubs an interception at the Super Bowl. An exaggeration? Watch this tale of Chaplin's Tramp trying to raise and protect a scruffy street orphan, and judge for yourself. Alas, all of the fame in the world couldn't keep Coogan from suffering the fate of so many exploited child stars. We're not talking obscurity here; we're talking *poverty*. All of

Coogan's well-earned millions were placed in a trust fund to be managed by his parents, but when he finally came of age, greedy mama and Coogan's stepfather were loath to part with a cent of it. By the time Coogan took them both to court (and won), he received barely $100,000 of the $4 million-plus owed him. His situation became so notorious it led to passage of the California Child Actors Bill—popularly known as the Coogan Act—which attempted ("attempted" is the operative word) to protect other juvenile actors from similar abuses. Coogan's screen popularity began to wane right about the time his voice was changing—not even front-page news of his marriage to Betty Grable when he was twenty-three could reignite his stardom—but he stayed active, in films and television, for the next six decades. In fact, it was once estimated that by the time of his death he had appeared in over thirteen hundred television programs. To TV-loving couch potatoes of the 1960s, he was best known as bald-headed, nasty-but-cuddly Uncle Fester in the popular television series *The Addams Family*.

25 On this day, in 1400, Chaucer died. In 1971, Communist China became a member of the United Nations.

Julia Roberts (b. *1967*),
U.S. actress

The left-handed actress—twice nominated for Oscars, for *Steel Magnolias* (1990) and *Pretty Woman* (1991)—has kept a diary most of her life and is known for taking her personal journal, which she privately titles "All the Makings of Insanity," with her at all times.

On this day, in 1881, the Gunfight at the OK Corral was fought.

Philip Charles MacKenzie *(b. 1949), U.S. actor and TV director*

Although left-hander MacKenzie did innumerable guest shots on TV through the late seventies and early eighties—in *Three's Company, Remington Steele, Cheers,* et al.—he became famous as the very flamboyant Donald, the swishy queen with the heart of gold, on the popular Showtime comedy series *Brothers* in 1984. After *Brothers'* cancellation, he all but abandoned acting and became one of the most prominent sitcom directors in Hollywood, working on *Roseanne, The Golden Girls,* and *Frasier.*

On this day, in 1492, Columbus became the first European to set foot on the island of Cuba. In 1904, the first section of the New York subway system was opened.

Terry Anderson *(b. 1947), U.S. journalist and Middle East hostage*

On the morning of Saturday, March 16, 1985, left-hander Anderson—the chief Middle East correspondent for the Associated Press—was kidnapped by Muslim extremists in West Beirut. "Don't worry," said one of the kidnappers, shoving a gun into Anderson's back. "It's political." Despite the odd attempt at reassurance, Anderson's wrists, arms, ankles, knees, and thighs were tightly bound with plastic tape, and a dirty blanket was thrown over his head. For the next 2,454 days—almost seven years—he lived in chains in a variety of squalid rooms in Beirut, was beaten, forced to listen while another hostage, CIA operative William Buckley, was tortured to death, endured the release of other Middle East hostages, one after another, until he was the only one left. His daughter was born—and lived the first six years of her life—while he was in captivity. He was finally freed on December 4, 1991. The wrenching details of his ordeal and survival are harrowingly related in his 1993 memoir, *Den of Lions*.

Marla Maples *(b. 1963), ex-wife of Donald Trump*

The former model abruptly rose from obscurity and became front-page fodder when she supplanted Ivana Trump in the marital affections of businessman Donald Trump. Maples and the tycoon have since divorced.

28

On this day, in 1886, the Statue of Liberty was dedicated. In 1958, Cardinal Roncalli became Pope John XXIII.

Bill Gates *(b. 1955), U.S. entrepreneur*

When Microsoft Windows was first released, the joke was that only left-handed Bill Gates would design a program in which you had to click "Start" in order to "Shut Down." As a boy, Gates was for many years an underachiever ("There was a whole period when I got terrible grades"), but he was always a voracious reader. "When I was young," he told one interviewer, "we used to read books over the summer and get little colored bookmarks for each one. There were girls who had read maybe fifteen books. I'd read thirty. Numbers two through ninety-nine were all girls, and there I was at number one. . . . I also liked taking tests. I happened to be good at it. Certain subjects came easily, like math. All the science stuff. I would just read the textbooks in the first few days of class."

Bruce Jenner *(b. 1949), U.S. Olympic decathlete*

Jenner was troubled by dyslexia as a child and started playing sports in part to help compensate for problems created by the condition. In

1976, at the age of twenty-six, he earned the unofficial title "World's Greatest Athlete" when he won the gold medal in the Decathlon at the Montreal Olympics. With his boyish good looks and disarming smile, he captured the imagination of the American public to a degree that was unusual even for an Olympic gold medalist. Soon after the games, he became a commercial spokesman for Wheaties; later, his fame helped him launch a fledgling movie career, including a role in the less-than-inspired film musical *Can't Stop the Music*, a 1980 "biography" of the disco group the Village People. Quipped critic Leonard Maltin, "Some people feel they *have* to see what the Village People and Jenner are doing in the same film."

On this day, in 1883, the Orient Express completed its first run. In 1929, the stock market crashed, in the financial collapse that triggered the Great Depression.

Winona Ryder (b. *1971*), *U.S. actress*

Even if you had never grasped the essential differences between left-handers and right-handers, you would know there was something special about Winona Ryder. It isn't that she's a great actress (she isn't, though she's come close several times). It isn't that she's a great beauty: Elle and Pamela Lee have nothing to fear from her. It isn't even that she has charisma, in the typical sense of the word: she is neither influential nor authoritative. What she has is intensity—and heart. So much heart that one eagerly overlooks all the technical imperfections in her performances in such films as *The Age of Innocence* and Francis Ford Coppola's *Bram Stoker's Dracula*: less polished, less convincing than many of her colleagues in both films, she nonetheless manages to be more *real*—a seeming contradiction that, in its own way, says *everything* about the differences between left- and right-handers.

Bill Mauldin (b. 1921), U.S. cartoonist

Mauldin first achieved fame for his *Stars and Stripes* cartoons detailing the often maddening and strenuous lives of army grunts during World War II; his specialty was slyly mocking the fatuity and noblesse oblige of military bureaucracy and the army brass. After the war, he continued to use cartooning to comment sardonically on the lives of soldiers: in this case, focusing on the troubled transition many GIs were experiencing as they reentered civilian life. By the 1950s, he had become one of the most widely syndicated cartoonists in the U.S., pillorying a wide spectrum of political figures, social issues, and foreign governments; he was especially famous for his frequently ironic commentary on the hypocrisy of the Soviet Union. He has been awarded two Pulitzer Prizes for his work.

Richard Dreyfuss (b. 1947), U.S. actor

Although Dreyfuss garnered critical attention for his eerily convincing portrayal of Baby Face Nelson in the John Milius "drive-in" classic *Dillinger* in 1973, his big break came when he was cast by George Lucas in the unexpected megahit *American Graffiti*. Roles in *The Apprenticeship of Duddy Kravitz* (1974), *Jaws* (1975), and *Close Encounters of the Third Kind* (1977) cemented his stardom.

30 On this day, in 1922, Mussolini became Prime Minister of Italy. In 1938, Orson Welles broadcast his now infamous radio play of *The War of the Worlds*.

Kurt Cobain (1967–1994), U.S. rock star

Today isn't Kurt Cobain's birthday, but it might as well be: this is the day he smashed his first guitar, at a Halloween dorm party at Evergreen State University in 1988. (For those who are overly fastidious,

Cobain's birthday is February 20.) Three years later almost to the day, Nirvana's major-label debut album, *Nevermind*, went gold. A month later, it went platinum. Cobain's troubled life—he dropped out of high school; he didn't just experiment with drugs, he *bathed* in them—shouldn't be seen as a blueprint for anyone seeking success in the music industry; the left-handed lead singer of Nirvana had a troubled psyche almost from the start. In death, he was elevated almost to sainthood by some: a symbol of adolescent nihilism, an angel of suicide. There were even conspiracy theories: he was *silenced*, man. All in all, that he killed himself at the age of twenty-seven with a self-inflicted gunshot wound to the head seems neither especially symbolic nor conspiratorial: it was just a terrible, stupid waste.

Herschel Bernardi *(1923–1986), U.S. actor*

The sometime film actor appearing in *Irma la Douce* (1963) and *Love with the Proper Stranger* (1964), as well as a handful of other movies, but was primarily known for his stage work, appearing on Broadway in *Fiddler on the Roof* and the musical *Zorba*. He was also the voice of the Jolly Green Giant and Charlie Tuna in television commercials.

31

Today is Halloween. It is also UNICEF Day. On this day, in 1517, Martin Luther nailed his Ninety-five Theses to the door of the Castle Church in Wittenberg, Germany, thus initiating the Reformation.

Michael Landon (1936–1991), U.S. actor

"Little Joe" wore his gun holster on the left on *Bonanza* for the fourteen years the show was on the air. He didn't pretend to be anything he wasn't. It was an inspiration to little boys everywhere—if "Little Joe" could be left-handed, why couldn't they?

Left-handers Born in
November

November: From the Latin novem—*"nine"—since it was, according to the ancient Roman calendar, the ninth month of the year*

1

Today is the Day of the Dead in Mexico. On this day, in 1755, Lisbon was leveled by one of the worst earthquakes in recorded history. In 1837, Mount Holyoke, the first women's college in the United States, opened its doors.

Fernando Valenzuela *(b. 1960), Mexican-U.S. baseball player*

Acclaimed as el Zurdo—"the Left-hander"—in his native Mexico, pitcher Valenzuela became famous for his notorious screwball, nicknamed "Fernando's Fadeaway," which had the eye-popping ability to veer unpredictably away from batters at the last moment. In 1981, after pitching eight shutouts and leading the Dodgers to a world championship, he became an international celebrity.

Bill Anderson *(b. 1937), U.S. country singer and songwriter*

"Whisperin' Bill"—as fans call him—is responsible for the hits "The Tips of My Fingers," "City Lights," "Slippin' Away," and "Mama Sang a Song." "I have worked for several years on writing a song about and for left-handed people," the country music legend told *Lefthander* magazine in 1994. "So hopefully we're going to have a left-handed song on the market soon."

Today is All Souls' Day. On this day, in 1889, North and South Dakota were admitted to the Union. In 1930, Haile Selassie became emperor of Ethiopia.

Greg A. Harris (b. 1955), U.S. baseball player

A switch-hitting, right-handed pitcher for the Montreal Expos, Harris stunned fans in the final inning of a September 28, 1995, game against the Cincinnati Reds when he started switch-*pitching*, alternating pitches between his right *and* left hands. Although the crowd-pleasing feat had been performed a few times previously—most notably by Tony Mullane in 1882 and Elton "Ice Box" Chamberlin in 1888—Harris was the first major-league player in 107 years to try it. To help him accomplish the feat, he used a six-finger, ambidextrous glove specially designed for the occasion; he later donated the glove to the National Baseball Hall of Fame and Museum. During a fourteen-year major-league career that began in 1981, Harris pitched for the Mets, Reds, Padres, and other teams. He retired in 1995. (See also January 30, August 10, and November 5.)

On this day, in 1957, Laika, a female Samoyed husky, became the first animal in space when she was launched into orbit aboard a Soviet spacecraft.

Jeremy Brett (1933–1995), British actor

Although the acclaimed, left-handed Shakespearean actor appeared in over forty films—including *War and Peace* (1956) and *The Medusa Touch* (1978)—he was primarily famous for two roles: as Freddy Eynsford-Hill (". . . knowing I'm on the street where you live") in the 1964 film *My Fair Lady*, and as Sherlock Holmes in the BBC

Sherlock Holmes series in the 1980s and the 1990s, later imported to the United States on PBS.

On this day, in 1922, King Tut's tomb was discovered. In 1979, Iranian militants seized the U.S. embassy in Tehran.

Captain Jean Danjou *(c. 1860), French soldier*

One-handed Captain Jean Danjou was a revered member of the French Foreign Legion in the mid-nineteenth century. Despite the fact that his left hand was a wooden prosthesis, he was renowned for his adventurousness and bravery. In the 1860s, Danjou fought in Mexico to help defend the ill-fated emperor Maximilian. Suddenly ambushed by nearly two thousand Mexican soldiers at an outpost near Camerone, Danjou and sixty-three of his men were hopelessly outnumbered. Danjou rejected Mexican demands that he surrender, and he and his fellow legionnaires fought to the death. Danjou's wooden left hand was later recovered by comrades from the site of the massacre and sent back to the legion's headquarters in Algeria—where it was proudly displayed for decades as a revered symbol of Legionnaire determination and honor.

5 Today is Guy Fawkes Day in England. On this day in 1605, thirty barrels of gunpowder were discovered beneath the British House of Parliament, planted there by religious conspirators who planned to blow up the building.

Paul Wittgenstein (1887–1961), Austrian pianist

After the first few moments of wondering how the devil he accomplished it, one almost forgot that one was listening to a player whose right sleeve hung empty at his side. . . .

—Music critic Lawrence Gilman, in a review
of a Wittgenstein concert in 1934

In 1913, Wittgenstein—the elder brother of renowned philosopher Ludwig Wittgenstein—made his concert debut as a pianist, in Vienna, to widespread critical acclaim. He was twenty-five and handsome, and as a member of the wealthy, erudite, and artistically gifted Wittgenstein clan, he seemed to have a secure, if not downright lustrous, future ahead of him. Less than a year after his concert debut, the young pianist was conscripted into the Austrian army, then engaged in fighting World War I. Almost immediately after assignment, he was hit by sniper gunfire during a skirmish in Poland. Despite the best efforts of the doctors, an infection quickly spread throughout young Wittgenstein's right arm, and the limb—to the horror of everyone who knew him—had to be amputated. All hopes of a continued concert career were shattered. "I cannot help thinking of poor Paul," brother Ludwig wrote in his diary. "How terrible! If only there is some solution other than suicide." Suicide was apparently the furthest thing from Paul's mind: while recovering from amputation, he devoted himself to exercises to strengthen the muscles and reflexes of his left arm. (Among other things, he learned to box one-handed.) He also began practicing—one-handed—at the piano for seven hours a day, and searched for left-handed piano works he might one day perform if he ever returned to the concert stage. Unfortunately, except for occasional short novelty pieces and simplistic exercises for beginning piano students, the existing repertoire of left-handed piano works was so limited as to be virtually useless to Wittgenstein's purpose. Finally, in 1928, he used some of his family's wealth (amassed in the Austrian steel industry) to commission celebrated French composer Maurice Ravel to write a one-handed piano concerto for him. "The concerto must not be a stunt," Ravel commented. "The listener must never feel that more could have been accomplished with two hands." In 1931, Paul Wittgenstein premiered Ravel's *Concerto in D Major for the Left Hand* to near ecstatic reviews. Although the actual composition was greeted with somewhat less-than-enthusiastic comments (several critics expressed serious reservations about it), Wittgenstein himself emerged as a miraculous hero, a figure of inspiration and hope amid the devastation and uncertainty that gripped Europe between the two world wars. His virtuosity was described as "amazing ... formidable even for a two-handed pianist." "His physical handicap was forgotten," said the *New York Times* after one Wittgenstein performance. "He showed commanding musicianship and played with an aplomb and gusto thrice admirable." Richard Strauss, Benjamin Britten, and Sergei Prokofiev also eventually composed "left-handed" piano works for Wittgenstein, as did a host of other composers who were moved by his courage and talent. (All in all, Wittgenstein was responsible for the addition of more than forty new piano pieces to the repertoire.) Meanwhile, the Ravel concerto slowly established itself as a mainstay of the concert hall, a minor masterpiece eagerly performed by a wide variety of concert pianists, including Gary Graffman (see October 14). In 1939, Wittgenstein immigrated to the United States and settled in New York City with his wife and children. He taught music there and continued to give concerts and recitals until his death in 1961.

Bill Walton *(b. 1952), U.S. basketball player*

The left-handed basketball champ—two-time NCAA champion with the UCLA Bruins, and two-time NBA World Champion with the Portland Trailblazers and the Boston Celtics—was one of the superstars of the game in the 1970s, and was inducted into the Basketball Hall of Fame in 1993.

On this day, in 1860, Abraham Lincoln was elected president. In 1923, the electric shaver was patented by inventor Jacob Schick.

Glenn Frey *(b. 1948), U.S. musician*

Best known as one of the lead singers of the Eagles—and famous for a solo career that produced such hits as "You Belong to the City," "Smuggler's Blues," and "The Heat Is On"—left-hander Frey has also had a notable acting career, guest-starring on *Miami Vice* in 1985 (in the episode that debuted the phenomenally successful "Smuggler's Blues"), as well in the film *Jerry Maguire*, with Tom Cruise, in 1996.

On this day, in 1874, the elephant became the symbol of the Republican party.

Billy Graham *(b. 1918), U.S. religious leader*

Graham once summed up his mission in life succinctly. "My one purpose," he said, "is to help people find a personal relationship with God, which, I believe, comes through knowing Christ." Though he has never wavered from that purpose, he has, along the way, provided solace, counsel, and meaningful advice to every U.S. president since Harry Truman, has done more than any other Christian leader to promote understanding among *all* religions (he was honored with the Torch of Liberty Plaque by the Anti-Defamation League in 1969), and has, through his weekly radio program, *Hour of Decision*, and through his numerous books, including the 1997 best-selling autobiography *Just As I Am*, given compassionate insight and guidance to millions, including large numbers of people who might otherwise have fled in dismay from anyone calling themselves an "evangelist." Small wonder that since 1955, he has appeared thirty-nine times on the Gallup poll's list of "Ten Most Admired Men in the World."

On this day, in 1895, X rays were discovered. In 1932, Franklin Delano Roosevelt was elected president.

Kurt Fuller (b. 1952), U.S. actor

Fuller has appeared in more than three dozen films, including *Ghostbusters II* (1989), *The Bonfire of the Vanities* (1990), *Wayne's World* (1992), *Calendar Girl* (1993), and *Stuart Saves His Family* (1995), as well as in the TV movies *Virus* (1995) and *Robin Cook's Harmful Intent* (1993).

On this night, in 1965, the largest power blackout in history hit the Northeastern U.S., depriving over 30 million people of power and stranding 800,000 commuters in New York subways for hours.

George Wood and Teddy Higuera (1858–1921)
and (b.1958), U.S. baseball players

There are two well-known ballplayers born on this day, exactly one hundred years apart. Wood, born in 1858, played major-league ball for twelve years, beginning in 1880; his teams included Worcester, Detroit, Philadelphia, and Baltimore. He finished his career with a .273 average and 601 RBIs. Higuera, born in 1958, was a left-handed pitcher for the Milwaukee Brewers from 1985 to 1994; in his best year, 1988, he had a 2.45 ERA. He retired with a 94–64 record.

10

On this day, in 1775, the United States Marine Corps was established. In 1989, the Berlin Wall was opened.

Russell Johnson (b. 1924), U.S. actor

To this day, there is an entire generation of TV viewers who can't go sailing for an afternoon without hearing in the back of their minds the cheerfully ominous lyrics, "A three-hour cruise, a *three*-hour cruise. . . ." Russell Johnson, of course, played the Professor on *Gilligan's Island*. (The Professor had a real name—Roy Hinkley—though it's difficult to recall a single episode in which it was mentioned). *Gilligan's Island* premiered in the fall of 1964, and the castaways from the *Minnow* remained stranded on their South Pacific island for three years; when the show was canceled in 1967, they were still there. (A highly successful 1978 made-for-TV movie, *Rescue from Gilligan's Island*, resolved their plight.) Left-hander Johnson continued working in Hollywood after the show's cancellation; he enjoyed, among other things, a brief stint on the TV series *Santa Barbara* in the mid-1980s. His priorities changed abruptly, however, in the early 1990s when his thirty-nine-year-old son, David, was diagnosed with—and later died of—AIDS. At the age of seventy, Johnson—devastated by the loss and infuriated by the stigma still attached to the disease and individuals with it—all but abandoned his acting career and redirected his energy to become a tireless AIDS fund-raiser and activist in Hollywood.

George II (1683–1760), King of England

If the British had assigned meaningful sobriquets to their monarchs as the French did, George II would have been known as George the Tremulous. The left-handed king lacked confidence—in part as a result of the fact that his father, George I, detested him—and the politics of his reign were dominated by ministers and advisers who bullied, strong-armed, and walked all over him. George's hopelessly swayable temperament—in a reign that lasted more than thirty years—provoked a kind of national irritation with monarchs in general in Britain and helped speed up the country's embrace of a constitutional monarchy.

On this day, in 1918, World War I ended with the signing of an armistice between Germany and the United States and the Allied governments of Europe.

Demi Moore *(b. 1962), U.S. actress*

Aside from being left-handed, Moore has the distinction of being the only movie star to have been born in Roswell, New Mexico, the dusty, UFO-centric town usually associated with alien autopsies and military cover-ups. In 1996—after nearly a decade of Hollywood megahits, including *Ghost* and *Indecent Proposal*—she became the highest-paid actress in history when she received a reported $12 million for her role in *Striptease*.

On this day, in 1946, drive-through tellers were first introduced, at a bank in Chicago.

Michael Moorer *(b. 1967), U.S. boxer*

On April 22, 1994, Moorer became the first left-hander to win the world heavyweight boxing title, in a decision against Evander Holyfield in a bout at Caesar's Palace in Las Vegas. He lost the title six months later, after being knocked out by George Foreman in the tenth round of their November 5 match.

13

On this day, in 1900, more than a hundred members of a Russian religious sect, the Brothers and Sisters of Red Death, burned themselves alive, believing that the world was supposed to come to an end that day.

Whoopi Goldberg
(b. 1955), U.S. entertainer

That Goldberg remains to this day one of the most popular—one of the most *beloved*—performers of her generation, despite having had a very uneven film career (punctuated by more than an occasional flop), is testament to the enormous charm and influence that left-handers can wield. Her one passionate pet peeve is intolerance, whether regarding race, handedness, or anything else: "Anything we don't understand, we want to eliminate. But I think people have to recognize that there is nothing you can do to stop people from living their lives. Either adapt or walk away. Move to another place where people will continue to be intolerant. Move to Iran."

Edward III (1312–1377), King of England

Edward's left-handedness wasn't confirmed until six centuries after his death. In 1953, archaeological evidence conclusively showed he had suffered a stroke that paralyzed the left side of his body and rendered it useless in later years. Until then, historians had known only that he suffered from an illness that took away his ability to write. By deduction, it became apparent that the king must have been left-handed.

Jean Seberg *(1938–1979), U.S. actress*

The stunningly beautiful actress appeared in the films *Bonjour Tristesse* (1958), *Breathless* (1960), *Lilith* (1964), *Moment to Moment* (1966), *Paint Your Wagon* (1969), and *Airport* (1970).

On this day, in 1864, General William Sherman began his march through Georgia after burning Atlanta.

Prince Charles *(b. 1948), heir to the British throne*

Since the death of his ex-wife, Princess Diana, in 1997, the philandering, plant-communicating, modern-architecture-loathing, left-handed Prince of Wales has become a more sympathetic figure in the public mind, having been cast in the role of a loving father trying to guide his now motherless sons into adulthood. Even Diana—whatever else she thought of him—repeatedly praised him as a "wonderful" papa. It may, in fact, be the role that Charles will be best remembered for, though his recent, controversial attempts to modernize the monarchy—bowing and curtsying to royalty would be optional, etc.—may also give him a significant niche in posterity. Among the many reforms he and his brother Andrew have been pushing for is a drastic reduction in the number of "official" H.R.H. titles by which each member of the royal family is known. In Charles's case, any reduction would be a welcome relief: his full title is Prince of Wales, K.G., K.T., G.C.B., P.C., Earl of Chester, Duke of Cornwall, Duke of Rothesay, Earl of Carrick, Baron of Renfrew, Lord of the Isles, and Prince and Great Steward of Scotland.

Brian Keith *(1921–1997), U.S. actor*

Left-handed character actor, veteran of more than a hundred films, often cast in Westerns—*Arrowhead* (1953), *The Hallelujah Trail* (1965), *Nevada Smith* (1966)—but equally comfortable in comedy (*The Russians Are Coming! The Russians Are Coming!*) and contemporary drama (*Reflections in a Golden Eye*). One of his best screen performances was as Teddy Roosevelt in *The Wind and the Lion*, in 1975. He was perhaps most famous as Bill Davis, the swinging bachelor guardian of three orphans—Buffy, Jody, and Cissy—on the popular TV series *Family Affair*, from 1966 to 1971.

15

Today is Shichi-Go-San, the children's festival, in Japan. On this day, in 1996, Michael Jackson wed wife number two, dermatologist's assistant Debbie Rowe.

Claus Schenk von Stauffenberg (1907–1944),
German officer and would-be Hitler assassin

Stauffenberg lost his right hand as a staff officer in a panzer division in North Africa in the spring of 1943. Whether or not the abrupt conversion to left-handedness suddenly made him come to his senses, he designed, during his convalescence, a plan to assassinate Hitler and redirect the energies of the German government; he was especially troubled by Hitler's brutality toward the Jews, and persuaded a cadre of equally disillusioned German officers to join him. His postconvalescence promotion to chief of staff of the German army provided him with the perfect opportunity to carry out his plan. At a general meeting at Hitler's headquarters in Wolfschanze, Stauffenberg left a briefcase with a bomb in it under the conference table and then walked out of the room on the pretext of taking a phone call. Meanwhile, other conspirators in Berlin were attempting a coup against high-ranking Nazi officials. Stauffenberg's bomb exploded, killing two of the men present; however, Hitler—though the explosion ruptured his eardrums and split the seat of his pants—survived. The coup in Berlin was also a failure. Stauffenberg and the other leaders of the conspiracy were shot before nightfall. Hitler ultimately came to suspect that thousands of others had taken part in the conspiracy as well, and an estimated five thousand people were eventually executed in connection with it.

16

Today is the feast day of St. Margaret of Scotland. On this day, in 1959, *The Sound of Music* opened on Broadway.

Tiberius *(42 B.C.–A.D. 37), Roman emperor*

Tiberius was not the kind of left-hander you wanted to drop in on unannounced. So paranoid, so corrupt, so utterly oblivious to the value of human life did he become in his later years that when a friendly foreign emissary casually stopped in at the royal palace on the island of Capri to say hello, said emissary was barely allowed to utter a benevolent word before Tiberius had him instantly whisked away, tortured for days, and then murdered in a particularly unsavory fashion. Tiberius acceded to the throne of Rome in A.D. 14, at the age of fifty-six, and at first seemed a wise, patient, and temperate emperor. He strengthened the military (though rarely misused it), and built up the empire's treasury and power, mostly by fair and evenhanded means. However, as time went on, his initiatives and laws became increasingly bizarre. In one edict, he outlawed the execution of virgins: thus, any condemned woman who was still a virgin had to suffer the added humiliation of being publicly raped by the executioner before the sentence could be carried out. Ravaged by syphilis in his final years— contemporaries describe his face as a mass of oozing pustules—he turned to prepubescent children to satisfy his sexual desires. And of the dozen or so villas he built for himself on the island of Capri, where he exiled himself from the age of sixty-seven until his death, virtually all were equipped with torture chambers, dungeons, and extravagantly designed orgy rooms.

17

On this day, in 1558, Queen Elizabeth I ascended the throne of England. In 1869, the Suez Canal opened.

Rock Hudson
(1925–1985), U.S. actor

Hudson went from capable contract player to adored movie star with a single performance: the penitent wild-playboy-turned-brilliant-surgeon in the 1954 four-hankie classic *Magnificent Obsession*. His salary nearly quadrupled, and the volume of his fan mail skyrocketed to more than three thousand letters a week. "Oh, those sad eyes!" one woman cooed in a letter to him. "When you looked at Jane Wyman," panted another, "I wanted to scream and deep down inside of me, I did!" Shortly after *Magnificent Obsession*'s premiere, one Hollywood gossip columnist wrote of Hudson, "He believes in fun babes. He believes in a goodnight kiss on the first date. He's leery of two careers in one marriage, but feels the future Mrs. H. should be hep to show biz." Of course, what millions of adoring fans probably didn't know was that Hudson was—left-handed. Hudson's left-handedness appears not to have played any significant role whatsoever in his life: not in his schooling, not in his slightly better-than-average athletic abilities, not in his acting career. Watch the otherwise almost unendurable *All That Heaven Allows* (in which he was paired with Jane Wyman again, this time as a virile, Thoreau-quoting gardener wooing a middle-aged socialite widow) to see him not only write with his left hand but saw, prune, hammer, and even use a butter knife left-handed as well.

On this day, in 1993, a new constitution was ratified in South Africa, giving basic civil rights to blacks for the first time.

Brenda Vaccaro (b. *1939), U.S. actress*

Left-hander Vaccaro is like a potent cappuccino. She either livens you up, makes you feel giddy and light-headed, makes you laugh—or she sends you clutching blindly for the nearest horizontal surface to collapse on with a troubled, overloaded stomach. In her first major film role, she played one of the first women to fall for Jon Voight's cowboy boots in John Schlesinger's X-rated *Midnight Cowboy*. Six years later, she was nominated for a Best Supporting Actress Oscar for her performance as Deborah Raffin's cheerfully ithyphallic best friend in *Once Is Not Enough*, based on the Jacqueline Susann potboiler about sex, the jet set, and beautiful women with father fixations. Perhaps the quintessential Vaccaro performance came in the underrated 1981 comedy *Zorro, the Gay Blade*: as the shrieking, jumpy wife of corrupt *gobernador* Ron Leibman, she alternately made one exasperated with her hyperactivity and then laugh with pleasure over her hilarious reading of simple lines like "My party—what's happening at my party?" A good cappuccino can affect you either way.

Today is Prince Rainier Day in Monaco. On this day, in 1863, Lincoln delivered the Gettysburg Address.

James Garfield (*1831–1881), U.S. president*

During his brief term of office, Garfield often amused visitors by sitting at his desk and writing classical Greek with his left hand while simultaneously writing Latin with his right. Unfortunately, he was shot four months after his inauguration in 1881—by a right-handed assassin who boisterously sang "I am going to the Lordy, I am so glad!" while ascending the gallows.

On this day, in 1920, the first municipal airport in the United States was opened, in Tucson, Arizona.

Estelle Parsons (b. 1927), U.S. actress

Left-handed character actress of stage and screen, most often cast as extroverted eccentrics or barely controlled hysterics. She won an Oscar as Best Supporting Actress for her portrayal of Clyde Barrow's raving sister-in-law in *Bonnie and Clyde* (1967) and received another Oscar nomination the next year as the religious fanatic in *Rachel, Rachel*. Beginning in the late 1980s, she was cast as Roseanne's grating mother in the hugely popular sitcom *Roseanne*.

Dick Smothers (b. 1939), U.S. comedian

An avid golf player, left-hander Dick was forced to learn to play the game right-handed as a boy because of the scarcity of left-handed clubs. He once confessed that in recent years he enjoys startling golf partners and spectators by alternating hands during a game, playing the first nine holes right-handed and the back nine left-handed.

On this day, in 1978, reports reached the U.S. of the mass suicide of more than four hundred men, women, and children—followers of cult leader Jim Jones—in Guyana.

Goldie Hawn (b. 1945), U.S. actress

The Oscar-winning comic actress has dealt with mild dyslexia for much of her life: "It hasn't stopped my growth or my thinking process. But I always remember numbers backwards." (So, incidentally, does her daughter.) Her early work, especially on the hit TV series *Rowan and Martin's Laugh-In* in 1968, typecast her as America's perennial dumb blond, an image it took years to scuttle. "Because someone has an optimistic outlook, because someone is hopeful, because someone likes to have fun, because someone is trusting and open, does not necessarily mean that someone is stupid," she has said.

Stan Musial (b. 1920), U.S. baseball player

"Stan the Man" started playing ball for the St. Louis Cardinals in 1941; it was an alliance that lasted for twenty-two years. His record speaks for itself: seven league batting titles, voted Most Valuable Player three times, a lifetime batting average of .331 on 3,630 hits. When Musial was moved to left field—an unusual position for a left-hander—the Cardinals managers cheerfully defended the action: "When a boy has baseball instinct like that Musial, he can make the plays upside down."

Laurence Luckinbill (b. 1934), U.S. actor

Prolific character actor who made his film debut in the 1970 movie adaptation of Mart Crowley's hit Broadway play *The Boys in the Band* and went on to memorable appearances in *Such Good Friends* (1971), *Cocktail* (1988), and *Star Trek V: The Final Frontier* (1989), in which he played Spock's brother, Sybok. Luckinbill, who is married to Lucie Arnaz, has also guest-starred on numerous TV shows, including *The Mary Tyler Moore Show*, *Murder, She Wrote*, and *Law & Order*.

Jim Bishop (1907–1987), U.S. writer

Bishop authored numerous best-sellers in the 1950s and 1960s—including *The Day Lincoln Was Shot* and *The Day Christ Died*—which sought, in a "docudrama" fashion, to relate the immediacy of historical events by concentrating on a twenty-four-hour period around them. A natural left-hander, he was switched to right-handedness at parochial school. He later wrote of the experience, "In Catholic schools at the time the nuns who had pledged their lives and souls to Christ were imbued with a will to share their suffering with students."

On this day, in 1928, Ravel's *Bolero* premiered. In 1963, President John F. Kennedy was assassinated in Dallas.

Ron Dean *(b. 1950), U.S. actor*

The left-handed character actor is a veteran of more than thirty feature films—including *Continental Divide* (1981), *The Breakfast Club* (1985), *The Color of Money* (1986), *Cocktail* (1988), *The Babe* (1992), and *Rudy* (1993)—but will probably always be remembered best as the detective with the bullhorn yelling "Get off the baby-sitter!" to Tom Cruise in *Risky Business*.

On this day, in 1996, actor Woody Harrelson and eight other people scaled the Golden Gate Bridge to protest redwood logging in California.

William H. Bonney, "Billy the Kid"
(1859–1881), U.S. outlaw

In the summer of 1880, Western outlaw Billy the Kid took time from his other activities—cattle rustling, gambling, murder—to have his picture taken at Fort Sumner, New Mexico. The resulting photograph—widely reproduced in newspapers and books—showed the Kid apparently wearing his holster on the left hip, giving rise to the widespread supposition that he was left-handed. In fact, what most people never realized was that the photograph was a tintype—a reversed image—and the holster was actually on Billy's *right* hip. Whatever the truth about Billy's hand preference, eyewitnesses attested to his deadly precision firing a gun with either hand or, on at least one occasion, firing two pistols at once, one in each hand. Before he was finally shot to death in 1881, at the age of twenty-one, Billy was reputed to have murdered over twenty men, though some authorities believe the actual figure was much smaller. He is buried in the Fort Sumner

Cemetery with the epitaph "The Boy Bandit King—He Died as He Lived."

Harpo Marx *(1888–1964), U.S. comic actor*

Harpo was the Marx brother with the curly reddish-blond hair (a wig) who never spoke, usually whistled, played the harp (he was self-taught), carried an old-fashioned taxi horn, and chased women. Okay, they *all* chased women—Harpo's the one who did it with the face of a demented child. His real name was Adolph. Some sources alternately give his birthday as November 21.

On this day, in 1963, John F. Kennedy assassin Lee Harvey Oswald was shot to death by Dallas night-club owner Jack Ruby.

Ted Bundy *(1946–1989), U.S. serial killer*

Offal, carrion, garbage, swill, slop, bilge, sewage, refuse, waste, dregs, rubbish, trash, junk, slime, sludge, mire, ooze, filth. Wretch, wastrel, degenerate, SOB, jerk, creep, louse, rat, hooligan, beast, viper, snake, worm, rotter, misfeasor, offender, evildoer. All of these words are listed as synonyms for "scum" in the fourth edition of the unabridged *Roget's International Thesaurus* (Harper & Row, 1977). The only one they missed was the name Ted Bundy.

On this day, in 1952, Agatha Christie's mystery drama *The Mousetrap*, destined to become the longest continuously running play in history, opened in London.

Helen Hooven Santmyer (1895–1986),
U.S. writer

The left-handed author is best known for her 1,300-page 1985 best-selling novel *And Ladies of the Club*, written over the course of fifty years.

On this day, in 1942, the film *Casablanca* had its world premiere, in New York City.

Daniel Davis (b. 1945), U.S. actor

A Shakespearean actor by training, Davis is best known as Niles, the glib, often acidic butler on the popular TV series *The Nanny*.

Vernon "Lefty" Gomez (1908–1989), U.S.
baseball player

Gomez compiled an enviable 189–102 record pitching for the Yankees from 1930 to 1942. However, he was at least as famous for his humor and antics as for his performance on the mound. He acquired the nickname "Goofy" after publicly announcing his latest "invention"—a revolving goldfish bowl that saved its occupants the necessity of swimming. He liked to tell fans that even his pet Chihuahua was left-handed. The proof, according to Gomez: "When the dog goes to the fireplug, he raises his left leg."

On this day, in 8 B.C., the Roman poet Horace died. In 1934, bank robber and killer Baby Face Nelson was killed by FBI agents in a bloody shoot-out near Fox River Grove, Illinois.

Jimi Hendrix (1942–1970), *U.S. rock star*

In 1967, guitar virtuoso Jimi Hendrix electrified crowds at the Monterey Pop Festival. He played the guitar not only with his left hand but with his left elbow, his teeth, his tongue, and, at one point, his crotch. He then doused the instrument with lighter fluid and set it on fire. For this and other revolutionary antics, the *New York Times* dubbed him "the black Elvis." One of the very few left-handed rock-and-roll stars to actually play guitar left-handed (his instruments were restrung to accommodate him), Hendrix mesmerized his followers with his often writhing, overtly sexual style of acid-rock showmanship. (His debut album, in 1967, was titled *Are You Experienced?*) The aphrodisiac quality and earsplitting volume of his performances made him public enemy number one to hordes of nervous parents who saw cultural Armageddon in his tendency to smash guitars onstage or simulate intercourse with them. The fact that he was also African-American (and that he "desecrated" "The Star-Spangled Banner" with a cacophonous, antiwar rendition of the anthem at Woodstock) put him in a league, in some people's minds, with the Black Panthers and FBI fugitive Angela Davis. Nowadays he's more likely to be acknowledged as a musical genius, for such hits as *Hey Joe*, *Foxy Lady*, and *Purple Haze*, and for his influence on virtually every rock-and-roll singer after him.

On this day, in 1925, Nashville's *Grand Ole Opry* debuted on radio.

Hope Lange (b. 1931), *U.S. actress*

The wholesome, blond, left-handed actress made her film debut in the 1956 Marilyn Monroe vehicle *Bus Stop* but scored her first real triumph the following year with an Oscar-nominated performance in the film version of Grace Metalious's then controversial novel *Peyton Place*. Although she appeared in a number of successful films after that—*The Young Lions* (1958), *The Best of Everything* (with Joan Crawford, in 1959), *Death Wish* (1974)—she ingratiated herself with an entire generation of TV viewers with her Emmy-winning performance in the sweet-natured hit series *The Ghost and Mrs. Muir*, which ran from 1968 to 1970.

29

On this day, in 1891, the first Army-Navy football game was played. In 1981, actress Natalie Wood drowned in the waters off Catalina Island, California.

Vin Scully (b. 1927), U.S. sports announcer

At Catholic school in the 1930s, Scully was regularly punished by the nuns whenever he tried to write with his left hand. One too many whacks with the ruler left his hand looking "chopped up" when he came home from school one day. His parents called the doctor, who in turn wrote a letter to the nuns at Scully's school. "He went through a great deal of reasoning," Scully said later, "as to why they shouldn't try to change me and among other things, he pointed out that it perhaps could cause me to stutter. Then he finished up the letter by saying something to the effect, 'and besides, dear Sisters, why would you want to change God's will?' " The nuns relented.

Chuck Mangione (b. 1940), U.S. musician

The Grammy Award–winning trumpeter and jazz composer is most famous for his megahit "Feels So Good"—"the song that put my daughters through college." Ironically, Mangione first took up the trumpet in his youth after seeing the film *Young Man with a Horn*, based on the life of another left-handed jazz great, Bix Beiderbecke.

Andrew McCarthy (b. 1962), U.S. actor

Teen heartthrob of the eighties, famous for his youthful roles, especially in adolescent angst films: *St. Elmo's Fire* (1985), *Pretty in Pink* (1986), *Less Than Zero* (1987), and others. Two of his most successful films were the comedies *Mannequin* (1987) and *Weekend at Bernie's* (1989), both of which precipitated sequels.

30 On this day, in 1939, the Russo-Finnish War began when the Soviet Union invaded Finland. In 1996, entertainer Tiny Tim died.

Ben Stiller (b. 1965), U.S. comedian-actor

Stiller's mother, Anne Meara (of the comedy team Stiller and Meara), is also left-handed. (See September 20.)

Ridley Scott (b. 1937), British film director

When Ridley Scott's *Blade Runner* was first released in 1982, a large number of prominent critics excoriated it. The film, they said, was obtuse, grim, self-conscious, and, good God, what is *with* all that endless rain, soot, and cobalt blue smokiness. Audiences, who initially lined up expecting another Harrison-Ford-dashing-to-the-rescue pic, were hardly more generous. What many people failed to appreciate on first viewing was that the film—which would launch a revolution in every visual art form, from rock videos to computer graphics to major motion pictures—was one of the most staggeringly beautiful ever made, right from its first zooming shot of the wrecked skyline of L.A. pierced by fleeting towers of shocking orange flames. The critics, as the film's reputation increased and its influence became widespread, began to abandon their original opinions and re-think their earlier denunciations. Left-handers are often in love with what they see, enraptured by the sheer experience of sight. It's one of the reasons they count among their ranks some of the most authoritative and powerful artists in history. Scott is no exception. Admittedly, he's made films whose scripts—either by misdesign or because of later interference—have left a lot, an *awful* lot, to be desired: *Legend* in 1985 and *1492: Conquest of Paradise* in 1992 are the two most obvious examples. Yet going to a Ridley Scott film specifically for the script seems as pointless and misguided as checking out a Matisse painting to see how the frame was put together. Among his other films are *The Duellists* (1977), *Alien* (1979), *Someone to Watch Over Me* (1987), *Thelma and Louise* (1991), and *G.I. Jane* (1997).

Left-handers Born in
December

December: From the Latin decem—"ten"—since it was, according to the ancient Roman calendar, the tenth month of the year.

1

Today is World AIDS Day. On this day, in 1955, African-American Rosa Parks was arrested for refusing to give up her seat to a white man on a Montgomery, Alabama, municipal bus, giving rise to the modern civil rights movement.

Richard Pryor (b. 1940),
U.S. comedian

"Man, you can *run* when you're on fire," Richard Pryor told audiences after the 1980 accident in which, while freebasing cocaine, he suffered third-degree burns covering one half of his body. Audiences laughed—albeit nervously—just as they had been laughing nervously at Pryor's stage routines for years, since he first started nightclub work in the 1960s. Pryor *makes* people nervous. His comedy is distinctly left-handed. it breaks boundaries. It doesn't break boundaries in polite increments: it breaks them by *decimating* them.

Lou Rawls (b. 1936), U.S. singer

The left-handed, Grammy Award–winning rhythm and blues singer is best known for his 1976 hit "You'll Never Find (Another Love Like Mine)."

Treat Williams (b. 1951), U.S. actor

Williams made his film debut as a falsetto-voiced detective in a gay bathhouse in the 1976 film version of Terrence McNally's play *The Ritz.* The film was a failure but five years later his career took an upward turn after his shattering performance as a New York City cop turned Justice Department informant in Sidney Lumet's critically acclaimed *Prince of the City.* He has also appeared in the films *The Pursuit of D. B. Cooper, The Men's Club,* and *Dead Heat.*

2

On this day, in 1804, Napoleon was crowned Emperor of France at Notre Dame Cathedral.

Monica Seles (b. 1973), Yugoslav-U.S. tennis player

Left-hander Seles became the youngest number-one-ranked tennis player in the world in 1991, when she was seventeen years old, a ranking she held for over three years, until—during a changeover while competing in quarterfinals against Magdalena Naleeva, in Hamburg, Germany—she was the victim of a knife attack from a deranged spectator. Her assailant, thirty-eight-year-old Steffi Graf fan Gunther Parche, plunged a nine-inch blade into Seles's back, just below the left shoulder blade. The attack sidelined her career for two years, as she recovered physically and—perhaps even more problematically—emotionally. Depression, anxiety attacks, and a shattering loss of self-confidence plagued her while she was sidelined from the game she loved. She finally returned to the court in 1995, winning first the Canadian Open, then the Australian Open in 1996, and ultimately almost two dozen more consecutive victories.

Today is the International Day of Disabled Persons. On this day, in 1910, the first neon sign was erected, in Paris. In 1967, the first human heart transplant was performed.

Julianne Moore (b. 1961), U.S. actress

"In grade school, I was a complete geek," Moore once told an interviewer. "You know, there's always the kid who's too short, the kid who wears glasses, the kid who's not athletic. Well, I was all three." She was also left-handed, which may or may not help to explain her obsessive drive to become an actress. In 1998, the left-hander was nominated for an Academy Award for Best Supporting Actress for her poignant performance as Amber in the critically acclaimed *Boogie Nights*.

Today is the Day of the Artisans in Mexico. On this day, in 1935, Parker Brothers introduced the board game *Monopoly*.

Wink Martindale (b. 1934), U.S. television personality

The perennial television game show host—as ageless as Dick Clark—has hosted *What's This Song?*, *Can You Top This?*, *Tic Tac Dough*, *Debt*, *Gambit*, *High Rollers*, *Trivial Pursuit*, *Boggle*, *Jumble*, and other popular game shows. His real name is Winston Conrad Martindale.

Thomas Carlyle (1795–1881), British historian and writer

A born right-hander, Carlyle experienced a violent deterioration in his health after the death of his wife in 1866, when he was seventy-one years old. Among other things, his right hand became progressively more infirm, often trembling uncontrollably. At first he tried writing with a pencil instead of a pen (for more traction on the paper), but that didn't help. Finally, when he was seventy-five, his right hand became completely paralyzed and useless. "My old right hand (and also my poor heart) has grown weary of writing," he confided to his brother in 1870. He was forced to become left-handed, though he eventually dictated his letters and other writings to a secretary.

Victor French (1934–1989), U.S. actor

On television, he was most familiar to viewers as Isaiah Edwards on the series *Little House on the Prairie* and Mark Gordon on *Highway to Heaven*, both series costarring his close friend (and fellow left-hander) Michael Landon.

5

Today is Discovery by Columbus Day in Haiti. On this day, in 1791, Mozart died. In 1933, Prohibition was repealed.

Angela Allen (b. 1929), U.S. script supervisor and continuity clerk

So deeply ingrained are the prejudices of society that one instinctively wants to write that Angela Allen was John Huston's right-hand man. Wrong on both counts. Neither right-handed nor a man, Allen first worked for Huston on the set of *The African Queen* in 1950. Despite the drabness of her official title—"continuity clerk"—she was, in fact, the individual who kept Huston's often manic intelligence under control so that both the script and the final film made sense. So indispensable was she to Huston's creative process that she went on to work with him on thirteen other films, including *Moulin Rouge* (1952), *Beat the Devil* (1954), *The Misfits* (1961), *The Night of the Iguana* (1964), and *Reflections in a Golden Eye* (1967). Her job description—to make certain there were no inconsistencies or errors of logic in the script, and to make detailed notes of each take so that when filming resumed, actors, burning cigarettes, and vases of flowers were all in the same place as before—hardly encompasses her duties helping Huston through hangovers, writer's block, and fits of artistic temperament. "I don't know how anybody makes a picture without Angela Allen," Huston once told an interviewer. She also provided her services on the sets of numerous other films, including—when she was in her late sixties—*Lost in Space* in 1998. Allen can be glimpsed on-screen in only one movie: she doubled for Katharine Hepburn in a handful of long shots in *The African Queen* when the star was indisposed.

Today is the Feast of St. Nicholas in Europe. On this day, in 1956, South African poet Nelson Mandela was imprisoned for political crimes against the state. In 1973, Gerald Ford was sworn in as U.S. vice president, after the resignation of Spiro Agnew.

Dick Gautier *(b. 1939), U.S. actor*

Handsome, muscular actor who made his film debut as the perennially shirtless Stefanowski in *Ensign Pulver* (1964), and who was a familiar face in films through the sixties and seventies, most notably in *Divorce American Style* (1967), *Billy Jack Goes to Washington* (1977), and *Fun with Dick and Jane* (1977). He is most familiar to TV watchers as Hymie, the robot agent on *Get Smart*.

On this day, in 1941, the Japanese attacked Pearl Harbor. In 1972, *Apollo 17*—the final manned mission to the moon—was launched at Cape Canaveral.

Larry Bird *(b. 1956), U.S. basketball player*

Bird played for the Boston Celtics from 1979 to 1992. During those thirteen years, the left-hander was NBA Rookie of the Year (1980), NBA All Star twelve times (1980–92), NBA All Star Game MVP (1982), playoff MVP in 1984 and 1986, and regular-season MVP in 1984, 1985, and 1986 (one of only three players in NBA history to win the award in three consecutive seasons)—and he achieved all of this left-handed, of course. "Bird was the embodiment of 'Celtics pride,' " one sportswriter has noted. "He was a classy, confident, hardworking player who thrived on pressure, and inspired teammates to excel." It was Bird who almost single-handedly lifted the Celtics out of their slump—including mediocre play and poor attendance—in the late 1970s; the Boston Garden was sold out for each of the final 541 games of Bird's career. Since retiring from active play in 1992, Bird has taken a coaching position with the Pacers.

Today is the Feast of the Immaculate Conception in Catholic countries. On this day, in 1984, the last episode of *Captain Kangaroo* aired on CBS.

Kim Basinger *(b. 1953), U.S. actress*

Although Basinger had already appeared in a handful of films in the early 1980s—and had done a layout in *Playboy* magazine as part of the publicity for the 1983 James Bond epic *Never Say Never Again*—it was her role as the glamorous femme fatale who tries to ruin Robert Redford's baseball game—and, by implication, lure him away from an honest life—in *The Natural* that first brought her to the attention of moviegoers. The camera loved her, especially under the graceful guidance of cinematographer Caleb Deschanel. Surprisingly, her next six films—including *Blind Date* (with Bruce Willis) and *My Stepmother Is an Alien* (with Dan Aykroyd)—were critical bombs, and that, combined with her growing off-screen reputation for being temperamental and high-handed, torpedoed her growing stardom. She was saved in 1989 by the box-office blockbuster *Batman*, in which she portrayed glamorous reporter Vicki Vale. Another string of flops followed, until the critically acclaimed *L.A. Confidential*, in 1997, for which she won an Oscar as Best

Supporting Actress. "I'm a highly, highly, highly creative person," she once said. "I write music all the time, I write scripts constantly, I run my own production company. . . . I'm also a very determined businesswoman. I've got a lot of things to do, and I don't have time to be classified as *difficult*, and I don't have time to care."

9

On this day, in 1854, Alfred Lord Tennyson wrote his poem "The Charge of the Light Brigade." In 1992, Princess Diana and Prince Charles announced their separation.

Sam Anderson (b. *1954*), U.S. actor

The left-handed actor has appeared in the films *La Bamba* (1987), *I Come in Peace* (1990), *The Puppet Masters* (1994), and *Forrest Gump* (as the school principal, in 1994), but is most recognizable for his role as Dr. Jack Kayson in the popular TV series *ER*.

Today is International Human Rights Day. On this day, in 1898, the Spanish-American War ended. In 1936, King Edward VIII abdicated the throne of England for the woman he loved, American divorcée Wallis Simpson.

Paul Assenmacher *(b. 1960), U.S. baseball player*

The left-handed specialty reliever has pitched for Atlanta, Chicago, New York, and Cleveland since joining the major leagues in 1986. Renowned for consistency, control, and reliability, as of 1998 he had a 58–40 win-loss record. Batters facing him in 1997 were unable to do any better than a .231 average.

On this day, in 1816, Indiana was admitted to the Union. In 1990, Donald and Ivana Trump were officially divorced.

Terri Garr *(b. 1949), U.S. actress*

Garr—who became one of Hollywood's most delightful almost-leading ladies in the seventies and eighties, through memorable roles in *Close Encounters of the Third Kind, Tootsie,* and other films—was the original bright, funny, bewildered-by-the-world actress. When Garr began appearing, with regularity, on lists of famous left-handers, no one thought anything of it: she *seemed* left-handed. Never able to perfectly verbalize her often passionate feelings (right-handers can be like a walking thesaurus in that regard: precise but sometimes insincere), always just a little out of sync with the world's sense of rectitude, and forever struggling to get people to acknowledge *her* point of view, *her* feelings, *her* way of doing things—if she wasn't left-handed, she certainly should've been. The moment of truth came in 1998, during—of all things—*Jeopardy!*, when Garr, as one of the celebrity panelists, moved to pick up her pen to play Final Jeopardy. Would it be with her right hand or her left hand? Which camp, after that night, would be able to claim her? Alas, without a moment's hesitation, she picked up the pen with her right hand and scribbled the question; we didn't even notice if she won the game or not. So, she joins the short list—including Marilyn Monroe and Olivia de Havilland—of mysterious figures who keep appearing on lists of famous left-handers for who knows what reason. We don't care. We can claim her if we want to. And we do.

 Today is the Fiesta of Our Lady of Guadalupe in Mexico. On this day, in 1800, Washington, D.C., officially became the capital of the United States. In 1925, the first motel opened, in California.

Kathleen Lloyd (b. *1951*), U.S. *actress*

Lloyd became a regular on the hit TV show *Magnum P.I.*, beginning in 1983, as Assistant District Attorney Carol Baldwin, a friend of Magnum's who often talked him into taking less-than-profitable cases. She has also appeared in the films *The Missouri Breaks*, *Take Down*, and *Best Seller*, as well as in the TV movie *The Jayne Mansfield Story* (as Carol Sue Peters) and *Sins of the Father*.

 On this day, in 1836, composer Frédéric Chopin met his future lover, French authoress George Sand, at a party in Paris. In 1928, the clip-on bow tie was invented.

Dick Van Dyke (b. *1925*), U.S. *entertainer*

The left-handed actor won three Emmy Awards for his classic TV series *The Dick Van Dyke Show*, which initially ran on network television from 1961 to 1966. His feature-film career—including *Mary Poppins* (1964), *What a Way to Go!* (1964), *Chitty Chitty Bang Bang* (1968), *Cold Turkey* (1971), and *The Runner Stumbles* (1979)—was only occasionally successful. In 1993, he returned to television in the popular mystery series *Diagnosis Murder*, costarring his son Barry, who is also left-handed. (See July 31.)

On this day, in 1799, George Washington died. In 1977, the film *Saturday Night Fever* had its gala world premiere.

George VI (1895–1952), King of England

A natural left-hander forced at an early age to write with his right hand, George suffered from a lifelong stammer. In 1951, just months before his death, he recorded his final Christmas Day address to the nation. Unfortunately, his stammer was even worse than usual, and (according to his assistant Michael Barsley, who later wrote the book *Left-handed People*) it was necessary to heavily edit the tape—deleting all the pauses, hesitations, and mispronunciations—before the speech was coherent enough for broadcast. Several sentences of the speech actually had to be redubbed: rather than embarrass the king by asking him to do it over, the missing sentences were dubbed by Winston Churchill, known for his not-always-kindly—but accurate—mimicry of the king.

On this day, in 1791, the Bill of Rights was ratified as part of the U.S. Constitution. In 1978, President Carter granted diplomatic recognition to Communist China.

Mo Vaughn (b. 1967), U.S. baseball player

One of the great sluggers of modern baseball, left-handed batter Vaughn joined the major leagues in 1991 and, playing for Boston, hit 190 home runs in his first seven years of play, with a peak .326 batting average in 1996.

On this day, in 1773, the Boston Tea Party was held. In 1951, the detective drama *Dragnet* debuted on TV.

Mike Flanagan (b. *1951*), *U.S. baseball player*

The left-handed pitcher played for Baltimore and Toronto from 1975 to 1992 and retired with a 167–143 win-loss career record.

 On this day, in 1843, Charles Dickens's *Christmas Carol* was published. In 1903, the Wright Brothers made their first successful flight, at Kitty Hawk.

Curtis Pride (b. *1968*), *U.S. baseball player*

Pride joined the major leagues, with Montreal, in 1993, then went to Detroit in 1996, to Boston in 1997, and finally joined the Braves in 1998. For several years, the left-hander felt that he would've found a permanent home with a major-league team if it hadn't been for his disability: Pride is deaf. "People always have a question mark over me because of my disability," he told one reporter. "It's frustrating. I want people to look beyond my disability and look at my abilities. I think I'm the equal of most guys as far as talent." Playing for Detroit in 1996—his best year—he had a .300 average, with 10 home runs and 31 RBIs. "I want to be known as a good ballplayer," he has said, "not just a deaf ballplayer."

18

On this day, in 1865, the Thirteenth Amendment, abolishing slavery in the United States, was ratified. In 1892, the *Nutcracker* ballet had its premiere, in St. Petersburg, Russia.

Betty Grable (1916–1973),
U.S. actress

It obviously wasn't Grable's hands that made GIs in World War II vote her their number one favorite "pin-up girl." And yet despite her own assertions—"There are two reasons why I'm in show business, and I'm standing on both of them"—it wasn't legs alone that accounted for Grable's success as an actress, singer, and comedian. Throughout her career—and even after—she remained as unpretentious, down-to-earth, and accessible as anyone who was once the movie industry's highest-paid star could be. Her first big success came in *Down Argentina Way* in 1940, when she replaced scheduled star Alice Faye (hospitalized with appendicitis) as the all-singing, all-dancing leading lady who falls in love with handsome horse breeder Don Ameche. (The film was also Carmen Miranda's first in the U.S.) Between 1940 and 1950, she made more than twenty films, including *Moon Over Miami, Four Jills in a Jeep, Pin-up Girl, Mother Wore Tights*, and *When My Baby Smiles at Me*. By the time she made the classic comedy *How to Marry a Millionaire* in 1953, her career was on the wane; far from resenting the constant upstaging of her costar, newcomer Marilyn Monroe, she encouraged Monroe to enjoy herself. "I've had my time," Grable told her. "This is your time now. Enjoy it for all it's worth." Grable retreated from films in the mid-fifties and took on stage and nightclub work instead. (She appeared in Broadway's *Hello, Dolly!*.) A lifelong chain-smoker, she died of lung cancer at a premature fifty-six.

Ty Cobb (1886–1961), U.S. baseball player

As a young man, Cobb accidentally shot himself in the left shoulder with a .22 rifle. The slug remained in him for the rest of his life, but it didn't stop him from batting—left-handedly—4,191 hits (second only to Pete Rose's 4,256) or from scoring 2,245 runs (still a major-league record). No player has ever bested Cobb's .367 lifetime batting average. In fact, Cobb created or tied more major-league records than any other player during his years with the Detroit Tigers. He's been called a Pete Rose with better hitting, slicker baserunning, and smarter accountants. Cobb was the first millionaire athlete, having amassed a fortune in General Motors and Coca-Cola stock. His benign nickname, "the Georgia Peach," hardly seemed to fit a man who was perhaps the fiercest competitor—and most disliked player—in the sport. Long on ambition and short on humor, he was arrested several times for getting into fights both in and out of the ballpark. On more than one occasion, he jumped into the stands to physically assault a heckling spectator. (He was suspended for ten days in 1912 after beating one spectator unconscious.) It was said that before a game, he even liked to sharpen the cleats on his shoes so that when he slid feet-first into a base he could inflict as much damage as possible on the defending baseman. His greatness as a ballplayer came not so much from raw power or natural talent as from a hardened determination and steely intelligence. He was a master strategist who stayed one step ahead of the competition, both at bat and as a base runner. He set numerous records for stealing bases and still holds the record for stealing home plate—thirty-five times. (He sometimes stole second base, then proceeded to third as the throw came in behind him.) Cobb dominated baseball from the turn of the century until shortly after World War I. Then the game changed forever. A "livelier" ball (one that could be hit out of the ballpark with some regularity) was introduced, and an even more monumental figure came onto the scene. The Babe Ruth era had dawned. (See February 6.) In 1936, Cobb became the first baseball player inducted into the Baseball Hall of Fame.

Paul Klee (1879–1940), Swiss painter

"Colour possesses me," the brilliant painter, poet, and violinist wrote in 1914, while painting watercolors in Tunisia. "[C]olour and I are one." As a boy, Klee read voraciously (belying the myth that all left-handers are poor readers), was a brilliant student violinist (belying the myth that left-handers can't really excel at a right-handed instrument like the violin), and wrote endless amusing short stories and poems, a talent inherited from his maternal grandmother, who was the family storyteller. He remained, at heart—despite his essential contentment—a daydreamer: a heavily patterned tablecloth in a café could drive him into a near hypnotic trance, and his ability to stare blissfully, thoughtlessly, at patterns or colors for long periods of time made him worry throughout his life that he was perhaps mentally deficient. At twenty-two, he fled the Munich Art Academy, bastion of stringent conformity and traditional artistic values. Klee began selling his own first paintings—brilliantly flowing abstracts, alive with motion and color—when he was in his mid-thirties. His reputation blossomed with each successive year, and by 1930 he was given an acclaimed exhibition at the Museum of Modern Art in New York. There was, incidentally, never any thought given to "correcting" his left-handedness in childhood. His mother (a graduate of the Stuttgart music conservatory) and his father (an opera singer turned music professor) believed that people were born with unique gifts and that to tamper with them defied common sense, not to mention the creation of God. No wonder Klee and his work were loathed by that most right-handed of twentieth-century regimes, the Nazis, who took considerable pleasure in publicly burning Klee's paintings and denouncing the artist as—what else?—a "degenerate." Blessedly, Klee himself was safely out of reach in neutral Switzerland.

19

On this day, in 1732, Benjamin Franklin published the first issue of *Poor Richard's Almanac*. In 1959, the last surviving veteran of the Civil War, Walter Williams—alleged to have been 117 years old—died.

Jean Genet *(1911–1986), French novelist and playwright*

To some, Genet is a literary saint, a renegade comparable to his American contemporary Allen Ginsberg: both ranted against the status quo (economic, social, moral), both explored taboo areas of human sexuality, and both aligned themselves with enough "suspect" radical causes in the 1960s to earn their own hefty FBI files. To others, Genet is a high-class, if somewhat giggle-inducing, pornographer, interweaving his lurid tales of prison sex and dockside prostitution with florid metaphysics, bombastic metaphors, and borderline stream-of-consciousness pretensions. (The English playwright Joe Orton, never one to suffer cant gladly, called Genet "the most perfect example of an unconscious humorist at work since Marie Corelli. . . . A combination of elegance and crudity is always ridiculous.") Since no revealing excerpt of Genet's writing would be appropriate in a book that might find its way into little hands, a brief quote will have to suffice. "Violence is a calm that disturbs you," he once wrote. "I recognize in thieves, traitors, and murderers, in the ruthless and the cunning, a deep beauty—a sunken beauty." His best-known works are the autobiographical novels *Miracle of the Rose* (1946), *The Thief's Journal* (1949), and *Our Lady of the Flowers* (1949).

Michael Dorn (b. *1952*), *U.S. actor*

The actor who became famous in the role of Lieutenant Worf on *Star Trek: The Next Generation*, starting in 1987, isn't certain if he's left-handed or ambidextrous, or belongs to some classification for which there is as yet no name. "I throw lefty," he told *Lefthander* magazine in 1993, "kick right-handed, write right-handed, and I eat both. When someone who knows me is setting the dinner table, I'll get asked, 'Michael, which hand are you going to eat with tonight?' *That's* when I get confused." Whatever he is, Dorn is happy with it. "Like with any artist," he has said, "it's an asset to be different."

Kristy Swanson (b. *1969*), *U.S. actress*

Swanson is best known for her performance in the title role of the hit 1992 vampire spoof *Buffy, the Vampire Slayer*, in which she drove stakes through the hearts of modern urban vampires—with her left hand, of course.

20

On this day, in 1965, *The Dating Game* debuted on television. In 1993, Donald Trump and Marla Maples were married. In 1996, astronomer Carl Sagan died.

Uri Geller *(b. 1946), Israeli self-proclaimed psychic*

Left-hander Geller achieved international fame in the late 1960s and early 1970s when he seemed to exhibit unique telepathic and psychokinetic powers: he became most famous for his apparent ability to bend spoons—later called "the Geller effect"—by mental exertion alone. Geller performed a variety of other impressive feats that garnered headlines around the world: using brain waves, he made broken watches spontaneously run again; he prompted Geiger counters to click wildly; one 1974 biography asserted that Geller had even, in private, dematerialized large objects. The handsome, photogenic Israeli claimed that his otherworldly talents were being beamed to him by an alien spaceship orbiting near the earth. Unfortunately for Geller his every move was being carefully watched and analyzed by magician and professional cynic James Randi, who, beginning in the late 1970s, began to show that virtually all of the clairvoyant's feats were replicable by traditional (if somewhat modified) sleight-of-hand techniques. One by one, many of Geller's previous adherents quickly changed their minds and offered public retractions of their earlier endorsement. Geller increasingly faded from the public eye, the market having quickly dwindled for his once phenomenally persuasive bull-shtick.

21

On this day, in 1913, the first crossword puzzle appeared, in a New York newspaper, the *World*. In 1937, the Walt Disney film *Snow White and the Seven Dwarfs* had its world premiere.

Joseph Stalin *(1879–1953), Soviet dictator*

Stalin was born right-handed. However, a congenital wasting syndrome made his right arm increasingly useless with age. He was forced to rely more and more on his left hand until, by the time of his death, he was entirely left-handed.

Dorothy Kamenshek (b. 1925), U.S. baseball player

It's doubtful that before the release of the 1992 film A League of Their Own more than a handful of Americans under forty had ever heard of the All-American Girls Professional Baseball League. Started in 1943, as a wartime substitute for major-league ball—many of whose best players were fighting in Europe and Asia—and as a morale-boosting entertainment for Midwest munitions workers, it initially consisted of only four teams and approximately sixty players. From the beginning, the "star" of the league was Dottie Kamenshek, a left-hander from Cincinnati who was only seventeen when she landed a spot on the Rockford Peaches. Her energy, talent, and drive inspired major leaguer Wally Pipp (who played first base for the New York Yankees) to remark that she was "the fanciest-fielding first baseman I've ever seen, man or woman." She was also one of the league's star batters: in 3,736 at bats she struck out only 81 times, and in 1946 she batted .316. Her powerhouse swing prompted an all-male minor-league team in Florida to try and buy her AAGPBL contract, without success. Kamenshek retired from the league in 1952 (as a result of back problems), made a brief comeback the following year, but—despite Wally Pipp's prediction that she would become the first woman player in the major leagues—she left baseball permanently, and moved to Southern California, where she became head of the Los Angeles Crippled Children's Services Department. (See also May 4 and February 18.)

On this day, in 1882, electric Christmas tree lights were invented. In 1965, the film *Doctor Zhivago* had its world premiere.

Steve Carlton *(b. 1944), U.S. baseball player*

Inducted into the Baseball Hall of Fame in 1994, left-hander Carlton played major-league ball between 1966 and 1988, most of those years for the St. Louis Cardinals, the Phillies, and the San Francisco Giants. He won the Cy Young Award in 1972, 1977, 1980, and 1982, and pitched his 4,000th strikeout in 1988. He was only the second player, after Nolan Ryan, to break Walter Johnson's career record of 3,508 strikeouts.

On this day, in 1823, the poem "A Visit from St. Nicholas"—beginning with the immortal line, " 'Twas the night before Christmas . . ."—was published for the first time, in a New York newspaper.

Brad Hall *(b. 1961), U.S. actor and writer*

The husband of *Seinfeld*'s Julia Louis-Dreyfus, left-hander Hall appeared as a regular on *Saturday Night Live* from 1982 to 1984 and appeared in the movies *Worth Winning* (1989) and *Bye Bye, Love* (which he also wrote and produced). He is also the creator of the TV comedy series *The Single Guy*.

On this date, in 1818, the Christmas carol "Silent Night" was performed for the first time. In 1951, Gian Carlo Menotti's opera *Amahl and the Night Visitors* received its world premiere, on NBC television.

Ehud, the Israelite warrior

Try to tear yourself away from shaking all those presents under the Christmas tree tonight, and instead take down your Bible and turn to the Book of Judges, chapter 3, verse 15—and read. And if anyone ever tries to tell you that *even the Bible* says left-handedness is a sin, tell them to do the same.

Today is Christmas Day in much of the Western world. On this date, in 1938, David O. Selznick announced that Vivien Leigh had been chosen to play Scarlett O'Hara in the film version of *Gone With the Wind*.

Kenny Stabler *(b. 1945), U.S. football player*

When he was first struggling to make it as a quarterback in the NFL, left-hander Ken Stabler was repeatedly told he had no future in professional football because he threw "with the wrong hand." The predictions proved premature: Stabler completed almost 60 percent of his passes (for 194 touchdowns) during his professional career, and led the Oakland Raiders to their 1976 Super Bowl victory. He once told an interviewer, "A guy will come up to me in a bar or somewhere and say, 'Hi, Ken, I'm a left-hander, too.' And it means something to me. I don't care how obnoxious he might be. I think, hey, he's not such a bad Joe. There's a bond there."

Annie Lennox (b. 1954),
Scottish singer

Lennox's technopop duo, the Eurythmics (with former boyfriend Dave Stewart), was wildly successful in the 1980s, for its extraordinary sound—as evidenced in number one hits like "Sweet Dreams (Are Made of This)" and "Would I Lie to You?"—and for Lennox's deep-rooted propensity for turning stage appearances into a kind of unpredictable and unrestrained performance art. When she performed live at the 1984 Grammys, she shocked some viewers by dressing with total and uncanny authority as a man, complete with slicked-back black hair. After leaving the Eurythmics in 1990, Lennox established a successful solo career for herself, first with the aptly named album *Diva* and later with such hits as "No More I Love You's," which won a Grammy in 1996.

Rickey Henderson (b. 1958), U.S. baseball player

On May 1, 1991, Henderson stole his 939th base, breaking Lou Brock's old career record of 938. "Lou Brock was a great base stealer," Henderson announced to his fans, "but today I am the greatest of all time." Henderson—a rare player who throws with his left hand but bats right-handed—prefers to steal bases by lunging headfirst at the sack. "When I was a little-leaguer," he told *Playboy* magazine in 1990, "Mom always used to say, 'If you don't come home dirty, you didn't play a baseball game.' So I always tried to slide so that I could go home dirty. That's why I started stealing bases."

On this day, in 1865, the coffee percolator was invented. In 1972, Harry S Truman died.

Marcelo Rios (b. *1975*), *Chilean tennis champion*

Left-hander Rios—often deemed a "deceptive" player for his uncanny ability to mislead opponents about his moves on the court—became the number-one-ranked men's singles tennis player in the world after beating Andre Agassi in the Key Biscayne final in 1997. He attributes much of his success to his left-handedness: left-handers, he has said, are "tough to play. . . . [I]t's really tough to read a lefty's game, where the ball is going."

On this day, in 1831, Charles Darwin boarded the HMS *Beagle* as naturalist on a five-year surveying expedition that would eventually lead to his theory of evolution.

Mick Jones (b. *1944*), *British musician*

The lead guitarist, and one of the founding members, of the rock band Foreigner—responsible for the hits "Waiting for a Girl Like You," "I Want to Know What Love Is," and "Feels Like the First Time"—is left-handed.

28

On this day, in 1846, Iowa was admitted to the Union. In 1869, chewing gum was patented.

Terry Sawchuk (1929–1970), *U.S. hockey player*

During his twenty-one years as a goalie in the National Hockey League, left-hander Sawchuk required more than four hundred stitches to his face and head; he also developed arthritis, shoulder trouble, and an abnormal forward curvature of the spine which eventually proved so agonizing he could only sleep a few hours at a time at night. In a sport that often seems like a testosterone-driven exercise in self-punishment, Sawchuk was the ultimate masochist: he gave his all to goaltending, and the spectacle of him diving after shots other goalies wouldn't touch called to mind medieval monks flagellating themselves in a compulsive drive toward inner perfection. He was, at the beginning of his career, a brilliant player: he was named Rookie of the Year and won the Calder Trophy in his first year of play, 1951, with the Detroit Red Wings. The brilliance continued throughout the years—though only in flashes toward the end—yet it was obvious to everyone that something wasn't quite right. As his career evolved, he became increasingly agitated, unhappy, bitter, and unbalanced. His mental deterioration—connected, at least in part, to the stress of play and his physical traumas—drove his fellow players to regard him with increasing wariness. In 1970, he moved in with one of his teammates, Ron Stewart. At their home one night, the two men got into a fight, and the argument turned brutally physical. Sawchuk had to be taken to the hospital, where he subsequently died as a result of complications arising from his injuries.

On this day, in 1845, Texas was admitted to the Union. In 1851, the first YMCA opened, in Boston.

Druon Antigonus, Flemish giant

Since there is absolutely no left-hander of note born on this date, it seems appropriate, now that our left-handed year is winding down, to pay our respects to Druon Antigonus, the legendary giant of Antwerp. Antwerp lies on an inlet of the North Sea at the confluence of four rivers—the Schelde, the Dijle, the Nethe, and the Rupel. According to legend, about two thousand years ago, the seaport was ruled by a giant, Druon Antigonus, who demanded that every mariner passing through pay him an appropriate tribute: fish, fur, money, food. Mariners who refused were quickly whisked off their feet by the colossus, and their right hands were chopped off. (According to legend, Druon himself was missing his right hand, the result of an unhappy encounter with another giant, Salvius Brabo.) In this savage way, Druon populated the coast of Belgium with untold numbers of suddenly left-handed sailors, and to this day, the official coat of arms of Antwerp prominently features two severed hands.

On this day in 1940, the first freeway opened in Los Angeles.

Matt Lauer *(b. 1957), U.S. television personality*

The left-handed cohost of NBC's *Today*—known for his friendly, unassuming air—was named one of *People* magazine's "50 Most Beautiful People in the World" in 1997.

Sandy Koufax *(b. 1935), U.S. baseball player*

Nicknamed "the Man with the Golden Arm," Koufax became, in 1971, the youngest player ever elected to the Baseball Hall of Fame. Between 1962 and 1966 (the year of his retirement), his win-loss record for the Dodgers was 14–7, 25–5, 19–5, 26–8, and 27–9. He retired from the game after doctors warned him he'd lose the use of his left arm if he continued pitching. "I have to drag my arm out of bed like a log sometimes," Koufax said. "I can actually hear liquid squishing round in my elbow, like there was a sponge in it."

Today is New Year's Eve in most of the Western world. On this day, in 1938, the first breath test for drunk drivers was used in Indianapolis.

Val Kilmer *(b. 1959), U.S. actor*

In recent years, Kilmer has become the Man Hollywood Loves to Hate. He once ranked fifth on a list of the "20 Meanest People in Hollywood," and for the last four or five years it's been impossible to pick up a magazine or supermarket tabloid without reading that he allegedly burned a camera operator's face with the lit end of a cigarette (on *The Island of Dr. Moreau*—Kilmer has denied the incident) or got into a shoving match with director Joel Schumacher on the set of the 1995 hit *Batman Forever*. "I don't like Val Kilmer," said John Frankenheimer, who directed him in the 1996 box-office disaster *Dr. Moreau*. "I don't like his work ethic, and I don't want to be associated with him ever again." Schumacher has had similar words for the star: he has characterized Kilmer in interviews as "childish and impossible" and "psychologically troubled." Kilmer—whose roles include the second-most-brilliant-man-in-the-world in *Real Genius* (1985), the second-best-fighter-pilot-in-the-navy in *Top Gun* (1986), singer Jim Morrison in *The Doors* (1991), Doc Holliday in *Tombstone* (1993), and legendary spy-for-hire Simon Templar in *The Saint* (1997)—is, at the very least, a kind of extremist. He is, according to Oliver Stone, who directed him in *The Doors*, "passionate about his work—with the wrong approach, you may see a side of him you don't like." Kilmer, in interviews, sums up his personality more succinctly: he often describes himself as "spiritually dyslexic."